How It Works®

Science and Technology

Third Edition

Marshall Cavendish
99 White Plains Road
Tarrytown, NY 10591

Website: www.marshallcavendish.com

Third edition updated by Brown Reference Group plc.

Library of Congress Cataloging-in-Publication Data
How it works: science and technology.—3rd ed.
p. cm.
Includes index.
ISBN 0-7614-7314-9 (set)   ISBN 0-7614-7333-5 (Vol. 19)
1. Technology—Encyclopedias. 2. Science—Encyclopedias.
[1. Technology—Encyclopedias. 2. Science—Encyclopedias.]
T9 .H738 2003
603—dc21   2001028771

Consultant: Donald R. Franceschetti, Ph.D., University of Memphis

Brown Reference Group
Editor: Wendy Horobin
Associate Editors: Paul Thompson, Martin Clowes, Lis Stedman, Dawn Titmus
Managing Editor: Tim Cooke
Design: Alison Gardner
Picture Research: Becky Cox
Illustrations: Mark Walker, Darren Awuah

Marshall Cavendish
Project Editor: Peter Mavrikis
Production Manager: Alan Tsai
Editorial Director: Paul Bernabeo

Printed in Malaysia
Bound in the United States of America
08 07 06 05 04   6 5 4 3 2

Title picture: Testing a new environment, see *Virtual Reality*

How It Works®

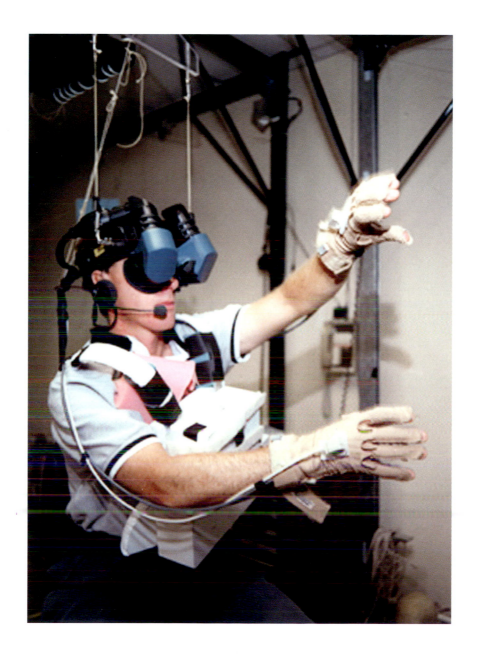

Science and Technology

Volume 19

Video Recorder

Zoology

Marshall Cavendish

New York • London • Toronto • Sydney

Contents

Volume 19

Video Recorder

The earliest video recording was made in 1928, when the British inventor John Logie Baird developed the Phonodisc, a 10 in. (25.4 cm) 78 rpm record, similar to the acoustic discs already being produced for conventional sound recording at that time. On the Phonodisc, a low-definition, 30-line television signal was recorded as a hill-and-dale modulation on the bottom of the groove. If replayed through a loudspeaker, the signal would have been heard as a warbling musical note. Despite its novelty, the Phonodisc failed to be a commercial success due to its poor image resolution. For the same reason, the 30-line television system was abandoned in 1936 in favor of the higher-definition, 405-line system.

Video recording was revived in the 1950s, when devices developed from audio recording machines were first used to record the information needed to reproduce black-and-white and color television pictures. The main challenge was

in recording all the information of a video signal: such signals cover a broad range of frequencies, sometimes as high as 6 MHz.

The first magnetic video machines recorded their signals longitudinally on magnetic tape—that is, as streams of magnetic fluctuations that followed the line of the tape. This arrangement was a direct application of audio recording techniques, where the frequency range is around 20 to 20,000 Hz. Since the range of frequencies in a video signal can be up to 300 times as broad as that of an audio signal, a challenge for video recording is to put information on tape at a correspondingly higher rate.

A further problem lies in recording the high-frequency components of a video signal, because the maximum frequency is dictated by the effective gap between the poles of the electromagnet that makes the recording. In fact, the minimum wavelength (which corresponds to the maximum

▲ A computer-based video-editing suite being used to compose a videotape for a television program. The screen on the right shows both the items recorded to date and the next piece to be spliced into the sequence. The left-hand screen shows the controls used for mixing the shots and adding various effects.

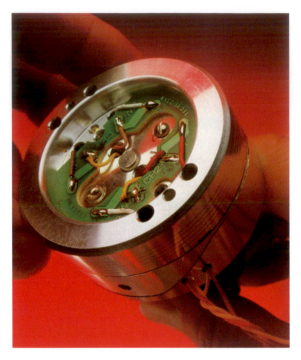

◀ A helical scanning drum is at the core of every VCR machine. Magnetic tape wraps around the drum in a spiral, and recording heads rotate inside the drum. The video signal is recorded in stripes as the tape moves.

circular shape by a vacuum guide. The drum rotated, powered by a small electric motor, so that its circumference wiped across the width of the tape as it passed. Four record replay heads, evenly spaced around the circumference of the drum, earned the name quadruplex for this type of system. The heads of this system scanned in turn across the width of the tape as it passed through the guide assembly. Just before one head left the top edge of the tape, the next head on the drum crossed the bottom edge; thus, there is always one head in contact with the tape. The resulting recorded stripes were essentially at right angles to the length of the tape, a slight tilt being caused by the movement of the tape during each pass of the head.

On the earliest quadruplex machines, signals were fed to the heads through slip rings on an extension to the motor shaft. Later machines used transformers to pass the signals to the rotating drum without requiring physical contact.

The exact rotation speed of the recording head depended on the broadcasting system. For example, the U.S. NTSC system uses 525-line images broadcast as "fields" of 262.5 lines each.

frequency) is just over half the gap between the poles. This problem can be overcome by using high tape-to-head speeds, since they make the effective gap smaller than the physical gap between the electromagnet poles.

Despite the technical challenges of video recording, a number of longitudinally orientated recording machines were manufactured in the early 1950s. In one type, tape speeds as high as 240 in. (20 ft.) per sec. (6.1 m/s) were used to capture the entire signal, including frequencies in excess of 1.5 MHz. In another, the signal was split into frequency bands and recorded by several heads in parallel tracks.

Ampex

The first commercial predecessor of modern video recorders was the Ampex Corporation's VR-1000, launched in 1956 and devised by a team led by Charles Ginsberg and Ray Dolby. Their machine revolutionized the television industry by allowing programs to be prerecorded and kept indefinitely on tape. Prior to 1956, all television had to be broadcast live. The first broadcast to use an Ampex VR-1000 took place on November 30, 1956, when a video recording was used to repeat to the West Coast of the United States a news program that had been transmitted three hours earlier on the East Coast.

The Ampex machine had a relatively low tape speed—15 in. per sec. (38 cm/s). However, it achieved a much higher tape-to-head speed by using a rotating drum to record the signal in stripes across tape that was 2 in. (5 cm) wide. The tape was guided across a rotating drum in the front of the head assembly and drawn into a semi-

▶ This quadruplex video recorder is typical of the machines that were once standard equipment in the television industry. Their introduction made it possible for programs to be recorded and edited before transmission.

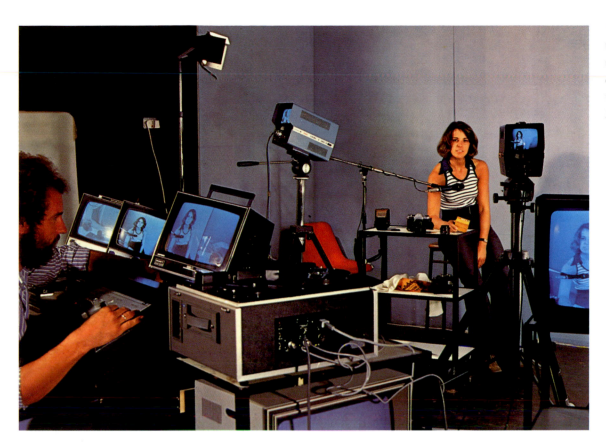

One field consists of the odd lines of the image, the other of the even lines. Alternating fields are broadcast at a rate of 60 Hz, so 30 frames are broadcast per second. European systems, on the other hand, broadcast 625-line images at 50 Hz. Hence, for NTSC the head rotated at 240 rps (revolutions per second), recording each field in 16 stripes; for European systems, a rotation speed of 250 rps recorded each field in 20 stripes, reflecting the larger field size. In both cases, the potential interference caused by changeovers between heads was avoided by synchronizing the speeds of the head and the tape so that the changeover occurred between lines. The effective tape-to-head speed using these rotation speeds was around 1,600 in. per sec., or around 90 mph (145 km/h). Hence, the system was able to cope with even the highest frequencies of the signal.

Quadruplex video recording was accompanied by three longitudinal tracks: an audio track on the upper edge that carried the sound information, a cue track between the audio and video tracks that helped when preparing the tape for playing, and a control track on the lower edge of the tape. The control track carried a simple sinusoidal signal whose frequency matches the rotational speed of the head—240 Hz for a 240 rps head, for example. On replay, the signal obtained from this control track was compared with a signal from a photoelectric sensor on the drive shaft of the rotating head assembly. Deviations between the two signals create error signals in the comparator that instruct the servomechanism to alter the speed of the head drive motor so as to reduce and eliminate the tracking error.

Frequency modulation

Early quadruplex machines suffered from a problem caused by the width of the frequency band that they recorded: the recording and playback sequence was approximately 10 billion times more efficient for the highest frequencies than for the lowest, and the electronics used to equalize the various parts of the signal were not able to compensate such massive differences. The result was a distortion of the image on playback.

The next generation of video recorders addressed the problem of bias toward higher frequencies by using frequency modulation (FM) to record signals at much higher frequencies than those used previously. The higher frequencies ensured a stronger signal on playback; the narrower frequency ranges of the FM signal required less equalization to compensate for bias in the recording and playback processes. Video signals require a certain amount of preprocessing before they are fed to the recording heads, however.

In FM recording, the input video signals are first used to modulate the frequency of a carrier signal at around 50 MHz. The resulting band of frequencies extends from 49.1 to 52.1 MHz, and since this range of frequencies is rather high for even the high tape-to-head speed achieved by quadruplex recorders, it is converted down to the range 6.3 to 9.3 MHz. The processed band of frequencies is fed simultaneously to all the recording heads, which then convert the original electric signal into a magnetic recording on the tape.

Apart from overcoming bias problems, the use of a frequency-modulated signal at several megahertz obviates some of the potential signal-error problems caused by variations in head-to-tape speed. It is not necessary to maintain an exact relationship between tape speed and head rotation during recording, and the control-track mechanism locates the heads immediately above the right portion of the tracks on replay.

Helical recording system

Although FM quadruplex recorders were standard equipment in the television industry for many years, they were never suitable for home-entertainment use. They were too complex and consumed too much tape to be considered for use in anything other than broadcast situations. Nonprofessional video recorders eventually came to be based on the helical recording system, which was developed at Ampex in parallel to the quadruplex system and launched around 1959.

Helical scanning is achieved by wrapping the tape around a drum in spiral fashion. The recording head rotates inside a drum split in two by a slot around its circumference. Thus, if the wrap angle is chosen with an appropriate angle of rise from one side of the drum to the other, the combination of the forward movement of the tape and the rotation of the head produces tracks aligned at a shallow angle to the length of the tape.

Several formats have been tried during the development of helical recording. Wrap angles vary from 90 degrees to 360 degrees around the circumference of the drum, and head assemblies can contain from one to four heads. Each track on the tape can have one or several television fields contained along its length. Reel-to-reel machines of this type for broadcast purposes use one-inch (2.5 cm) or two-inch (5 cm) tape running at a speed of 9.4 in. per sec. (24 cm/s). The head-to-tape speed is typically 70 ft. per sec. (21.38 m/s), and the video signals are recorded at around 5 MHz. Units of this type offer broadcast-quality recordings of color and monochrome signals.

Cassette systems

The operation of a reel-to-reel recorder is complicated by the need to thread the tape into a complicated path through a series of guides and rollers and around the head drum. Hence, a major factor in the domination of the home-entertainment market was the introduction of video cassettes. The cassette system took the threading-up operation out of the hands of the operator and made loading a tape simply a case of inserting a cassette and letting the machine do the rest.

In the cassette system, the feed and take-up reels are contained in the cassette. They remain locked when out of use but engage with drive wheels in a video machine and become free to turn when a pin in the machine enters a release mechanism in the cassette. The same mechanism releases a protective flap that covers the stretch of tape that runs along the inside of one edge of the cassette between pins that guide it to the reels.

When a cassette is inserted into a video recorder, a transport mechanism pulls it into the machine, drops it into the playing position, and opens the protective flap. A threading mechanism then draws a loop of tape out of the cassette and

▼ This machine combines a DVD player with a high-specification VHS-HQ (high quality) recorder.

TRANSVERSE AND HELICAL SCANNING

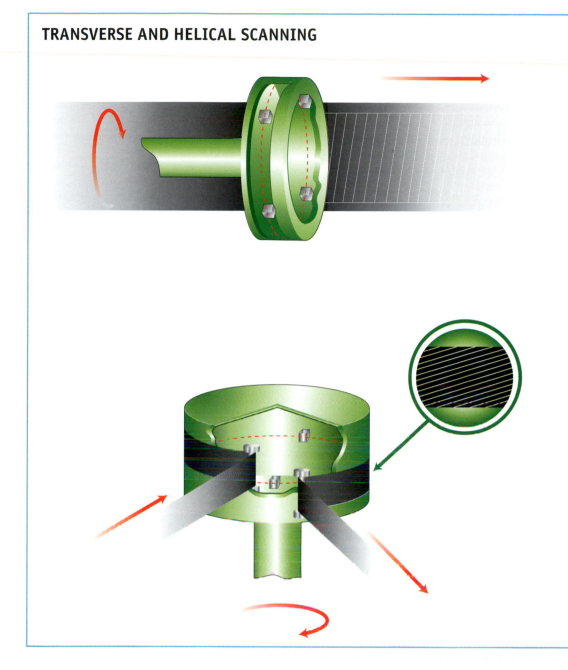

A great challenge in the development of video recording was to find a means of recording data at the necessary rate without resorting to impractically high tape speeds. The two methods that found success in this respect both use heads that rotate to increase the speed of relative motion between the head and the tape. Transverse scanning (top) uses four recording heads mounted in a cylinder that rotates to record tracks almost perpendicular to the direction of motion of the tape. It uses vacuum guides to hold the tape in the shape necessary to maintain contact with the rotating head. This system is also called quadruplex recording. Helical scanning wraps the tape at an angle around a drum (bottom). Rotating heads inside the drum record shallow-angled tracks on tape.

positions it around the drum. On playing, a capstan-drive mechanism pulls the tape around the drum at constant speed and tension.

One of the earliest cassette systems was the Sony U-matic, introduced in the early 1970s. The U-matic cassette was 8.6 in. (21.9 cm) wide by 5.4 in. (13.8 cm) deep by 1.1 in. (3.1 cm) thick and contained tape ¾ in. (1.9 cm) wide. The tape speed was 3.7 in. per sec. (9.5 cm/s), the tape-to-head speed was 26.3 ft. per sec. (8.54 m/s), and the maximum playing time was one hour. The standard version of the system found semi-professional, commercial, and limited home use, while a high-performance version, which used the same cassettes but was otherwise incompatible, was used for broadcast applications only.

Sony's efforts to develop the U-matic system to be better suited for home use resulted in the Sony Betamax system, launched in 1975, which used ½ in. (1.25 cm) tape. The Betamax cassette measured around 6 in. (15.5 cm) by 4 in. (9.5 cm) by 1 in. (2.5 cm) and contained up to three hours of tape when run at standard speed.

A year after its launch, the Betamax system had to face strong competition from a new rival—JVC's new format, VHS (video home system), which now completely dominates the VCR (video cassette recorder) market. VHS uses a larger cassette than Betamax, and its dimensions of 7.3 by 4.1 by 1 in. (18.7 x 10.4 x 2.5 cm) can contain enough tape for four hours of standard play.

Although both systems use helical-scan recording, they are incompatible. Betamax has a larger head drum, which gives a faster head-to-tape writing speed, even though the tape speed is slower than that of VHS. Its longer playing time was one of the main reasons for the eventual victory of VHS in the consumer market.

VHS characteristics

VHS uses twin-head helical scanning to record on and play back from tape that is ½ in. (1.25 cm) wide. The track angle is 5.96 degrees to horizontal, and each track carries one field of an interlaced frame. For NTSC, this requires the heads to rotate at 30 rps, or 1,800 rpm. The signal that synchronizes the start of each new field when shown on a screen is frequency modulated on a carrier frequency of 3.4 MHz; the luminosity signal, which shows how brightness varies through a field, is frequency modulated on a carrier at 4.4 MHz. Color information, or chroma, is recorded as an amplitude modulation of a 629 kHz carrier.

Signals for recording are encoded from the output of a receiver in the VCR, which takes television signals from an antenna, or from a satellite or cable decoder. On replay, video signals can be decoded and reconstructed in a form that can be read by a television receiver, in which case they are fed to the receiver through the antenna socket. Some receivers can process video signals directly, in which case a dedicated cable makes the connection between the VCR and the receiver.

Most VHS VCRs now have three tape speeds. The standard speed is 1.3 in. per sec. (3.3 cm/s), long play is 0.66 in. per sec. (1.7 cm/s), and extended play is 0.44 in. per sec. (1.1 cm/s). Standard play uses one pair of heads, while long and extended play modes use a second set of heads that record narrower tracks to fit onto the slower-moving tape. A single static head is used to erase tapes for rerecording. This head precedes the helical drum in the tape's path.

Audio signals are recorded on two longitudinal channels along the edge of the tape, and they are read and recorded by an audio-recording head through which the tape passes after it has passed over the helical drum. A control track is recorded parallel to the audio tracks and instructs the tape-speed selector as well as the tracking-control mechanism that synchronizes the heads with recorded tracks on the tape. Manual tracking control alters the synchronization of the head rotation relative to the recorded control track.

Auxiliary features

As VHS matured as the standard for the consumer market, manufacturers strove to win customers by including ever more sophisticated features to enhance the appeal of their products. The basic fast-forward and rewind mechanisms were supplemented by search features that allowed the recorded picture to be viewed while moving through the tape at high speed and by freeze-frame and slow-motion features, which allow a recording to be examined in detail.

Other features seek to help consumers who are unfamiliar with technical devices and can be baffled by the apparent complexity of setting a VCR to record unattended under timer control from television stations. They include bar-code scanners, mounted in remote-control handsets, that read start and finish times from bar codes printed on a sheet. In another system, start and stop times and the channel number can be programmed by entering a simple string of digits.

Digital video

The clarity of digital signals and their resistance to interference made the introduction of digital technology to video recording inevitable. At the start of the 21st century, the digital video market finds itself in a state similar to that of the video market of the late 1970s, with competing formats vying to be accepted as the standard.

One typical format, called DV (for digital video), uses ¼ in. (6.35 mm) tape that moves at 0.74 in. per sec. (1.9 cm/s); multihead helical scanning at 150 rps (9,000 rpm) achieves a head-to-tape speed of 32.5 ft. per sec. (9.9 m/s). Each field is segmented into 10 tracks that carry the digitized information for 26.25 lines each. There is no control track, and two audio tracks are recorded into the ends of the video tracks, rather than as separate longitudinal tracks along the edge.

The video and audio signals are digitized by sampling: the sampling rates are 13.5 MHz for the yellow signal, 3.375 MHz each for the red-minus-yellow and blue-minus-yellow signals, and 48 kHz for the sound. After compression, these sampling rates produce a data stream of 25 megabits per second to be recorded on tape.

◄ This mobile VHS video cassette player has been developed for use in cars. The unit features a fold-down color LCD (liquid crystal display) screen and is run from the car's cigarette lighter.

SEE ALSO: ANALOG AND DIGITAL SYSTEMS • AUDIO AND VIDEO RECORDING • DIGITAL VERSATILE DISC (DVD) • MAGNETIC TAPE AND FILM • MOVIE PRODUCTION • TELEVISION CAMERA • TELEVISION RECEIVER • VIDEO CAMERA

Virtual Reality

◀ This montage shows a VR user against the background of a virtual battlefield. The red rings signify centers of military activity, and the inset views show the status of the virtual forces available to the battle coordinator in the training exercise.

Virtual reality (VR) is a technology that allows humans to interact with computers in such a way that the user can visualize and manipulate complex data through an artificial environment. The aim of VR is to immerse the user in that environment so that he or she is not directly aware of the participation of the computer.

Virtual reality presents data in forms that mimic everyday sensations of sight, sound, and touch, and the user feeds information to the computer in equally "natural" ways—by pressing a button seen in the virtual environment or by speech, for example. A variety of peripheral devices, including goggles, helmets, gloves, and body suits, enable the user to experience the virtual environment and to instruct the computer.

One of the main fields of application of VR is in training: users can become accustomed to risky procedures, such as surgery or the operation of a fighter aircraft, without endangering humans or expensive equipment. Virtual environments can also have characteristics difficult or impossible to create otherwise in the everyday world, a zero-gravity environment that allows astronauts to practice handling tools in space, for example.

Forms of virtual reality

A number of systems aim to provide a realistic environment, but the distinguishing characteristics of virtual-reality systems are real-time three-dimensional (3-D) graphics and a response to user actions that results in a sense of immersion. Many VR systems rely purely on sight and sound to create the immersion experience, and some stimulate the sense of touch through the use of special gloves. Smell is much harder to stimulate satisfactorily, although some success might be expected in coming years with the development of fledgling systems designed to release odors in response to instructions contained in websites—the smell of coffee from a coffee trader's website, for example. The sensations of temperature and movement through space are possible to simulate but tend to be omitted from VR systems.

Cab simulators. Cab simulators are direct descendants of one of the principal technological ancestors of virtual reality—the flight simulator. Simulators were developed in the late 1920s to train pilots in the handling of airplanes while still safely on the ground. These machines were able to pitch, yaw, and roll, but they had no provision for simulating the view outside the cockpit.

As airplanes became more complex, simulators evolved to match their capabilities, but they still lacked visual feedback. The first move to resolve this deficiency came in the 1950s, when the first video cameras began to be used, and multiple-angle views could be controlled by the pilot moving the control stick. In the 1960s, computer-generated scenery started to replace film. Early simulators of this type were little more than head-mounted displays with tracking systems, but they evolved into simulators in which the user sits inside a cab mounted on a number of hydraulic rams. The interior of the cab has fittings and instrumentation identical to that of the aircraft cockpit, locomotive cab, car, or spacecraft interior that is being simulated, and monitors replace the windows of the real system. During simulations, the view from these "windows" changes in a real-time response to the driver's actions, and the hydraulic rams move the platform accordingly. Sound effects make the experience complete.

Artificial reality. Artificial, or projected, reality was first developed in the 1970s. One system, called Videoplace, consists of two rooms covered with wall-sized video screens, each with a video camera and a computer. The users can see colorized silhouettes of themselves projected onto the artificial environment of the video screen rather than seeing the world through the computer. Another system, the Mandala machine, also projects the user's video image but analyzes the user's motion and arranges sounds, graphics, and video effects in response. Video mapping systems such as these work in only two dimensions, however, and their effects give the impression of the user being part of a video game.

▼ The astronaut Michael Foale practicing a maneuver for a space shuttle operation using VR. The head-mounted device uses cathode-ray tubes to project images in front of the astronaut, who gives commands to the computer via a microphone. Data gloves give him the feeling that he is handling actual pieces of equipment when in reality there is nothing there at all.

Telepresence. Telepresence is an immersive technology that links remote sensors in the real world, such as video cameras and microphones, with the senses of the human operator. These sensors may be mounted on robots, as has been done in NASA research projects for planetary exploration, or on endoscopes used in surgical investigation. In some cases, force sensors on clasping devices at the remote location return force-feedback signals to levers at the user end. This arrangement allows the user to grasp remote objects without using excessive force.

Desktop VR. Also called window-on-the-world systems, desktop VR uses a large computer screen rather than a headset to display the virtual world. This system is useful for business purposes, since it enables groups of people to view the virtual world at the same time. The effect can be augmented by wearing liquid crystal display shutter glasses synchronized with alternating left-eye and right-eye views to give a 3-D perspective, and sole users can benefit from the addition of a head tracker that adjusts the display to the perspective of the individual user.

Visually coupled display. A visually coupled display is a truly immersive form of VR; the user wears a head-mounted display and stereophonic headphones. Sensors track the motion of the user's head and change the display accordingly. A variation is the "cave" environment, in which the user is surrounded by multiple large display screens. Cave rooms give the impression of being in a very large space while the actual physical surroundings are quite small.

Effectors

Effectors are the interface devices that allow the user to interact with and experience the virtual world. They are classified here according to the human sense that they stimulate.

Vision. The visual component of virtual reality is by far the most important factor in determining whether or not VR users feel truly immersed in a scene. Virtual images can be viewed through head-mounted displays (HMDs)—goggles or helmets—or on one or more static screens. HMDs provide a stronger sense of immersion in the VR environment, but they are often cumbersome and their weight can be a distraction for the user. Static screens produce less convincing VR, but they allow more freedom of movement and can be shared by several users at one time.

HMDs are helmets or goggles that usually hold a small video display in front of each eye to provide stereoscopic vision; some HMDs have a larger single screen but without stereoscopy. The screens use either LCDs or small cathode-ray

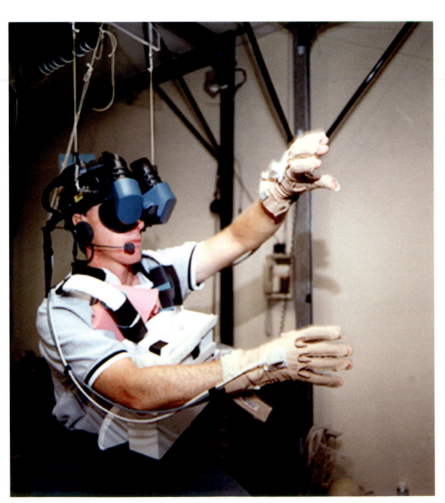

tubes (CRTs). Optical systems enlarge the horizontal scope of the field of view from the 140 degrees of the VR display to the full 180-degree view of normal human experience. The optics also make it easier to focus on the display, which is too close to the eyes for unaided focusing, and they completely fill the field of view, and thus reinforce the impression of immersion.

Boom HMDs, also called head-coupled displays, have viewing and tracking devices mounted on a movable support frame. The support allows the display to use CRTs, which give better resolution than LCD screens but are heavier. The viewing device has six degrees of freedom (6 DOF) —it can move along the three perpendicular dimensions of space as well as being able to rotate around axes along those dimensions. Tracking sensors monitor the position and orientation of the user's head through movements in the joints of the support boom and thus provide instructions for the graphics processor to modify the view displayed on the screen.

The mechanical linkages of booms tend to impede user motion, and alternative tracking systems have been developed so that the HMD need only connect to the processor through a flexible cord. Inertial trackers are accelerometers that work well in detecting rotational motion but are less useful for linear motion. Movements in three dimensions are detected by transmitting pulses of light, magnetism, or ultrasound between transducers and sensors mounted on the HMD and in its surroundings. Position is then calculated by triangulation or, in the case of light, by correlating the timing of detected flash with the positions of the LEDs illuminated at that time.

Hearing. After vision, sound is the next most important component of a VR system. Because sound is processed in a different part of the brain than vision, it can be used in VR to provide clues about the environment without overloading the visual system. In the real world, surfaces make different sounds when an object impacts them—an object dropping on a hard surface makes a different sound than when it drops on a soft surface, for example—so a virtual world needs to mimic such difference so as to give the impression that the virtual world has a physical presence. This impression is reinforced by sound effects that reflect how the user is manipulating the object, such as dragging, dropping, smashing, or switching it on. Sound cues are also useful as warnings to prevent the VR user from bumping into walls.

Sound quality makes an important contribution to the experience of VR—with monaural sound the perception of a scene is less convincing than with full stereo. NASA's Ames Research

▲ A head-mounted display and virtual-reality gloves under test at NASA's Marshall Space Flight Center as part of the CAVE (computer applications and virtual environments) program. It is hoped that VR will cut development costs by allowing virtual models of equipment to be tested in virtual mockups of planned but as yet unbuilt spacecraft.

Center pioneered the development of 3-D sound for use in VR, serving to provide users with clues as to the positions of objects relative to the user in the environment. One of the first applications to use this technology was a simulator for training pilots to avoid air collisions. The pilots could hear approaching aircraft and learn to take the appropriate evasive action.

Touch. The sense of touch is another key part of making a VR experience seem real. Haptic perceptions—those of touch—rely on two types of feedback: tactile feedback, which is the sensation of surface textures arising from the pressure on the skin, and force feedback, felt by muscles and joints when an object is handled.

Touch is a difficult sense to simulate, and none of the devices currently available can replicate the same degree of sensitivity as the human hand and skin. At present, this lack of tactile feedback creates a major problem in sustaining the illusion that an object has been touched, since a hand appears to pass through virtual objects, making them easy to overlook unless some form of warning, such as a noise, is given. Development work is in progress on tactile sensors that can replicate feelings of roughness or smoothness using tiny fingertip vibrators so that the VR user feels that he or she has touched a real object.

Input mechanisms

In addition to effectors, two-way interaction with a virtual environment requires channels through which the user passes information to the processor. As of 2002, the disparity in the sophistication and capabilities of the input devices available or in development was vast.

The simplest devices for intuitive interaction with virtual worlds include the mouse, the trackpad, and the joystick. These devices operate in

▲ A VR data glove used to control and mix electronic music. The colored lines show the paths of the composer's fingers as detected by sensors in the glove. The computer follows the movements of the glove and interprets the music according to the shapes the composer makes with his hand.

two degrees of freedom (DOF), corresponding to back-and-forth and left-to-right motions, and their actions can be combined with the pressing of buttons to select and deselect objects in the field of view. As such, these input devices are restricted to simple actions—moving an object from one place to another without affecting its orientation, for example—and it is easy to learn how to use them.

Developments from these devices work with three DOF (forward or backward, up or down, and left or right) or even six DOF (with the addition of yaw, pitch, and roll) to allow movement without constraint. To achieve six DOF, an isometric device, which can look like a ball atop a stick or a puck on a metal base, measures the amount of force exerted by sensors located in the base of the device. Such devices work best in stationary environments, where they can be used for changing a viewpoint or moving an object. A six DOF mouse has electromagnetic, gyroscopic, or ultrasonic tracking added to an ordinary mouse.

Other input devices with six DOF include button-activated wands. To navigate the environment, the wand is pointed in the right direction and advanced by clicking a button. Objects are selected by pointing, which targets a virtual laser beam onto any object in its path, and clicking.

More sophisticated input devices rely less on conscious manipulations of the input device. One such device, the head-tracking mechanism, has already been mentioned in the context of head-mounted displays. In fact, head-tracking devices collect information on head movements that are essentially subconscious reactions to elements within the virtual environment. Whole-body tracking extends such monitoring with the use of body suits in which sensors measure the angles at critical body joints, such as those of the fingers,

wrists, and knees. These sensors can be resistive, mechanical, or fiber optical, and they create a map of the user's body that is used by the computer. Position and orientation sensors at key points on the body, such as the wrists, provide the computer with detailed information on the movements of limbs as they perform specific actions. Yet more detailed tracking of conscious gestures of the hands and fingers, such as pointing, is achieved by the use of glove-mounted sensors. They also provide information by which the computer "knows" how an object in the virtual environment is being handled.

Another form of data input is by spoken commands in response to voice-synthesized prompts. It is useful because the low resolution of HMDs makes text hard to read, and data gloves—when worn—prevent users from typing keyboard commands. Hence, the computers of many VR systems are programmed to respond to voice commands and to produce spoken information.

As of 2002, biosensors were still in development. They process the electrical signals picked up from muscles by dermal (skin) electrodes. If placed near the eyes, biosensors detect movement of the eye muscles as they search the environment. Biosensors could let users navigate by directing their gaze and select objects by blinking. When these developments mature, they will bring an enormous improvement in accessibility for people with restricted capacities for movement.

Networks provide another channel for the information from which virtual environments are created. In applications such as virtual reality teleconferencing, also called teleimmersion, this information includes instructions for creating representations of remote speakers within the virtual environment as perceived by each user.

Creating a virtual environment

At the heart of any VR system is a huge amount of processing power to run the sound, image generation, and sensory feedback components with the minimum of delay between responses. This delay must be less than 100 milliseconds (0.1 s) if the environment is to to appear as "real time." Thus, the video component of a VR system must be able to generate frames at a rate of at least 10 fps (frames per second). Motion still appears jerky at this rate, however, and a smooth representation requires much faster frame rates, such as those of movies (24 fps) or television (30 fps).

The rate at which new frames must be generated makes the scale of the processing challenge for VR systems enormous, since each frame must be redesigned according to actions within the virtual environment and changes in the perspective of the user, and there is no recourse to prerecorded frames. For this reason, the most sophisticated VR systems require processing power equivalent to dozens of personal computers working together, although less ambitious VR applications can be run on a single desktop computer. In either case, it is this ability to change direction and view objects from different perspectives that differentiates VR from noninteractive video.

Video component. The video component is the most complex and, in terms of processing power, the most demanding part of VR. The key elements of any scene are the background, the lighting, and objects. The objects in a scene may move of their own accord in response to interactions with the user, or they may be avatars (representations of users) that follow the user's moves.

The background is the least dynamic element of a VR scene, yet even it must be mapped in such a way that its presentation can change with the user's perspective. Thus, a three-dimensional "sculpture" of the background, stored as a database of the 3-D coordinates of representative points in the surface of the background is required. In the case of wholly computer-generated backgrounds, these coordinates derive from the graphics programs that produce the background images. Where the background is taken from a real scene, the coordinates are obtained by comparing the images from several cameras with different perspectives of the scene.

The images that represent objects in the scene are mapped in essentially the same way as background images, but there must also be programming to imbue the objects with their required behavioral properties. An unsupported ball will appear to accelerate toward the ground under the force of gravity, for example, by applying the appropriate equations of motion to its coordinates, which then become time dependent. On reaching the ground, the same ball must bounce, with the height of the first and successive bounces determined by the elasticity of the collision (a joint property of the ball and the ground surface). Hence, various parameters of elasticity must be included in the equations of motion. In principle, the shape of the ball should be made to deform through the course of each bounce, but doing so would mean an extra drain on processing resources, so such details are likely to be overlooked until much faster and more powerful processors are affordable than at the present time.

In addition to the point of view of the user and the adherence of objects to the laws of physics, user actions determine how the surface coordinates of avatars and other objects in the scene change from frame to frame. Body movements of avatars are determined by inputs from sensors in body suits and gloves, and movements of objects depend on how they are grabbed by a virtual hand or otherwise selected and moved.

Once the processor has calculated the positions of all the elements in a VR frame, their coordinates in space are converted into coordinates that refer to the user's position as the origin. (In stereoscopic VR this conversion happens twice—once for the left-eye perspective, once for the right.) The next step is to eliminate all the points that are hidden from the virtual eyes by intervening objects. This step reduces the amount of data that must be processed in subsequent stages.

At this point in processing, the virtual scene consists of polygonal frameworks based on the object and background coordinates, together with information on the colors of surfaces and the positions of light sources in the virtual scene. The process of rendering puts skins on these frameworks and then colors and lights each polygonal section of skin according to its position and orientation. The extent of rendering depends heavily on the processing power available, since the whole process of putting an image frame together must be completed within the interval between frames. Whereas full rendering can produce well textured surfaces in which the boundaries between surface polygons are smoothed over, it is usually necessary to compromise the quality of rendering to meet the required frame rate.

◀ A virtual Porsche auto engine being worked on by engineers. The model is programmed to alter the performance of the engine according to the actions of the engineers, so it is a useful training tool.

Some savings in processing time can be made by using texture maps, which consist of areas of an image that have been prerendered for various viewing orientations, so the processor merely looks up the appropriate view for a given frame, rather than rendering from scratch.

Sound and touch. Separate rendering applications look at the action in each frame and produce instructions for loudspeakers (including subwoofers for rumbles and vibrations) and force-feedback effectors. The haptic aspect of rendering is the least mature—the most sophisticated systems to date use force effectors in gloves and exoskeletons to reproduce contact forces, but the development of touch-rendering applications will have to await the development of suitable touch effectors for the time being.

Related technology

A number of computer applications in use or in late development stages employ aspects of virtual reality without attempting to create a wholly immersive environment. These technologies are aimed at fields as diverse as leisure, scientific research, and military applications.

Virtual modeling. Virtual models use the rendering and variable perspective aspects of VR to produce on-screen models that can be viewed from a variety of angles or even viewed from within. Such models enable scientists to view spatial models of molecules based on the computed variation of electron density around their framework atoms, and they make it easier to see the potential for interactions between molecules with more ease than ever before. Virtual modeling of buildings and machines provides a tool for architects and designers to show their proposals to prospective clients. Even more sophisticated are physiological models that allow doctors and surgeons to develop their diagnostic skills by palpating (feeling) virtual growths and tumors.

Augmented reality. Also called mixed reality, augmented reality (AR) superimposes elements of virtual reality onto images of the real world. This combination is useful when the user needs to retain awareness of the real world while accessing data pertinent to the activity in hand. In one form of augmented reality, users wear transparent head-mounted displays onto which diagrams, 3-D plans, and other data are projected; in another form, the same data is added to a video image of the view from the user's standpoint.

The U.S. military is sponsoring research into head-mounted displays for ground forces that could project intelligence-gathered information about strategic sites and weak points onto real-time video or image-intensified views. Position-tracking information for such systems could come from a global positioning system (GPS) used in the high-accuracy military configuration.

Foreseeable civilian applications of augmented reality include virtual tour-guide systems, in which information related to specific sights enters the view. Engineers and mechanics could use AR to call up lists of parts, instruction manuals, and schematic diagrams related to the equipment under repair. Similarly, surgeons could call up CAT (computerized axial tomography) scans and real-time ultrasound images while operating.

Outdoor position tracking could use a GPS, and indoor tracking systems already exist that use ceiling-mounted grids of LEDs flashing in sequence as a reference for user-mounted sensors. The requirement for clumsy HMDs is a major limitation, however, and work has been in progress to develop lightweight eyeglasses with lateral projectors that bounce virtual images off their lenses onto the user's retinas.

▼ This life-size mockup of a Level 5 air-traffic-control tower at NASA's Ames Research Center, California, uses virtual reality to observe the behavior of real-life air-traffic-control staff in lifelike situations.

SEE ALSO: Cathode-ray tube • Computer • Computer graphics • Feedback • Flight simulator • Liquid crystal • Mouse and pointing device • Multimedia

Viscosity

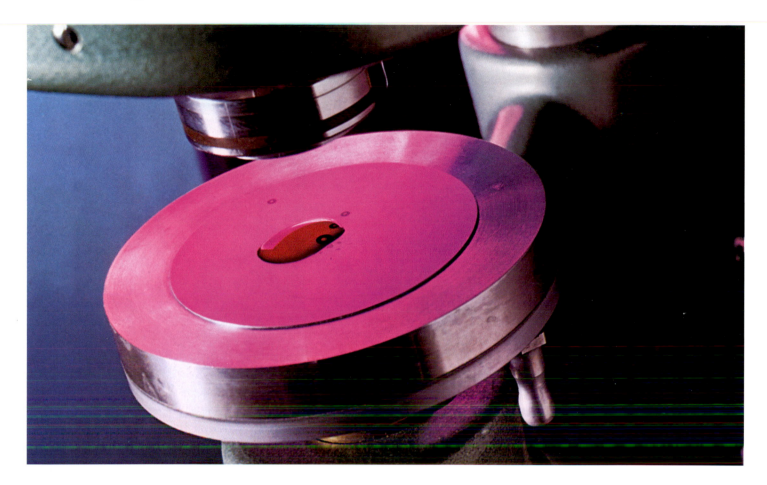

Viscosity of a fluid (a liquid or gas) is its resistance to flow. It is a form of internal friction that results from collisions between the molecules and intermolecular attractive forces, such as the van der Waals force and hydrogen bonding. In the case of fluids composed of larger molecules, these may include forces due to the entanglement of chains.

Viscosity characteristics

If a fluid is placed between two parallel plates, separated by a distance, d, and moving relative to one another at a velocity, v, the force per unit area, F/A, required to keep them moving is given by the equation

$$F/A = \mu v/d$$

where μ is the viscosity coefficient. The flow characteristics depend on how μ varies with v/d, which is the viscosity gradient in the fluid.

Newtonian fluid. A Newtonian fluid—named for the British scientist Isaac Newton, who formulated the earliest quantitative theory of viscosity—is one whose viscosity coefficient is constant at all shear rates. A fluid that has this type of behavior flows as soon as an external shear stress is applied; Newtonian fluids include liquids such as water and ethyl alcohol (ethanol).

Thixotropic fluid. A thixotropic fluid is one whose viscosity diminishes as the rate of shear increases. Such a fluid becomes more free flowing as a result of agitation but regains its initial consistency when left to stand for a while. Thixotropy occurs in liquids whose molecules develop an attraction for one another with time. Shear breaks down these short-range attractions, the viscosity being thus reduced; standing allows the attractions to develop again, so viscosity rises.

Thixotropic materials include some paints and printing inks. Thixotropy is a useful characteristic because the application technique—by brush in the case of a paint, say—imposes high shear that reduces the viscosity such that the paint flows. Immediately after application, the viscosity build due to thixotropy prevents the wet paint from running. This is the basis of nondrip paint.

Dilatancy. Dilatancy, or shear thickening, is the property of materials that become more viscous as the rate of shear increases. An example of a dilatant fluid is a paste of cornstarch in water. The paste pours (low shear) with relative ease, but attempts to throw it out of its container (high shear) cause it to form a semirigid gel. Other examples of dilatant fluids include latexes of the type used to make emulsion paint. At rest, these

▲ A cone-and-plate viscometer is a handy device for measuring viscosity at high shear rates. The sample is seen here on the plate. The cone is at the end of a rotating shaft that presses down on the sample. Viscosity is measured by the amount of resistance to the rotating shaft.

liquids consist of coiled polymer molecules in a water-based fluid. As the polymer molecules have little affinity for water, they remain tightly bundled and do not interact with one another. The application of shear causes the polymer bundles to unravel, so they start to become entangled with one another and viscosity increases.

Laminar and turbulent flow

There are two basic types of fluid flow: laminar and turbulent. In laminar flow, the fluid can be considered to move as a series of layers, called laminas, parallel to the direction of flow. Each lamina moves relative to its neighbors in an orderly manner, and there is a difference of velocity between adjacent layers that constitutes a velocity gradient. The conditions for laminar flow exist when a fluid flows through a capillary tube, for example. Beyond a critical velocity gradient, flow becomes disorderly and is said to be turbulent. This critical velocity depends on the nature of the fluid, in particular, on its viscosity. Techniques for the quantitative measurement of viscosity require laminar flow characteristics.

Quantitative measurement

In the first theory of viscosity, Newton postulated the existence of a proportionality between the shear stress imposed on a fluid and the velocity gradient perpendicular to its flow. The proportionality constant is a characteristic property of the fluid— its coefficient of viscosity.

▶ In this device, a precise amount of liquid flows through a capillary tube under gravity. The time taken is measured as an indication of its viscosity.

▼ The tables at left compare the viscosities of various liquids and gases. The diagrams to the right of the tables are of three types of viscometers.

In 1843, the French physician and scientist Jean-Léonard-Marie Poiseuille extended the theory to the laminar flow of liquid through a horizontal pipe under the influence of a pressure difference between its ends. The liquid layer in contact with the tube wall is considered to be at rest, and successive laminas move with increasing velocities up to a maximum at the center of the tube bore. Poiseuille derived a formula for the rate of flow through a tube in terms of the diameter of the tube, the pressure difference, and the

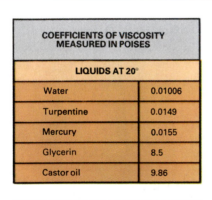

COEFFICIENTS OF VISCOSITY MEASURED IN POISES	
LIQUIDS AT 20°	
Water	0.01006
Turpentine	0.0149
Mercury	0.0155
Glycerin	8.5
Castor oil	9.86

GASES AT 20°	
Air	1.81×10^{-4}
Hydrogen	0.88×10^{-4}
Nitrogen	1.74×10^{-4}
Helium	1.97×10^{-4}
Carbon dioxide	1.46×10^{-4}

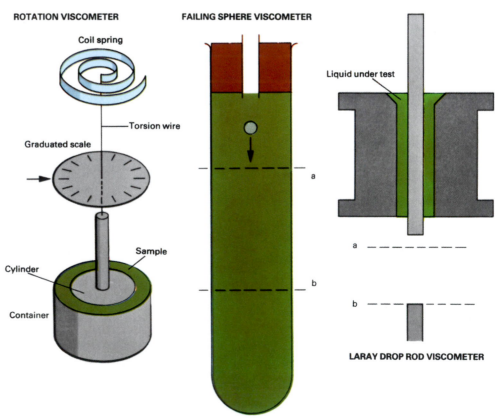

viscosity coefficient. This contribution to the study of liquid flow is commemorated in the unit of the coefficient of viscosity, the poise.

A further development in quantitative viscosity determination was made in 1850 by the Irish physicist George Gabriel Stokes. He showed that an object, allowed to fall freely through a viscous liquid, accelerates initially before reaching a steady velocity known as the terminal velocity. The downward force of gravity is then exactly counteracted by the upward forces of liquid viscosity and upthrust. The coefficient of viscosity of a given fluid is then determinable from the terminal velocity of the falling object.

When the effect of gravity on a liquid is significant, such as when considering flow through a nonhorizontal tube, it is convenient to define a kinematic coefficient of viscosity, obtained by dividing the Poiseuille coefficient by the liquid density. The unit of this coefficient is the stoke.

Viscosity measurement

In practical situations, it is often sufficient to compare the viscosities of fluids rather than to actually measure the viscosity coefficient. Instruments called viscometers are used for this purpose. Viscometers are calibrated using standard oils of known viscosity, and all measurements must be taken at an established standard temperature appropriate to the application, since viscosity drops off rapidly with increasing temperature.

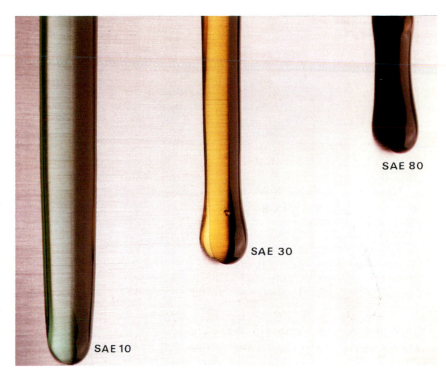

SAE 80

SAE 30

SAE 10

▲ Here the differences in viscosity between three grades of engine oil are evident from the different speeds at which they flow down a metal plate.

A wide variety of viscometers are in current use. They are based on the rate of flow through a narrow tube or orifice, the terminal velocity of an object falling through a liquid, or the resistance of the liquid to an object rotating in the liquid.

A typical and widely used example of the first type is the Ostwald viscometer, in which viscosity is measured in terms of the time taken for a predetermined volume of liquid to flow through a vertical capillary tube. Another type of viscometer, widely used in the paint industry, is the efflux cup. It consists of a metal cup with a conical base. The cup is filled, and the liquid then drains through an orifice in the base. The time taken for the cup to empty is a measure of viscosity.

In the second category, the time taken for a heavy object to fall through a predetermined distance in the liquid is used to compare liquid viscosities. An example is the falling-sphere viscometer, in which ball bearings drop through liquid in a transparent column, and the time taken to pass between two marks is measured.

The third class, that of rotational viscometers, is possibly the most important group of viscometric instruments. They measure the drag experienced by an object rotating in a liquid as an indication of viscosity. In one type of rotational viscometer, a cylindrical metal spindle rotates in the test sample. Different spindle diameters are used for different viscosity ranges, smaller diameters being used for highly viscous liquids.

FACT FILE

■ Xanthan gum, a polysaccharide produced by growing a bacterial culture on glucose, can raise the viscosity of water by more than 100,000 times when used in a concentration as low as 0.5 percent.

■ Emulsan is a biopolymer that reduces viscosity. Employed in the cleaning of oil vessels, it has extremely large molecules, a thousand times the size of those in conventional surfactants, and forms oil-in-water rather than water-in-oil emulsions.

■ Dextron, a polysaccharide used as a thickener in the food industry, is also used in a mixture with water and a suspended abrasive to keep industrial cutting and grinding machinery free of fouling. Drilling muds, mixed with Dextron, are used to cool heated rock-drill bits during drilling.

SEE ALSO: Lubrication • Newton's laws • Paint

Vitamin

Vitamins are small molecules that the human body needs for certain important chemical reactions to take place. If a person has a vitamin deficiency, normal body functions can break down and make that person more susceptible to disease. Vitamins were unknown in the 19th century, although a century earlier, the efficacy of fresh citrus juices in preventing the disease scurvy had been demonstrated in the British navy.

The word *vitamin* was first coined by the Polish chemist Casimir Funk, who isolated vitamin B_1 (thiamine) in rice in the early 20th century. Between 1915 and 1945, more than 50 compounds were identified as vitamins. Many have since been discounted, leaving only thirteen.

▼ Vitamins in crystal form seen under a microscope using polarized light for extra clarity. They are: vitamin C (left), vitamin B_1 (center), and vitamin B_6 (right).

The tiniest amounts of these vitamins—a few milligrams or less—taken daily, have cured devastating diseases such as beriberi, rickets, and scurvy in a way that at first seemed almost miraculous. Vitamins' curative powers have led to exaggerated claims being made for their ability to cure or prevent everything from the common cold to cancers and heart disease. The truth of these claims about vitamins continues to attract interest both from the public and from the medical profession.

Classification of vitamins

Vitamins are divided into two groups—fat soluble and water soluble. The fat-soluble vitamins, which can be stored in the liver (and can be poisonous if taken in excess), are A, D, E, and K. The water-soluble vitamins, which are usually excreted from the body and so do not accumulate, are the B-complex and C vitamins.

Fat-soluble vitamins

Vitamin A (retinol) is found in some animal foods and is produced from beta carotene in some plants. One of its main roles is the production of retinal, which is very important for effective vision. The body cannot produce retinal without vitamin A, and without retinal, the eyes cannot see.

Vitamin D (calciferol) is normally supplied by sunlight. Rickets, a bone deformation caused by vitamin D deficiency, was common among children in British cities where smog blocked the sunlight. Cod liver oil, which contains substantial quantities of vitamin D, was found to be an effective cure. Cleaner air has mediated the need for this supplement.

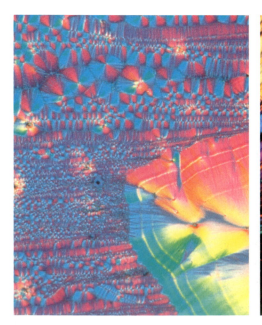

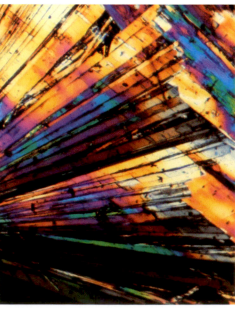

THE VITAMINS

Vitamin	Deficiency symptoms	Good sources
A (retinol)	Night blindness, slow growth, aggravation of lung diseases, rough dry skin, blindness	Liver, fish, dairy produce, eggs, carrots, green vegetables (particularly spinach), margarine
B_1 (thiamine)	Memory and appetite loss, digestive disturbances, fatigue, nervousness, beriberi	Whole grain cereals, fortified breakfast cereals, flour, potatoes, meat, milk, peas, beans, brewer's yeast, wheat germ, yeast extract
B_2 (riboflavin)	Cracked corners of mouth, dizziness, light sensitivity, eye fatigue, poor digestion, slow growth	Milk, meat and offal (particularly liver), eggs, green vegetables
B_3 (niacin)	Appetite loss, headaches, depression, loss of memory, nervous disorders, pellagra	Lean meat, fortified breakfast cereals and bread, eggs, milk products
B_6 (pyridoxine)	Associated with fatigue and depression; low levels sometimes found in women who are pregnant or have a hormone problem	Most foods—particularly liver, yeast, cereals, bread, milk products, eggs
B_{12} (cyanocobalamin)	Fatigue, loss of memory, pernicious anemia, degeneration of nerve cells	Dairy and animal products (particularly liver)
Folic acid	Digestive disturbance, growth and sleep problems, megaloblastic anemia (enlarged blood cells)	Most green leafy vegetables, variety meats, pulses, bread, oranges, bananas
Pantothenic acid and biotin	Very rare	Most foods
C (ascorbic acid)	Anemia, bleeding gums, scurvy	Fresh fruit (particularly citrus), vegetables, potatoes
D (calciferol)	Bone deformity (rickets and osteomalacia)	Cod liver oil, egg yolk, oily fish, butter, and margarine; most important source is sunlight
E (tocopherol)	Hemolytic anemia in premature infants	Most foods, particularly cereal products, vegetable oils, wheat germ, eggs, nuts
K (menaquinone)	Problems in the blood-clotting process	Dark green vegetables, liver; made by bacteria in the intestine

The role vitamin E (tocopherol) plays in the human body continues to be studied; some scientists claim that therapeutic doses of vitamin E can help prevent heart disease. Others have not supported this theory, though there is agreement that intermittent claudication (cramplike pains in the legs caused by defective arteries) and retrolentral fibroplasia (blindness in premature infants) are helped by doses 20 to 40 times the recommended dietary intake.

Vitamin K (menaquinone) is made by bacteria in the intestine and can also be obtained from green leafy vegetables and liver. It is important for blood clotting.

B-complex vitamins

There are eight B vitamins: thiamine, riboflavin, niacin (also known as nicotinic acid and nicotinamide), pyridoxine, folic acid, cyanocobalamin, pantothenic acid, and biotin. They have several useful functions in the body, including the breakdown of glucose (which provides energy) and the breakdown of fats and proteins (for normal functioning of the nervous system). The B vitamins are also important for the healthy maintenance of the stomach and intestinal tract, skin, hair, eyes, mouth, and liver. Although they are water soluble, small amounts of the B vitamins are also stored in the liver.

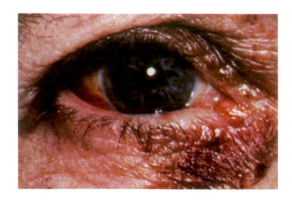

▼ Pellagra is a disease that occurs as a result of a deficiency of niacin (nicotinic acid). It causes dermatitis on parts of the body exposed to sunlight, nausea, diarrhea, depression, and weight loss.

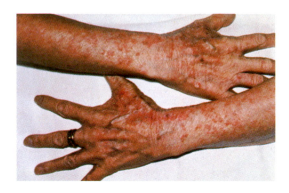

◀ Skin hemorrhages and bleeding gums are typical problems caused by too little vitamin C. Scurvy was a particular problem on long sea voyages until it was discovered that citrus fruits could prevent symptoms from occurring.

Vitamin C

Perhaps the best-known vitamin is vitamin C (ascorbic acid), which comes from fresh fruit and vegetables. Among other functions, it is important for the formation of collagen in the body. Collagen is a fiber contained in connective tissue, such as the skin. Humans are one of the few animals that do not produce their own vitamin C.

The American chemist Linus Pauling put forward the theory that large doses of vitamin C help prevent infections, especially colds, and prolong the lives of patients who are terminally ill with cancer. However, scientists who disagree argue that high doses of vitamin C may actually be harmful.

Because vitamin C is water soluble, some believe that taking large doses is safe. In fact, high doses of vitamin C without medical supervision can lead to serious health effects, including the formation of kidney stones, abnormal heart rhythms, and a toxic release of inorganic iron, which can be fatal.

Use of vitamin supplements

Many cancer treatments, as well as the disease itself, can alter the metabolism of patients and harm their absorption of nutrients. This malnutrition greatly reduces the chances of any therapy to succeed, and research has shown that patients may benefit from special supplements of vitamins

▶ Rickets, a disorder in bone formation, is caused by a deficiency of vitamin D, whose main source is sunlight. Children living in smog-filled towns and cities where very little sunshine penetrates were once frequent victims of rickets, which is often characterized by bowing of the legs.

A, thiamine (B_1), and C. In a similar way, alcoholics, who are often deficient in vitamins owing to a poor diet, can benefit from massive injections of thiamine, which can arrest the brain damage caused by heavy drinking.

Another area where vitamin therapy may be helpful is in the prevention of congenital (existing at birth) neural defects such as spina bifida (incomplete development of one or more of the vertebrae) and anencephaly (failure of the brain to grow in the embryo). Doctors now recommend that pregnant and lactating (breast-feeding) women increase their daily intake of folic acid.

As people age, it becomes more difficult for their bodies to absorb and use vitamin B_{12}. Doctors recommend that people over 60 have their levels checked to see if they need a B_{12} injection.

Although there is a medical consensus that good health should begin with a well-balanced diet, the efficacy of therapeutic doses of vitamins to treat disease is still being debated.

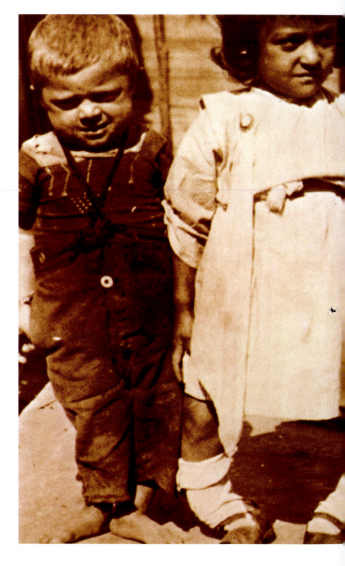

SEE ALSO: CELL BIOLOGY • DIGESTIVE SYSTEM • ENZYME • FAT • FOOD PROCESSING • NUTRITION AND FOOD SCIENCE • PROTEIN

Voice Recognition and Synthesis

Human speech is a complex process involving not only the vocal cords but also the mouth, nose, lungs, and connecting air passage. Voice recognition uses computers to recognize human speech, which the computer then converts into a printed text or uses to carry out certain procedures, such as the opening of a security door or the turning on of lights. Voice synthesis carries out the opposite function of turning printed words or words held in a computer memory into speech.

Voice production

Speech sounds are produced in two ways, both of which involve the controlled flow of air from the lungs, either out through the lips and nostrils or just the nostrils (as when humming), past a variety of constrictions.

A sustained vowel (for example, *ee* in *sheep*), called a voiced sound, is produced when the vocal cords are set in vibration. This vibration is the product of muscular control of the vocal cords and of air flow through the larynx. The vibrations of the vocal cords cause a series of brief interruptions of the airflow through the cords, and the resultant pulses of air are perceived as the pitch of the voice.

Unvoiced sounds (such as *sh* and *p* in *sheep*) are caused by constrictions in the mouth, at the teeth or at the lips. These constrictions may be complete and of short duration, as in *p*, or incomplete and sustainable, as in *sh*. In both instances, the sound results from air turbulence at the site of the constriction; the vocal cords play no part in the production of the sounds. As in the case of voiced sounds, the shape of the mouth affects, through the excitation of resonances, the produced sound. It is, of course, possible to produce an unvoiced type of sound, such as *s*, at the same time as a voiced sound, resulting in, for example, *z* as in *zoo*.

Voice recognition

Two main methods are used for voice-recognition programs; template matching and feature analysis. Template matching is the simplest and most accurate method but also the most limited. A microphone is used to convert speech into an analog electric signal, which is then converted into a digital signal and stored in a memory. The computer then matches this digitized speech pattern to digitized examples of words in its memory. This system has the disadvantage of being speaker dependent, that is, the voice-recognition system will recognize words spoken only by a specific speaker. This method requires the speaker to "train" the program to understand his or her voice, a process that involves reading a text that may take anywhere between 30 and 50 minutes to complete. Once done, however, the program will be able to recognize the speaker's words with an accuracy of around 95 percent.

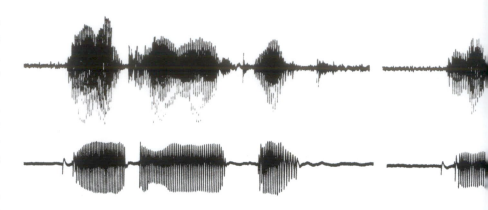

Speaker-independent systems use feature analysis to recognize words. This process involves the use of mathematical relationships called Fourier transforms and another speech analysis technique called linear predictive coding (LPC). These systems enable the program to understand different voices and accents, but so far, feature analysis has proved limited in its ability to understand a wide range of words and consequently has a limited range of applications.

Another important aspect of voice recognition is whether the program can understand continuous speech or is able to recognize only discrete speech, where each word is spoken separately and distinctly. Programs that understand continuous speech are easier to use but have proved difficult to create and have therefore been expensive to produce. However, programs such as Dragon's Naturally Speaking and IBM's Via-Voice, which understand continuous speech, have become widely available at low cost.

Applications

Voice recognition is finding increasing use in information technology and communications, such as in computer programs that allow the operator to use his or her voice to write and edit text, create spreadsheets, send e-mails, and perform a variety of other tasks. This application of voice recognition is particularly helpful for people who have difficulty using keyboards, such as those with a physical disability or an injury that prevents them from typing, and people who have difficulty reading and writing, such as those with a learning disability. Most systems require the user to wear a speaker and microphone headset, which reduces the number of errors by eliminating extraneous noise. When voice-recognition systems first became available they were expensive and not very effective. Current programs, however, are much easier to use and are designed in different versions for both professional and home use. Voice recognition is also used in voice-

▼ An operation to remove a patient's gall bladder being performed using a voice-recognition system linked to a robot named Zeus. The doctors sit at a computer in a control room and give the robot verbal instructions on the next step of the procedure. This system can improve the ability of doctors to perform very precise minimally invasive surgical procedures.

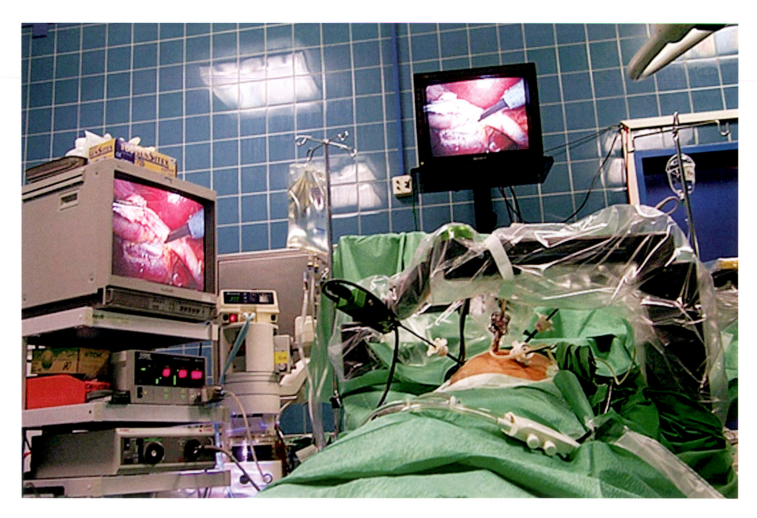

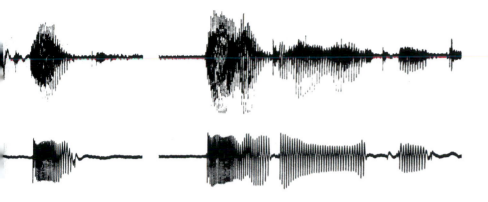

activated telephone systems, such as those in which the caller is requested to speak a particular number to connect them to the correct operator. Security systems have also been developed that operate only in response to particular voices. A further application is the use of voice recognition to operate a variety of different devices within the home. Home Automated Living (HAL2000), for example, works on a home computer and can be use to activate lighting, climate control, telephone, security, home theater, and the Internet. Voice-recognition systems may also be designed to produce synthesized speech to acknowledge the performance of a requested action, for example, or to help the user through a series of required tasks.

Speech synthesis

Because speech synthesis has only to reproduce written words, it is easier to achieve than voice recognition. A voice-synthesis program will possess a broad vocabulary stored in its memory and information on how to reproduce these words as sounds. The program must also possess information on intonation, word stress, speed of pronunciation, and the order in which words may occur. Individual phonemes are sometimes modified by the phonemes surrounding them, so the program must be able to accommodate these subtleties. Some words, such as *desert*, also have a different stress when used as a noun or a verb. Therefore, to pronounce the word correctly, the voice-synthesis program must include information on grammar and be able to assess the way the word is being used in a given sentence.

Applications

Voice synthesis has a variety of applications, such as in the reproduction of written words for blind and partially sighted people and for devices used in language learning. In the case of language learning, the speech may be produced at varying speeds to enable the learner to become familiar with the pronunciation and intonation of words as they appear individually and in sentences.

▲ An oscilloscope may be used to provide traces of the wave forms produced by speech. The analysis of such wave forms is important in the development of computer software systems that can recognize spoken words and reproduce them.

Internet dictionaries also now provide voice-synthesized production of words.

Universal translators, currently under development in the United States, will enable a person to speak into a small handheld device that will automatically translate the language of the speaker into one of a variety of other languages. The computer will then produce a spoken translation using voice synthesis. These devices will be especially useful to military personnel for communicating with people who do not speak their language. They will also be useful for tourists, customs agents, and phone operators.

Voice synthesis is also very useful for people such as the British physicist Stephen Hawking and others who, through illness, have lost the ability to type or to speak. Hawking now produces spoken words using a program called the Equalizer created by a U.S. firm, Works Inc. Words are selected from a computer screen by pressing a button or by head or eye movements. The selected words can then be printed out, stored in the computer's memory, or be produced orally using a speech synthesizer made by Speech Plus.

▼ These dog-like robots possess stereo microphones in their ears, which they use in conjunction with voice recognition software to hear, understand, and respond to a variety of words, including the name given to them by their owner. If the robot understands a word or phrase the "horn" on top of its head lights up.

SEE ALSO: ACCESSIBILITY AID • COMPUTER • INFORMATION TECHNOLOGY • OSCILLOSCOPE • SOUND • SOUND REPRODUCTION • SPEECH AND LANGUAGE • VIRTUAL REALITY

Voltage Regulator

A voltage regulator is any device that when included in an electric circuit maintains a steady voltage under a range of operating conditions. Among the most important applications are those in battery charging systems in automobiles.

The output of generators used in automobiles to provide the electric current to charge the battery rises with increasing speed. Engine speeds can vary from 1,000 to more than 15,000 revolutions per minute, so the output from the generator would vary widely if not controlled in some way.

The two forms of generators used in automobiles, DC generators (dynamos) and alternators, require different controls, but the principle of control is the same. In both cases, the generator field current is reduced as the voltage rises and increased as the voltage falls. DC generators use electromagnetic controls, and alternators now use electronic controls.

When the generator is charging, current flows into the battery, but when the generated voltage drops below that of the battery, it is necessary to prevent the battery from discharging through the generator windings. The alternator contains rectifier diodes, devices that let current flow only one way. A DC generator does the same thing with an electromechanical cut-out switch.

The cut-out mechanism is an electromagnetic relay connected across the output of the DC generator, and the normally open spring-loaded contacts of the relay are connected between the generator output terminal and the battery. When

the generator voltage rises sufficiently, the relay contacts close—and charging current flows from generator to battery. A heavy series coil, connected in the generator to the battery lead, is wound around the relay shunt coil to assist in holding the contacts closed when current is flowing from the generator to the battery. When the generated voltage falls, there is a momentary flow of current from battery to generator. This flow causes the series coil to oppose the shunt coil—the contacts open and prevent discharge of the battery.

The voltage regulator could also be an electromagnetic relay connected across the generator output. Its contacts control the DC generator field supply and are normally closed. As the voltage rises, the electromagnet attracts the armature carrying the moving contact, and the field circuit is broken. The generated voltage falls immediately, so the contact is released. The circuit is completed again, thereby remaking the contacts, and the procedure is repeated.

If the battery is in a low state of charge, the current generated could be sufficient to damage the windings of the generator. To prevent damage, two alternative forms of control are used. The first employs an additional series coil wound around the regulator shunt coil. When a heavy charging current flows through it, the series coil assists in the opening of the contacts and reduces the regulating voltage; the voltage reduction in turn reduces the flow of current. The second type of control employs another set of contacts in

▲ An early electronic voltage regulator, unmounted (left) and mounted (right). No current regulator is necessary.

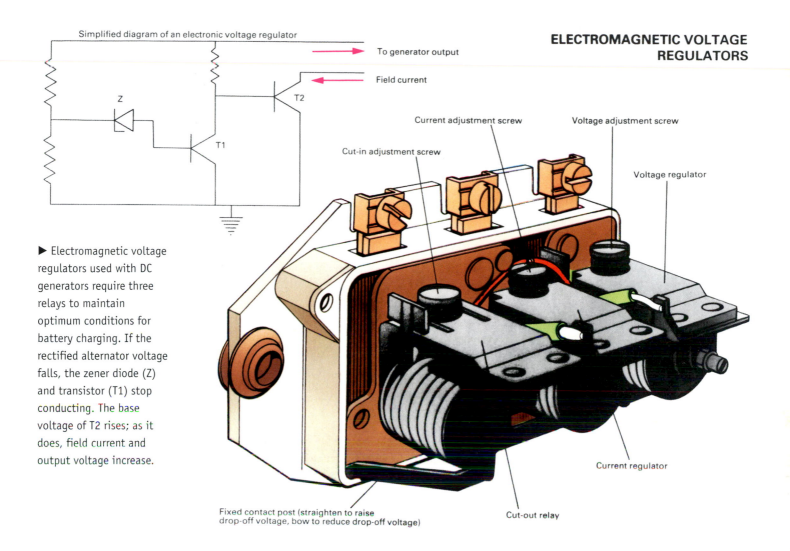

Simplified diagram of an electronic voltage regulator

To generator output

Field current

Z

T2

T1

ELECTROMAGNETIC VOLTAGE REGULATORS

Current adjustment screw

Voltage adjustment screw

Cut-in adjustment screw

Voltage regulator

Current regulator

Cut-out relay

Fixed contact post (straighten to raise drop-off voltage, bow to reduce drop-off voltage)

▶ Electromagnetic voltage regulators used with DC generators require three relays to maintain optimum conditions for battery charging. If the rectified alternator voltage falls, the zener diode (Z) and transistor (T1) stop conducting. The base voltage of T2 rises; as it does, field current and output voltage increase.

▶ An electromechanical current-voltage regulator.

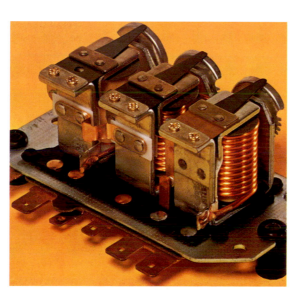

series with the voltage regulator contacts. These contacts are controlled by an electromagnet activated by the load current. If a heavy load current flows, the contacts open before the voltage-controlled contacts, and the generated voltage is reduced below the nominal setting.

The alternator is called a self-regulating machine because, for a particular voltage, there is a limit to the current that will be generated, an amount determined at the design stage, so there is no need for a current-limiting device in the control. In addition, the output is fed through diodes, which allow current to flow only in one direction, and this feature makes a cut-out unnecessary—the only control needed is a voltage regulator.

This regulator is usually electronic and is made of a transistor, which acts as a switch, and a control circuit containing a zener diode, which conducts only when the voltage reaches a predetermined value. When this voltage is reached, the current flows in the diode and makes the control transistor conduct. This diverts the base current away from the field supply transistor, which in turn reduces the field current. The field current reduces until the load on the system balances at the voltage set by the zener diode breakdown voltage. Extra circuits are included to make the field-control transistor switch on and off quickly so that the average current produced is the amount needed to balance the system and there is no overheating.

Zener diode

Zener diodes are semiconductor devices named for an American physicist, Clarence Zener, who conducted the early studies of the phenomenon on which the operation of such devices depends. They possess the useful property that, under certain conditions, they will provide a variable current at a fixed voltage.

The zener diode finds important and extensive application in electronic circuits such as voltage reference sources and constant voltage sources in regulated, stabilized DC electricity supplies. If a supply is unregulated, the output voltage varies as the load power from the circuit varies. Also, in the case of a rectified electricity supply, the DC output voltage varies as the alternating current (AC) supply changes, and particularly in semiconductor circuits, the DC output voltage varies with temperature.

◀ Digital multimeters, which measure current, voltage, and resistance of a circuit, use zener diodes as voltage references.

Design of the zener diode

A simple electricity supply might consist of a DC voltage supply, a resistor, and a zener diode. The resistor and zener diode are placed in series across the voltage supply, with the load (requiring a stable voltage) in parallel with the diode. If the load requires more current, the zener diode takes less, the voltage being maintained as long as sufficient current flows through the diode to maintain the zener voltage.

The materials silicon and germanium, which are insulators in their pure state, can be rendered electrically conducting by the addition of carefully controlled amounts of specific impurities—a process called doping.

The inclusion of impurities such as phosphorus, antimony, and arsenic results in the crystal having extra electrons, as compared with the pure material. These extra electrons are relatively free to move through the material and contribute to electric conduction. Because of these excess electrons (negative charge carriers), the semiconductor is referred to as n-type.

If the elements boron, aluminum, indium, or gallium are introduced as impurities into the host material, the result is a material deficient in electrons. The sites of these absent electrons can be regarded as holes in the lattice that behave as positive charges, because the neighboring electrons are attracted toward these vacant sites. The resulting semiconductor is p-type material.

The *p-n* junction

When the impurities are doped into a single piece of semiconductor in such a way that a p-type region is directly next to an n-type, there is a certain probability of some of the electrons from the n-type material diffusing across the p-n boundary, or junction. As a result, the p-type material acquires a negative charge. Similarly, holes from the p-type material diffuse into the n-type material, and a positive charge results. A potential (voltage) barrier therefore develops across the boundary and prevents further movement of electrons and holes. The region of the junction is termed the *depletion layer* because of the diffusion of charge.

If an external voltage is applied across the junction in a sense opposite to that of the barrier potential, the internal barrier is reduced, enabling a large current to flow. The junction is then described as being biased in the forward direction. If the externally applied voltage is in the same sense as the internal potential barrier, this barrier is intensified, and current flow is extremely small. The junction is then said to be reverse biased. This asymmetry of conduction characteristics accounts for the use of the p-n junction as a diode in rectifiers.

The zener voltage

When the voltage applied in the reverse direction exceeds a certain level, depending on the design characteristics, the reverse current flow is observed to increase rapidly. This phenomenon is the breakdown of the diode. At the breakdown voltage, the electric resistance of the device becomes variable, and the result is a constant voltage characteristic whatever the current flowing through the diode.

Appropriate selection of material and impurity level enables the design of units for which breakdown occurs at reverse voltages ranging from about three volts to several hundred volts.

Explanation of the breakdown

The original theory postulated by Zener to explain the observable breakdown of the diode proposed that the sudden rise in current at a certain critical voltage is due to the rupture of the bonds between atoms and electrons in the boundary region between the *p*-type and *n*-type semiconductors. He postulated that this rupture is caused by the high intensity of the electric field in this region resulting from the combined, additive effect of barrier potential and the applied reverse voltage. Such disruption of bonds would make an increased number of electrons available to participate in the conduction process.

This effect described by Zener is now known to be significant only in diodes with breakdown voltages below about six volts. In the usual *p-n* junction, the original theory is found to be less satisfactory as an explanation of breakdown than the theory of avalanche breakdown here described.

Avalanche theory

In so-called avalanche diodes, the electrons and holes whose motions give rise to the very low reverse current in the diode, are accelerated to high kinetic energies by the reverse potential applied. At a critical strength of the electric field, the moving charges acquire sufficient energy to knock electrons out of the normal chemical bonds in the material. Each such event gives rise to a new electron–hole pair.

The resulting free charge carriers are also accelerated by the reverse potential and in turn generate more electron–hole pairs by subsequent collisions. This accumulative process is known as avalanche multiplication, and its effect is that the current rapidly increases.

Although breakdown is known to occur in these different ways under different conditions, the term *zener diode* has become universally applied to all breakdown diodes regardless of the precise conditions under which they are operated.

Temperature dependence

The temperature dependence of the breakdown, or reference, voltage of a zener diode is a matter of great importance in its design as a circuit element but additionally provides information as to the nature of the physical process responsible for the breakdown phenomenon.

By defining a temperature coefficient as the percentage change in reference voltage per degree Celsius rise in temperature and measuring this temperature coefficient as a function of current through the device, it is found that the temperature coefficient may be either positive or negative. In general terms, for breakdown voltages above six volts, when avalanche multiplication accounts for the physical behavior, the temperature coefficient is positive. When zener breakdown occurs—that is, below six volts—the temperature coefficient is negative.

In order for the field intensity at low voltages to be sufficiently high for bond disruption to occur, a very narrow depletion layer is required. Increase of temperature increases the electron energy, and therefore less applied voltage is required to pull them from their binding positions in the crystal and render them available for conduction. The zener breakdown voltage thus decreases with increased temperature, accounting for the negative temperature coefficient.

If the *p-n* junction has a wide depletion layer, as determined by the doping level (impurity content), there is a low field intensity, and breakdown occurs by the avalanche mechanism. In this condition, a temperature increase causes increased vibrations of the atoms of the crystal and hence an increased probability of collision between the atoms and the accelerated charge carriers. There is therefore less chance for these electrons and holes to gain sufficient energy between collisions to initiate the avalanche process. Thus, increasing the temperature necessitates an increase in the required avalanche voltage and hence the positive temperature coefficient.

Provided that the current through the device is controlled, zener diodes provide a wide range of reproducible reference voltages. By careful design and selection of the impurity level, any desired reference voltage from three volts to several hundred volts can be provided by these devices.

▼ Many of the components of this long-distance telephone exchange printed circuit board are zener diodes, which are used to stabilize the voltages in the circuit. Zener diodes are also incorporated in the power supply device in the top right-hand section of the circuit board, where they regulate the voltage of the power supply and thus prevent its variance from a mean level.

SEE ALSO: CONDUCTION, ELECTRICAL • DIODE • ELECTRICITY • ELECTRONICS • GENERATOR • INSULATOR, ELECTRIC • RESISTOR • SEMICONDUCTOR • SILICON • TRANSISTOR

Warehousing

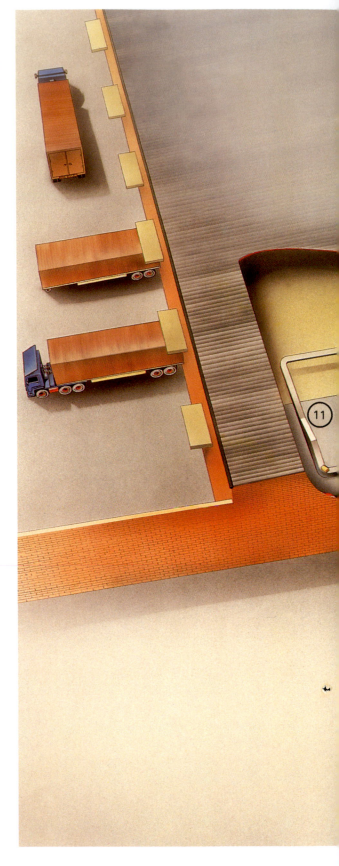

◄ A warehouse containing abrasive blasting materials to be allocated. Modern warehouses have largely computer-controlled precision racking and fire-safety systems.

Technology has revolutionized methods of warehousing. Planners no longer think of a warehouse merely as a building to put things in—they see it as a machine for the storage, retrieval, and control of the flow of production materials to the factory or as a sophisticated center for distribution.

An automated storage/retrieval system (AS/RS) consists of a store served by storage and retrieval machines and by conveyors—all controlled by only a few workers and computers. Indeed, one-person warehouses are now practicable. An AS/RS offers advantages of speed of action, rapid production of up-to-the-minute data, and improved security against theft. It also leads to much cheaper operation costs and more efficient use of space.

The idea of devising a warehouse system to fit an existing building is generally out of favor. Instead, the system is planned first, and the architects and builders must work around it.

Many of the most recent warehouses are not conventional, free-standing structures but hang from their own racking systems. These steel storage racks, which may be more than 100 ft. (30 m) high, actually support the roof and carry the stresses of the enveloping walls, a method of construction that allows great savings in erection time and cost. In the United States, there is the added advantage that the Internal Revenue Service rules that such a structure depreciates as equipment rather than as a building, a saving on tax bills.

The concentration of huge amounts of valuable materials in an AS/RS brings with it the danger of large-scale losses during a serious fire. Planners, therefore, use a variety of techniques to prevent and control the spread of fire. Sprinkler systems, built into the warehouses, bring fires quickly under control in areas where the storage

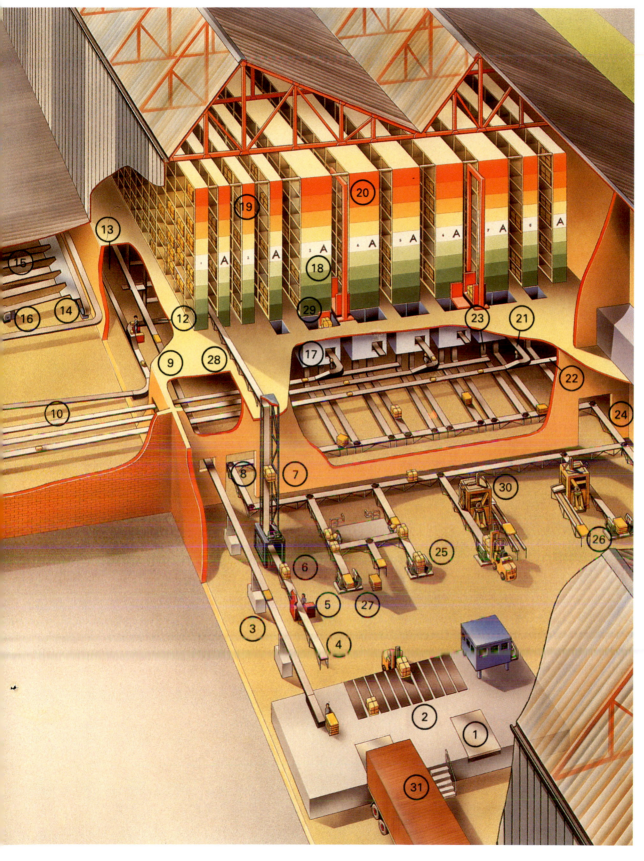

racks are less than about 23 ft. (7 m) high.
However, conditions may modify their effectiveness—in particular, the combustibility of the stored
materials, the storage density, and the levels and
distribution of the sprinklers themselves. In many
warehouses, sprinklers are sited in zones so that
they respond to a fire in their immediate locality.

Many local departments recommend the
installation of high-expansion foam devices. They
are very efficient and cause less damage to most
types of stored items than a soaking with water.
Also, curtains of glass-fiber material, which are
lowered automatically from the roof to isolate a
fire from neighboring racks, may be installed.

Smoke ventilators are built into the roofs of most new warehouses. Smoke and radiation detectors activate an automatic, zoned firefighting response in the building and, at the same time, alert the nearest fire-control officers.

Precision racking

The storage structure in an AS/RS depends on the use of palleted, or binned, loads held in high racks. The aisles between them are only a few inches wider than the palleted loads themselves. The clearance between the machinery that serves the racks and the storage system itself is critical, and makes the installation of the units a matter of precision engineering. A tolerance of about 2 in. (5 cm) in any plane is the limit in constructing the frames for the stacks.

The racks are free-standing structures of steel on whose verticals the architect marks a line and relates it to a datum level fixed off the site. This enables the warehouse manager to check on settlement caused by the great weight of material pressing down on the racks and on the foundations.

In the narrow aisles between the stacks run the storage and retrieval machines. They are double-masted cranes that run on heavy-duty undercarriage wheels with supporting rollers at each side. A pair of powerful travel motors drives the crane along the aisle, and telescopic forks extend to either side of the lifting carriage powered by a couple of hoisting motors. Yet another motor drives the telescopic arms that slide under the pallets to support the load.

The machine, locked into its upper guide rail, forms a rigid frame for lifting and shelving operations. It travels along its aisle at speeds up to 500 ft. (152 m) per minute and hoists or lowers pallet loads at more than 120 ft. (37 m) per minute. When storing pallets, the cranes carry them to their correct positions in the racks, the forks extend to place the load in position, and the crane moves to its next task. To retrieve a pallet, it operates in a similar way, carrying the load to the end of a spur of racks and lowering it onto a conveyor, which takes it to waiting delivery trucks.

Various devices serve to carry palleted loads from the spurs to dispatch stations. In a warehouse where employees called pickers make up loads consisting of many different items, conveyors and carousels may help in their work. The carousels are endless loops of conveyors combined with turntables and elevators. A carousel may form a vertical loop, running along a rack, descending to picking stations, and then moving back to the rack again. It runs continuously as the pickers choose items from their lists and pack them ready for dispatch.

Driverless transport

Forklift trucks may take materials that are ready for their journey to a dispatch point or a factory floor, but this function is increasingly fulfilled by driverless, battery-powered vehicles. Computer controlled and activated from an operating console, these vehicles function in different ways. Some use an optical device to scan and track a line painted or taped to the floor.

Most warehouse systems planners, however, prefer to install wire tracks for guidance, as they are more durable. A wire loop is buried about 0.5 in. (13 mm) beneath the floor and fed with a 10 kHz alternating current from a high-frequency transmitter to create a magnetic field. Each vehicle has a scanner with two antennas in which the magnetic field induces a high voltage. The voltage level is governed by the lateral distance of the antennas from the wire. An electronic device measures and compares the voltages picked up by each antenna and adjusts the vehicle's steering to keep the voltages equal. Infrared sensors at stopping points along the route halt the vehicle, which waits until the operator at the computer control panel tells it to move on to the next point.

The controller may select a route that takes the vehicle past a spur where a crane may lower pallets into trailers pulled behind it. Alternatively, the vehicle may be equipped to store and retrieve pallets. The computer prevents collisions from taking place, and the vehicles are programmed through their own microprocessor units to return to a battery-recharging station when their power supply starts running down. They move at speeds of up to nearly 4 mph (6 km/h) and can be programmed to open and close doors if they need to pass fire barriers or enter and leave cold storage.

Computerized coordination

Sophisticated AS/RS systems, which are fully programmable, belong more in the realm of robotics than of mere automation. A modern AS/RS system is fully programmable, and it governs so much of the warehousing operation that it has been likened to a gigantic robot with its limbs turned inward.

When such a system is integrated with a manufacturing process, it is called an in-process S/R (storage/retrieval) system. In many warehouses, the in-process S/R system consists of racks that are serviced by a worker operating an S/R machine. The worker picks components from pallets or bins, and the machine transfers them to the end of a spur, where a conveyor takes them to be assembled in another part of the plant.

The picker receives instructions through a computer terminal sited on board the machine. It gives information on which components to select, how many are needed, and where to find them. The operator can also record any shortages he or she notices via the computer keyboard.

The computer system in the Avon Corporation warehouse in Chicago works in several ways. It controls and distributes manufacturing materials and products, as well as organizing the flow of incoming raw materials and the shipping of consignments. The computer control of this giant machine, which is 426 ft. (130 m) long, 164 ft. (50 m) wide, and 75 ft. (23 m) high, enables the company to quickly extract data on its raw materials' holding in relation to production requirements and shipping products to its markets.

The small processors on the S/R machines communicate with a minicomputer, which acts as an equipment controller and can remotely control all the equipment in the system. The chain continues as the equipment controller links with a larger minicomputer, which produces an inventory of the system's input and output as well as other data essential for decision making by management. In turn, this minicomputer may feed and respond to the overall corporate computer system. In this way, the AS/RS and in-process S/R systems merge with the entire corporate function.

In hot countries, certain kinds of warehouses pose particular problems for the storage of perishable goods. A warehouse in Dhahran, Saudi Arabia, designed by the U.S. company Munck Systems Inc., supplies a wide range of foodstuffs to about 60 clients. The extreme environment in which it operates makes internal temperature control imperative. Of the ten aisles serving the stacks of this huge rack-supported structure, five are for frozen goods kept at −18°F (−28°C), two for frozen or refrigerated goods, and three for refrigerated foods only.

Each picking station has its own computer terminal, which tells the operator the items he or she must select and place on the pallet ready for dispatch. When the operator completes the order, a task-completed button is pressed to instruct the computer to update its inventory.

The AS/RS computer system at the Dhahran warehouse embraces a larger number of responsibilities than most systems of its kind. In addition to the general control and information functions, it makes regular checks of temperature and humidity in the racks, even monitoring the temperature of the subsoil outside the building as an indication of changes in external conditions that might affect the stored food. The computer can also arrange the automatic transfer of stock from one aisle to another. Its comprehensive report on conditions and holdings within the warehouse is made to the corporation's central computer daily.

Cutting the cost

In countries where trained personnel is hard to find but where large sums of money are available for expensive projects such as the Dhahran warehouse, the efficiency of the AS/RS is a good choice. Many businesses elsewhere cannot find the necessary capital to build their own large warehouses, and other companies might not be quite large enough to generate the levels of turnover to warrant such expense.

One solution to this problem is to have large warehouses that are available to a variety of different users. Outside of Oslo in Norway, there is a warehouse built on three levels in an unused quarry. Twenty-four stacker cranes serve its racks, and over 75 trucks and narrow aisle stackers move items in and out of the system.

This ingenious arrangement of services is available to manufacturers and distributors to rent. They can also use the other related facilities, such as banking, letter and parcel mail service, a travel bureau, and a computer inventory printout service.

Road vehicles entering the complex are met at a checkpoint, where data relating to the client company and the vehicle load are fed into the computer system. By the time the truck arrives at the business end of the approach tunnel, coded labels are waiting for its load of goods, which are palleted and carried to their racks. In this way, the advantages of the kind of large-scale mechanized warehousing used by large businesses are made available to smaller companies.

◀ A computer used in warehouse stock control. Recording the arrival and departure of goods helps to ensure cost-efficient use of storage space.

SEE ALSO: Computer • Conveyor • Freight handling • Information technology • Mass production

Warship

Up to World War II, the world's navies had fought in conventional naval battles, conducted at relatively close quarters with heavy guns. This tactic had led to the favoring of large warships such as the battleship and the slightly smaller cruiser. They had a displacement of more than 60,000 tons (54,000 tonnes), carried very large guns, 12 to 18 in. (305–460 mm), and had an enormous thickness of armor plating—for example, the huge Japanese battleship *Yamato* of World War II had 25 in. (63.5 cm) armor plating in parts of the turrets and superstructure. It became apparent during World War II that naval warfare had changed, with less emphasis given to sheer seaborne hitting power and much more to air power. A few torpedoes dropped from small, comparatively cheap aircraft could sink the largest and most expensive battleship. Aircraft range, performance, and armaments were constantly increasing and so was the technology of the aircraft carrier. Many of the naval battles of the Pacific campaign were fought entirely by aircraft, without warships of either side coming anywhere near each other.

The type of armaments a nation stocks, however, is determined by the type of war it envisages for the future, and estimates do vary. During the 1980s, the U.S. Navy took its four most sophisticated battleships out of storage. These ships first came into service during World War II and between them had already experienced several phases of decommissioning and recommissioning. For the most recent recommissioning, they were reequipped with Tomahawk cruise missiles (which can hit targets hundreds of miles away), Harpoon sea-skimming antiship missiles with a range of 70 miles (113 km), and newer defensive systems; the ships were made the core of four battleship groups. The reason for their revival was their immense firepower—each of their nine 16 in. (406 mm) guns could project a 2,700 lb. (1,225 kg) shell 20 miles (32 km), a feat of great value in coastal bombardments. They also provided good platforms for helicopters. However, the high running costs of these ships, large staffing requirement, and the greater effectiveness of modern cruisers and destroyers led to these battleships once more being decommissioned in the early 1990s.

The other very large warships—up to 97,000 tons (87,300 tonnes)—are aircraft carriers, which must be of a fair size simply to have enough space on the flight deck for takeoff, landing, and parking of aircraft and below deck for storage,

fuel, and spares. The U.S. Navy, for example, has been equipped with enormous nuclear-powered carriers. A typical modern navy consists, apart from aircraft carriers, of frigates, guided-missile destroyers, assault ships, patrol boats (or corvettes), minesweepers, and submarines.

Construction

The hull of a warship is prefabricated and of all-welded construction with T-bars for stiffening in the longitudinal direction. A grillage hull structure is the best design to resist shock from underwater explosions. It is formed by passing the T-bar longitudinally through the larger transverse frame, forming squares of stiffening to support the shell plates. The grillage structure gives the most efficient form of stiffening for minimum weight. High-strength steel is used in regions of the hull where there are great stresses, to reduce the likelihood of cracks. To prevent corrosion, the steel is shot blasted to remove mill scale and rust, and then it is painted and used in the construction. Some parts of the vessel particularly susceptible to corrosion are shot blasted and sprayed with zinc after construction. Weight can be saved by using aluminum for the superstructures, but it must be restricted to areas not likely to be subjected to blast, because it has a low melting point. Abrupt changes in the shape of superstructures, such as the forecastle and the long midship superstructure, cause a loss in strength, and for this

▲ Six F14A Tomcats fly in formation over the USS *Nimitz*, a nuclear-powered aircraft carrier. The *Nimitz* has an angled flight deck, 1,092 ft. (333 m) long, which enables aircraft to land in rapid succession. Four elevators transport aircraft to and from the flight deck. Fuel and munitions are stored in the lower regions of the vessel.

reason, gradual changes are made by sloping the ends of these structures.

Watertight subdivision, which is essential to keep the ship afloat in the event of damage, is achieved by including a number of watertight transverse bulkheads, longitudinal bulkheads, decks, and watertight flats. The transverse bulkheads are usually stiffened vertically and the plates that make up the bulkhead are welded together horizontally. The T-bar longitudinals are connected strongly to the bulkheads with stiffeners to help integrate the structure. Access through the bulkhead is often necessary, so watertight doors are fitted. They must be above the deep-waterline level, and all watertight compartments not normally occupied are closed when the vessel is at sea.

Lattice masts were common on many vessels, but the weight of modern equipment, such as the large radar scanner, has led to the introduction of the plate mast, which is stronger and less prone to vibration. The inside of the mast protects the cables and junction boxes that are used to connect the antennas and radar.

Frigates

Originally, frigates specialized in one primary role: antisubmarine, antiaircraft, or aircraft direction. Several frigates may be required at one time to cover all of these duties, so today the Oliver Hazard Perry class of guided missile frigate is designed to be much more versatile. Other types, such as the Garcia and Bronstein class, were used as fleet escorts, owing to their higher speed and superior weapons capability.

▼ The electronic warfare module of the USS *Kitty Hawk* aircraft carrier where the advanced combat direction system (ACDS) is used to integrate the ship's sensors, intelligence sources, and weapons.

The Perry-class guided missile frigates carry a single missile launcher, which can fire both Standard medium-range surface-to-air and Harpoon surface-to-surface missiles—the magazine carries 36 Standards and four Harpoons. There are also two triple-torpedo tubes. The principal gun is a 76 mm, which fires up to 90 rounds a minute. A 20 mm gun is also fitted aft above the double hangars, which house two light airborne multi-purpose system (LAMPS) helicopters carried as added antisubmarine defense.

The overall length is 445 ft. (135.6 m), and full load displacement is 4,100 tons (4,166 tonnes). The main engines are two General Electric gas turbines capable of giving the frigate a top speed of 29 knots. It also has two retractable auxiliary propeller pods, which can be deployed aft of the sonar dome. They improve berthing capability and provide get-home power in the event of the failure of the main engines or propeller shaft.

A modern frigate is capable of running in a closed-down condition in the event of a nuclear attack. This mode of operation is possible because there are contingencies to prevent contamination through the ventilation systems. In the upper structure of a frigate, it is usual to have a radar room, communications control room, electronic warfare office, enclosed bridge, and computer rooms. No. 1 deck accommodation consists of the wardroom, officers' and petty officers' berths, galley, recreation rooms, and sick bay. No. 2 deck is subdivided into gun bays, power rooms, gunners' stores, weapons spare gear store, senior and junior ratings commissary, galley, scullery, missile magazine, ship control center, engineers' workshop, and accommodation for junior ratings. The No. 3 deck contains the sonar instrument room, junior ratings' mess, refrigeration stores, and fuel stores. In the bottom of the vessel are the magazine and diesel oil tanks; there is also provision for the storage of helicopter fuel, lubricating oil, and the sonar system.

Guided-missile destroyers

The guided-missile destroyer (GMD) is larger than a frigate and often approaches the size of the older conventional cruiser. The U.S. Navy's Kidd class, for example, has a full displacement of 9,783 tons (8,804 tonnes). Its armaments include two 5 in. (130 mm) guns, eight Harpoon surface-to-surface missiles, LAMPS helicopters with homing torpedoes to act as an antisubmarine weapon, and the new threat upgrade (NTU) antiair warfare (AAW) system, designed to meet the technological requirements of 21st century battles. Kidd-class destroyers are 563 ft. (171.6 m) long and have a top speed of around 33 knots. The crew of

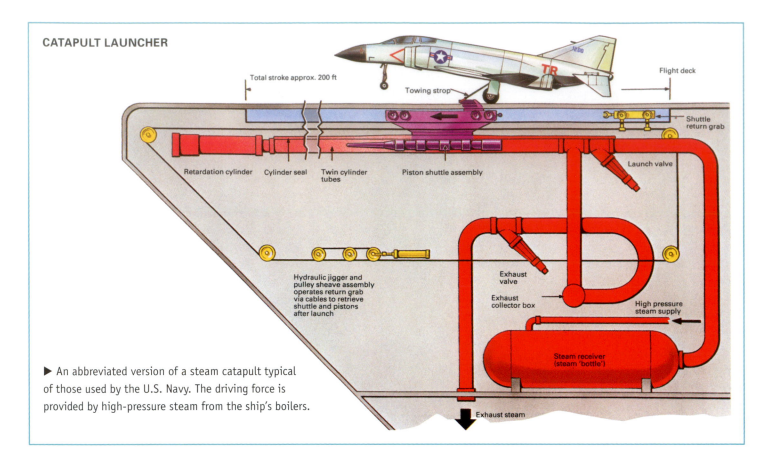

CATAPULT LAUNCHER

Total stroke approx. 200 ft

Towing strop

Flight deck

Shuttle return grab

Retardation cylinder

Cylinder seal

Twin cylinder tubes

Piston shuttle assembly

Launch valve

Hydraulic jigger and pulley sheave assembly operates return grab via cables to retrieve shuttle and pistons after launch

Exhaust valve

Exhaust collector box

High pressure steam supply

Steam receiver (steam 'bottle')

Exhaust steam

▶ An abbreviated version of a steam catapult typical of those used by the U.S. Navy. The driving force is provided by high-pressure steam from the ship's boilers.

20 officers and 318 enlisted personnel have fully air-conditioned living and working spaces.

The U.S. Navy's more recently designed Arleigh Burke class is designed with a collective protection system against nuclear fallout and chemical or biological agents. Each ship's crew is protected by double air-locked hatches. There are fewer accesses to weather decks, and the air pressure in the interior of the ship remains higher than that outside, to prevent contaminants from leaking in. All incoming air is filtered, and greater reliance is placed on recirculating air inside the

ship. Exposed decks are designed simply to allow nuclear fallout to be washed off easily.

The main propulsion comes from four General Electric gas turbines fitted with a closed-cycle energy-recovery system, which uses the heat of the exhaust gases to heat steam to drive an extra turbine.

The entire ship, with the exception of the aluminum funnels, is constructed of steel. To provide added protection against attack, the bulkheads are made with double-spaced steel plate, and the combat system equipment rooms are shielded

◀ The USS *Anzio* (far left), seen here on maneuvers in the Baltic Sea, is a Ticonderoga-class guided-missile cruiser with a displacement of 9,600 tons (8,640 tonnes) and an overall length of 567 ft. (189 m). Cruisers are multi-mission ships used primarily in battle force roles. They are equipped with Tomahawk missiles, which give them additional long-range strike capabilities.

with Kevlar. Displacement is 8,300 tons (7,470 tonnes), and the ship's length is 505 ft. (154 m) overall. Each ship carries 23 officers and 300 enlisted personnel. The single 5 in. gun and the two 20 mm guns are controlled by the Seafire laser system. The ship also carries Harpoon and Tomahawk surface-to-surface, standard surface-to-air, and ASROC antisubmarine missiles—as well as being fitted with two triple-torpedo tubes. The ship's hull is designed with a large water-plane area that improves the ability of the ship to move at high speeds in rough seas.

Assault ships

Assault ships are used to transport and land heavy military equipment and personnel when there are no port facilities. The vessel carries two types of landing craft, one for personnel and light equipment and the other for tanks and other heavy vehicles. An assault ship can carry four of the large landing craft in a floodable dock compartment at the end. Troops are transferred to landing craft from No. 1 deck when the craft is lowered from the davits and bowsed into (held against) the ship's side to prevent relative motion. Inside the dock there are batten boards to prevent damage to the landing craft or the ship, and there is a sloping apron up to the tank-deck level to act as a beach to reduce the wave motion in the dock and as a hard loading area for the landing craft. The apron is made of steel gratings. A hinged gate is used at the aft end to close the dock.

◀ A standard missile being launched from the USS *Thach* during a missile test exercise. This Oliver Hazard Perry-class frigate uses SM-1 MR (medium range) standard surface-to-air or surface-to-surface missiles, which can be used against ships and aircraft and also against other missiles.

▼ A Ch-46 Sea Knight helicopter delivers supplies to the USS *Constellation*, a Kitty Hawk-class aircraft carrier. The green jerseys indicate that these crew members are in charge of arresting gear, catapults, and cargo handling.

The dock floor is above the waterline, and the space is dry during transit, but for a seaborne assault, the ballast tanks in the vessel are quickly flooded to bring the ship down to a deep draft and so flood the dock. Vehicle spaces are well protected by steel bulkheads, and the ventilation system is designed to remove fuel vapor and dangerous gases.

The vessel is heavily stiffened to withstand the variations in loading due to ballasting and cargo movements. No. 2 deck, over the dock, must withstand the dynamic weight of the helicopter and requires heavy deck beams for support, because pillars cannot be used in that region. The tank deck is supported by rows of pillars fitted in the vehicle space below, which are in turn supported by the bottom structure in the ship; ballast tanks are arranged over the length of the bottom structure, with fuel tanks and stores in the center portion. The flight deck can be used for extra vehicle storage if required.

Steam turbines are used for main propulsion, and the engine room is below the vehicle deck. Accommodation is sited forward and in the superstructure, and various stores are arranged on lower decks. These ships are equipped with medical facilities and double as offshore hospitals.

Aircraft carriers

Aircraft carriers are complex ships with special requirements. Their decks must be well above the waterline so that aircraft can land in bad weather,

and they must be clear, with the bridge and funnel, if there is one, on the starboard side. The hangar deck must be a clear space with a depth extending through two decks. To avoid passing the boiler uptakes through the hangar deck, they are led across to the starboard side and then up to the funnel.

Armaments to protect the the U.S. Navy's 97,000-ton (87,300-tonne) Nimitz class of aircraft carriers consist of three Basis Point Defense Missile Systems with Sea Sparrow missiles and 85 aircraft. Two pressurized-water nuclear reactors drive four turbines, providing the carrier with a top speed of over 30 knots and generating 8,000 kW of electrical power. These aircraft carriers have a total height from keel to mast of 244 ft. (74 m) and a width of 257 ft. (78 m). The flight deck of a carrier must be long enough—1,092 ft. (333 m) in the case of the Nimitz class—to give sufficient landing area aft and catapult length forward to accelerate the heaviest aircraft.

A crew of between 5,000 and 6,000 personnel is necessary for such large vessels, and because of the complexity and scale of operations, a system of color coded uniforms is worn by the flight deck crew to make their function easily recognizable. Yellow is worn by officers and aircraft directors; green is for arresting-gear and catapult crew, purple for fuel handlers, brown for chock and chain runners, red for ordnance handlers and crash and salvage crew, and blue for tractor drivers.

The large crew of Nimitz-class carriers are provided with many of the amenities available in a small town, such as a post office with its own ZIP code, a library, a hospital, a fire department, two barbershops, and their own newspaper.

Four elevators serve both ends of the hangar for transportation to and from the flight deck. To maintain the aircraft, several workshops are arranged around the hangar on the port and starboard sides of the ship. Aircraft munitions and aircraft fuel are stored in lower regions of the vessel to give maximum protection. The sides of the ship are compartmented, and vulnerable areas are protected by 2.5 in. (6.3 cm) thick plating.

The 4.5-acre (1.8 ha) flight deck has four catapults, each of which can accelerate a 37-ton (33-tonne) jet to 180 mph (288 km/h) in around 300 ft. (91 m). At the aft end of the catapult, protection from the jet blast is necessary to prevent following aircraft from being damaged by hot exhaust gases. The deck panels must also be water cooled in this region to prevent overheating.

Firefighting arrangements on these vessels are extremely important, and the hangars can be quickly drenched by a sprinkler system operated from remote-control pumps.

Steam catapult

The steam catapult was first used experimentally aboard the British light fleet carrier HMS *Perseus* in 1949. In 1953, it was adopted by the Royal

◀ The British Navy's HMS *Ark Royal* is an Invincible-class through-deck carrier designed specifically for vertical and short takeoff and landing (V/STOL) aircraft, such as the Harrier AV8. *Ark Royal* also carries AEW Sea King helicopters. The raised ski jump enables short takeoff runs with full payload capacity.

◄ An F/A-18C Hornet is readied for launch as it sits on a catapult on the flight deck of the aircraft carrier USS *Enterprise*. This carrier is 1,101 ft. (336 m) long and carries 85 aircraft.

Navy as the standard replacement for earlier systems, which used compressed air to accelerate the aircraft to flying speed, and was shortly afterward chosen by the U.S. Navy for installation on its carriers. Installations vary from ship to ship, but the one installed on the ships of the U.S. Navy's Nimitz-class carriers is typical: four C13 Model 1 catapults, each 310 ft. (94.5 m) long, can apply more than 4 g (g is a measurement of acceleration equivalent to that of Earth's gravity) acceleration to the heaviest aircraft operated from the ships.

Each catapult consists of two piston-and-cylinder combinations lying alongside one another in the fore-and-aft direction of the deck. The two pistons of each catapult are connected by means of a keyed joint, in the center of which is an upright girder called a shuttle. The shuttle has rollers that run along guide rails fixed under the deck. On the shuttle is a towing block that projects up through a slot in the deck. To launch an aircraft, steam is released into the cylinders, driving the pistons (and shuttle) forward. The slots in the cylinders (along which the joint connecting the pistons and shuttle runs) are normally sealed by a flexible metal strip. During launchings, as steam pressure drives the pistons through the cylinders, the sealing strip is moved from its seat ahead of the connecting joint and reseated behind it by special devices attached to the piston assemblies. These prevent the steam pressure from falling as the pistons travel forward. Each cylinder is 18 in. (45.7 cm) in diameter.

At the end of their travel, the shuttle and pistons are brought to rest by means of a retardation cylinder in the bow of the ship. Because it lies on its side and not vertically, the retardation cylinder has to be kept full of water by means of a spray system that directs a jet of fluid spirally around its inside walls. After launch, the pistons and shuttle are pulled back to the starting point by a cable-and-pulley-block system.

Steam is supplied to the catapults from steam receivers—referred to as "bottles"—which are kept filled by the ship's boilers. A system of valves is used to control the flow and pressure of steam supplied to the catapults; the heavier the aircraft being launched, the higher the steam pressure required.

▼ The USS *Benfold*, an Arleigh Burke-class destroyer, fires its 5 in. (12.7 cm) Mk 45 lightweight gun.

Arresting mechanism

When an aircraft lands on an aircraft carrier deck, its speed has to be cut from perhaps 150 mph (240 km/h) to rest in about 200 ft. (60 m). The aircraft may well weigh up to 37 tons (33 tonnes), so the kinetic energy—the energy of motion—to be dissipated is considerable.

At the same time, the retardation must be smooth: there must be no sudden snatch, which might break the pilot's neck, overstress the aircraft's frame, or disturb its landing path. Ideally, the retardation should be progressive, starting from nothing, building up to a maximum, and then remaining constant until the aircraft finally comes to a standstill.

Arresting mechanisms are designed to achieve this aim, and in principle, they all operate in the same way. At its tail end, the aircraft is fitted with a hinged hook that hangs below the level of the wheels of the aircraft during the landing run. As the plane comes in over the deck, the hook engages with a steel arresting wire stretched across the deck and raised a few inches by bow-shaped steel springs to allow the hook underneath. The ends of the arresting wire are connected to the energy-absorbing gear.

One widely used system is based on the ram effect of a piston pushing hydraulic fluid through a control, or throttling, valve. As the arresting wire is pulled out, it runs through a series of guiding pulley wheels—or, in naval terms, sheaves —which transfer the movement to the ram through a series of pulleys mounted on both the fixed cylinder and the moving ram housed below the carrier deck.

Movement of the main arresting wire by, say, a distance of 16 ft. (5 m) moves the final pulley, which is coupled to the piston, by only 1 ft. (30 cm). This reduction in movement keeps the size of the piston within bounds and gives a useful mechanical advantage.

The retarding force is actually the hydraulic pressure in the cylinder, which depends on the ram speed. As the aircraft and therefore the ram slows, this force would decrease. So that the retardation remains constant, the control valve is arranged to provide greater restriction as more wire is pulled out. This device can be adjusted to allow for different weights of aircraft.

The outflow from the hydraulic cylinder goes into a chamber, where it compresses a gas to store the energy. This energy is used to reset the system and pull the arresting wire back to its original position, the compressed gas forcing the hydraulic fluid back into the cylinder with the aid of a pump to overcome the energy losses in the system.

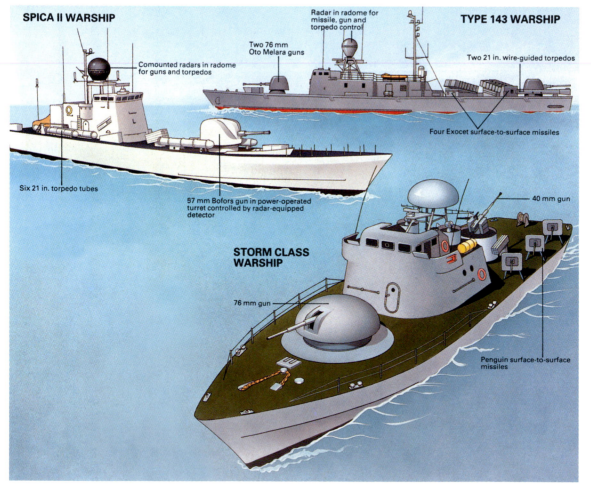

SPICA II WARSHIP

Comounted radars in radome for guns and torpedos

Two 76 mm Oto Melara guns

Radar in radome for missile, gun and torpedo control

TYPE 143 WARSHIP

Two 21 in. wire-guided torpedos

Four Exocet surface-to-surface missiles

Six 21 in. torpedo tubes

57 mm Bofors gun in power-operated turret controlled by radar-equipped detector

STORM CLASS WARSHIP

76 mm gun

40 mm gun

Penguin surface-to-surface missiles

◀ Far left: The Swedish Spica class II is armed with six 21 in. torpedo tubes and one 57 mm gun. The warship can reach a top speed of 40 knots. Left: The German Type 143 fast-attack craft is armed with four Exocet surface-to-surface missiles and two 76 mm guns. The craft's top speed is 38 knots. Bottom: A Norwegian Storm-class craft capable of carrying six Penguin surface-to-surface missiles equipped with 397 lb. (180 kg) warheads; the other armament includes one 76 mm and one 44 mm gun.

Resetting at speed is important when a large number of aircraft have to be landed in a short time. After an aircraft has landed, the arresting wire is inspected quickly for faults and then is pulled back tight across the deck, the whole operation taking only about 20 seconds.

Patrol boats

Patrol boats are used by many nations for police work along their coasts and for rescue operations. Some vessels have antisubmarine weapons and are well armed with guns. The majority are very fast, and some are fitted with hydrofoils. Many are powered by gas turbines. A conventional gunboat will have accommodation for officers and senior and junior ratings. The gun is armed from a revolving magazine below deck at the forward end. The operations room, enclosed bridge, and radio room are situated on the strengthened deck aft of the gun. Twin diesels are used to power the boat, and the engine room contains two alternators and a control room with the main switchboard. Some nations have vessels that are between the size of a frigate and a patrol boat. These vessels, corvettes, can perform most of the peacetime duties of a frigate with greater economy, while providing training for naval personnel.

Minesweepers

Minesweepers are small vessels—the U.S. Navy's Osprey class of coastal mine hunters, for example, has a displacement of 893 tons (907 tonnes) and is 188 ft. (57 m) long. The main function of minesweepers is to clear shipping lanes into port by sweeping and recovering mines. Equipment on board the vessel must be able to deal with the several types of mines.

Buoyant mines connected with a wire to a sinker are moored to the seabed and will explode on contact with a ship's hull. The minesweeper's paravane will cut the wire holding the mine, and it can then be destroyed by gunfire when it floats to the surface. An influence mine will explode when the magnetic field of a ship comes into the vicinity. These mines are destroyed by trailing a cable well astern carrying a pulsating electric current supplied by the generator on the minesweeper. Acoustic mines will explode from the noise made by a ship, usually by the propellers. This type of mine is destroyed by a drum with a noise generator that is towed some distance behind the minesweeper. Some mines may be activated by the pressure change in the sea as a ship passes overhead.

The hull of a minesweeper must be made from a nonmagnetic material to avoid activating magnetic mines when sweeping. Many of these vessels are made from wood and aluminum. The U.S. Navy's Avenger class of mine-countermeasure vessels are made with wooden hulls sheathed with fiberglass. Minesweepers' hulls are also made of glass-reinforced plastic (GRP). The lightness and nonmagnetic properties of plastic make this material ideal for the construction of minesweepers.

SEE ALSO: Boat building • Gun • Mine, explosive • Missile • Navigation • Rudder • Ship • Sonar • Torpedo

Washing Machine

◀ Front-loading washing machines are more expensive to purchase than top loaders but are becoming increasingly popular owing to their lower water and energy consumption.

In the latter half of the 19th century, a forerunner of the washing machine was developed in the form of an octagonal wooden washing box, often associated with a mangle to wring the articles after washing. The box was first filled with hot, soapy water, and then the clothes. The box was rotated by means of a handle, which tumbled the clothes. This principle of tumbling the laundry inside a cylinder is the basis of modern washing machines, for both home and industrial use, although other designs are also employed. Two basic types of cylinder washing machines are available: top loading, or vertical axis, machines; and front loading, or horizontal axis, washing machines (HWMs).

Top-loading washing machines

The most widely sold type of washing machine in the United States is the top loader, which is designed to handle up to about 9 lbs. (4 kg) of washing. The articles are placed in a perforated steel drum that revolves in an outer container; the top is closed and the appropriate wash cycle pre-set on a timer. Program selection is by means of a dial, by push button, or by keyplate. The program timer enables a combination of factors, such as presoaking, water temperature, number and length of washes and rinses, and the length of spin to be selected according to the amount of soiling and the type of fabric—cotton, wool, synthetics, and so on—or its colorfastness.

After selecting the program, the machine is switched on, and water enters through an automatic water valve, which cuts out when the pressure switch sends it a signal. The pressure switch consists of a diaphragm that is forced upward by air pressure in the water-level tube from the outer drum until it trips a microswitch, completing the electric circuit and closing the valve. The water level, low for washing robust fabrics and high for washing delicate fabrics and also for rinsing, is preset for a particular wash by the program timer. The two water levels are attained by means of different microswitches in the pressure switch.

The program is controlled either by a single face cam or about 15 to 20 edge cams, driven by a synchronous motor. Each of the 15 to 20 cams has a characteristic profile enabling it to be examined by spring contacts for selection of a particular operation, which may be, for example, the length of a washing or rinsing cycle or the changeover to spin or the opening of the water inlet valve. Various operations may, however, work simultaneously—such as the filling of the machine with water and the turning of the washing drum.

The face cam serves a similar purpose, but it is contoured with various precisely shaped humps that guide the functions.

Apart from the synchronous motor to run the program controls, there is also the washing-drum motor, which can be made to reverse the direction of drum rotation continuously during washing and rinsing. This motor also operates spin drying by centrifugal action, rotating the drum at speeds up to 1,100 rpm. Wastewater from washing, rinsing, and spinning is removed by the drain pump.

Most automatic washing machines in the United States use hot and cold water supplies, whereas some European machines rely only on the cold water supply, the required heating being done by the elements in the machine. In all cases, the actual water temperature is controlled by a thermostat.

Most countries lay down standards of both electric and mechanical safety. For example, the door is automatically locked once a machine is in operation and is released only on completion of the program and following a short time lag by means of an electromagnet.

Horizontal-axis washing machines

Horizontal-axis washing machines account for over 90 percent of washing machine sales in Europe and are becoming increasingly popular in the United States. With a front-loading machine, the clothes are placed in a horizontal drum, which requires less water and therefore uses less energy to heat the water. In addition, less detergent is necessary in front loaders, and faster spin speeds as more of the detergent is removed during rinsing and more of the water is removed in the final spin, and thus, drying time is reduced. Currently, front-loading machines are more expensive to purchase than top loaders, but higher cost is compensated for by the reduced running costs of horizontal-axis machines as well as their reduced impact on the environment.

One development of the front-loading washing machine is a design produced by Dyson that instead of one drum has two counterrotating horizontal drums. Two drums create a motion that flexes fabric and thus helps the detergent to penetrate the weave and clean more efficiently. Another design places the drum at a 15-degree angle for easier loading and unloading.

Fuzzy logic

An improvement in the design of automatic washing machines has been the introduction of a computer technology known as fuzzy logic.

▼ Sales literature depicting the components of a fully automatic washing machine. Clothes are loaded in through the top of the machine, and a suitable program is selected. When the machine is switched on, water enters through an automatic valve that closes when the tub is full. A central agitator, run by an electric motor, moves the clothes around in the water. A heavy-duty pump removes water from the machine at programmed times in the washing machine cycle.

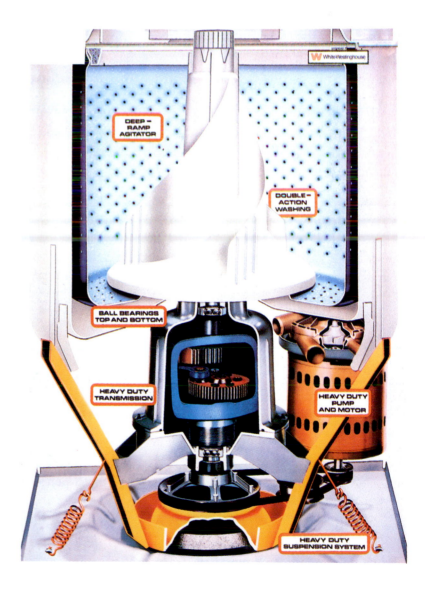

Conventional computers use a system of binary logic, in which information is represented as a series of zeros and ones. Fuzzy logic systems, however, use a multivalue logic in which levels of approximation may be represented. Information acquired in this way can then be combined to produce a logical inference. In washing machine control, this technology is employed to produce the optimum washing cycle for an individual washing load. Sensors in the washing machine are able to measure, for example, the volume of clothes and the level of transparency of the water and from the transparency estimate the amount of dirt in the water; the dirtier the clothes, the lower the level of transparency. The water reaches saturation when the level of dirt in the water ceases to increase. This process occurs more slowly when the dirt is made of grease, because grease does not dissolve in water as easily as other types of dirt. From the volume of clothes, level of dirt, and the time taken to reach saturation, a device called the fuzzy controller can estimate the optimum wash time for a particular load of washing.

Twin tubs

Semiautomatic washing machines, such as twin-tub models, comprising separate wash and spin containers, are still manufactured in some countries. Twin-tub machines incorporate a drain pump, and washing and rinsing times can be preset on a timer. The washing tub must always be filled with water to the prescribed level for each

◀ Below left: An energy-saving loading door, which registers the size of a wash. Above left: A dispenser for bleach and fabric softener. Bleach is diluted in the outer tub before it come in contact with the clothes; fabric softener is automatically added later, at the programmed time in the washing machine's cycle. Above center: The wash is rinsed with the help of lint-ejector vanes, which thoroughly remove suspended particles of dirt. Above: The user can set a control to measure the correct amount of water into the tub.

▶ This front loading washing machine manufactured by Dyson uses two counterrotating drums (visible through the transparent door), which have the effect of flexing the clothes as they are washed. This action enhances the ability of detergents to penetrate the weave of a fabric and so results in a cleaner wash.

wash and rinse. The washing is suspended in the water and agitated, for example, by an impeller or a pulsator on a central shaft or a central paddle. The centrifugal action of the spinner in a twin-tub machine is very efficient, as the spinner rotates at up to 3,000 rpm.

Green machines

A number of attempts have also been made to produce washing machines that are environmentally friendly. Automatic washing machines, for example, are available that are designed to use less water or that have short-cycle options. One recent development in washing machine technology is the Midas produced by Daewoo of Korea. This machine uses electrolysis to filter a variety of components out of tap water to produce ionized water, which is then used to dissolve dirt and disinfect clothes instead of detergents, which are potentially harmful to the environment. The manufacturers claim that the cleaning power of this machine is 15 to 20 percent greater than conventional machines and that it also uses less water. This machine also kills over 90 percent of the bacteria in clothes and so avoids some of the skin problems associated with these bacteria. Skin problems associated with the use of detergents are also avoided. Future developments in washing machine technology are likely to focus on improved efficiency and environmental impact.

SEE ALSO: Detergent manufacture • Dry cleaning • Electric motor • Laundry • Soap manufacture • Switch • Thermostat • Valve, mechanical • Water

Waste Disposal

Waste is an inevitable fact of life. Food consumption, for example, produces refuse ranging from banana skins to Styrofoam burger cartons. Play, study, and work creates garbage—think about every magazine that ends up in the trash, along with the endless sheets of computer paper and the packaging from compact discs and other products. The manufacturers of consumer goods produce waste daily on behalf of the consumer in their offices and production plants.

All these activities produce municipal solid waste (MSW)—better known as garbage or trash—that would accumulate and threaten public health if it were not dealt with. The activity that clears up this mess is called waste management. It consists of waste disposal and waste recycling.

History

Although drainage systems for sewage have been in existence for at least 5,000 years—there were sewers at Nineveh in Mesopotamia (present-day Iraq) around 3000 B.C.E.—organized procedures for the disposal of refuse or solid wastes are a comparatively recent invention. When the refuse produced by primitive communities became too offensive to live with, there was always the simple expedient of moving on to another site. Often, however, communities stayed where they were and caused a gradual rise in the ground level as refuse accumulated around them.

Of course, primitive garbage was mainly biodegradable—exceptions include the fragments of ceramics that archaeologists study today—whereas a significant proportion of modern waste consists of plastics that, left alone, would stay intact for millions of years. This fact, coupled with the increasing sizes and densities of urban societies, has exacerbated the need to deal with the castoffs of daily living. Figures from the U.S. Environmental Protection Agency (EPA) show that the scale of this task reached 230 million tons (209 million tonnes) per annum in 1999 for the United States alone and continues to grow.

Removal

Waste disposal consists of three tasks: removal from the source of waste, storage, and final disposal. For the average citizen, the solution to the waste disposal problem continues to be represented by the garbage collector. Labor for collection and transportation makes up most of the expenditure—in the United States, nearly 80 percent of the cost of waste disposal arises from the collection and transfer of refuse. From the house-

holder's point of view, probably the most significant event in the history of waste disposal has been the requirement in some communities of standard covered containers or tied plastic bags.

The first custom-built collection vehicle made its appearance in 1922. Collecting vehicles now incorporate two-way tipping, compaction, side loading, and other hydraulically operated features designed to increase collection efficiency, both in terms of the rate at which a single vehicle can collect waste and the amount it can store.

▲ Many refuse dumps have special days when householders can bring half-used cans of paint, solvents, oil, and other substances banned from inclusion in collected garbage. They can then be recycled or disposed of in a controlled manner that will not pollute landfill sites.

MUNICIPAL WASTE INCINERATION

One of the greatest problems in disposing of municipal waste is its sheer volume, particularly where the opportunities for opening new landfill facilities are scarce. Incineration is a highly effective means of reducing the bulk of waste—by up to 90 percent—and the heat it produces can be put to use.

The three basic stages of incineration are primary combustion (drying and ignition), secondary combustion, and clinker burnout. Associated operations include the delivery and segregation of waste prior to incineration, the treatment of combustion gases before their release to the environment, and the exploitation of waste heat to produce steam for heating and power generation.

The process starts with the delivery of municipal waste in refuse trucks. In one plant layout, refuse trucks approach the incinerator on a ramp that leads up to the edge of a huge concrete bunker. There they add their contents to the stockpile of refuse awaiting treatment. In some plants, refuse is grabbed by a mechanical claw and fed direct to the incinerator. In others, it is segregated into materials for recycling and for combustion.

The purpose of waste segregation, apart from the recovery of recyclable materials, is to reduce the amount of noncombustible material that has to be dried and heated to ignition temperature, thereby saving heat that would otherwise be lost. Ferrous metals (iron and its alloys) are easy to extract, since they can be picked out by spreading the waste on a conveyor belt that passes under an electromagnet. Other noncombustible materials can be collected

by other techniques, hand sorting, for example. Segregation usually occurs in a recycling plant near the incinerator and is followed by shredding to make the material easier to burn. The product of segregation and shredding is called refuse-derived fuel, or RDF.

Refuse and RDF contain some moisture, especially from food waste—potato peelings and traces of liquids left in drinks containers, for example. This moisture must be removed before the combustion begins, and the drying is done by heat from refuse and fuel that are already burning. Air preheated by combustion gases can be used to dry waste before charging, but it is more usual to dry waste on automatic grates inside the incinerator. In this case, waste is tipped at the top end of a sloping grate and is dried by the hot combustion gases as it moves down the grate.

The combustion process is often aided by the addition of a fuel, such as oil or coal. Air for combustion is blown in through the gate and can be preheated by heat exchange with the exhaust gases to assist the drying and combustion processes. Temperatures at this stage need to be more than 1400°F (750°C) for effective combustion to occur, and some authorities require that the temperature of combustion gases remains above 1750°F (950°C) for two seconds or more to discourage harmful or even toxic products of partial combustion from forming.

The final stage is burnout, in which the combustion of the slower-burning components of the refuse mix finally comes to an end. It should occur before the solid product of combustion,

▶ This diagram shows a typical layout for a municipal waste incinerator. Its waste heat can be used to produce steam for industry, for district heating systems, or even for generating electricity.

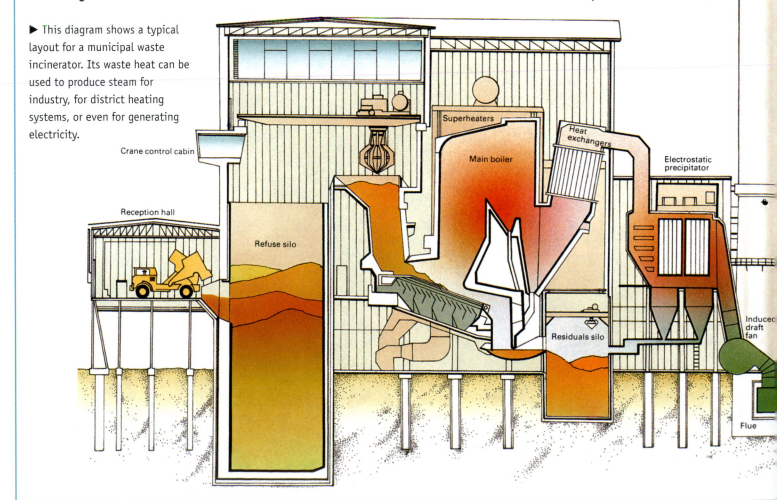

Crane control cabin

Superheaters

Heat exchangers

Main boiler

Electrostatic precipitator

Reception hall

Refuse silo

Residuals silo

Induced draft fan

Flue

called clinker or bottom ash, drops off the end of the grate. The factors that determine whether combustion is complete at this stage include the temperature profile of the incinerator, the feed rate, and the time taken for material to traverse the grate. The main components of clinker are the minerals left after the organic component has been eliminated by burning. If unsegregated waste is used, the content of metals, glass, and pot will be higher than if RDF is used. The physical form of clinker depends on combustion conditions and incinerator design. If the temperature exceeds around 1800°F (1000°C), some components of the ash start to melt. The ash then runs through the grate and forms granules if it drops into a trough of cooling water. Under most circumstances, this form of clinker is easier to handle than powdery ash.

Normal requirements are that clinker should contain no more than 0.3 percent putrescible material (unburned organic waste) and less than 5 percent free carbon (char). If the clinker contains significant amounts of toxic materials, such as heavy metals, it must be handled as hazardous waste and buried in appropriately secure landfill sites; otherwise, clinker can be buried in normal landfill or used as a filler for construction work.

The other waste stream from an incinerator is formed by fly ash and waste gases. Fly ash can be collected by cyclonic filters, electrostatic precipitators, and bag filters. It is then united with the bottom ash. The gases consist mainly of carbon dioxide and water vapor (from combustion) and oxygen and nitrogen (from the air feed). Of these, only carbon dioxide is of concern, since it is a greenhouse gas. Minor components of the gas stream—but of more serious environmental impact—can include carbon monoxide (poisonous); oxides of sulfur and nitrogen (SO_x and NO_x—acid-rain gases); polycyclic aromatic hydrocarbons (potential carcinogens, or cancer-causing agents); and polychlorinated hydrocarbons, such as polychlorinated biphenyls (PCBs), dioxins, and dibenzofurans—all of which are carcinogens. The formation of carbon monoxide can be avoided by ensuring that the incinerator receives enough air for complete combustion so that any carbon monoxide burns to form carbon dioxide. Oxides of sulfur can be absorbed on lime (calcium oxide) in desulfurization equipment, and nitrogen oxides can be reduced to nitrogen by injecting ammonia into the waste gases.

All the organic compounds in the waste gases—including those that contain chlorine and other halogens—would be converted into carbon dioxide and hydrogen halides (which would absorb on the lime if the incinerator conditions were always adequate for their complete combustion). However, there is a risk of incomplete combustion—and the formation of toxic compounds—if the incinerator design or operating conditions allow combustion gases to follow relatively cool paths, or if a sudden change in the feed rate or quality of fuel causes a drop in overall temperature. Hence, incinerators are often fitted with activated-charcoal filters that scrub organic compounds from the waste gases after they have passed through bag filters.

Some waste-disposal agencies are now turning to fluidized-bed combustors as alternatives to grate incinerators. In these combustors, the refuse burns as it falls through a bed of sandlike material

▲ Smoke is a form of waste that indicates a poorly run furnace. Modern incinerators burn refuse cleanly, and any smoke particles are trapped from the flue gases before their release to a smokestack. The white clouds seen issuing from incinerators are mainly condensing steam.

that is kept bubbling by an updraft of hot air and combustion gases. The motion of the bed material encourages combustion by scouring combustion products from the surfaces of burning particles and allowing more oxygen to get to them. Also, the bed is a reservoir of heat that prevents rapid fluctuations of temperature, so it is easy to keep the bed in a condition that promotes full combustion. Finally, addition of lime to the bed traps sulfur oxides and removes the need for separate desulfurization equipment. Clinker falls to the bottom of the bed, where it is removed together with bed material and separated before the bed material is reinjected.

Heat from incinerator gases is used to produce steam in a boiler. That steam can be used to heat houses and offices, or it can be used to run a combined heat and power (CHP) plant, which uses the steam to drive turbogenerators—producing electricity that can be sold—before it is used for heating.

Public and political opinion on the environmental impact of waste incineration is divided, however. Some people argue that a well-run incinerator spares the environment by reducing the area of land needed for refuse dumping while producing heat and power as a bonus. Others argue that emissions of greenhouse gases and, potentially, of toxic products make incinerators environmental liabilities that should be shut down at once. Perhaps because of this debate, the amount of refuse incinerated annually in the United States has remained at around 15–20 million tons (14–18 Mtonnes) since 1990 and is declining, whereas total waste is increasing toward 240 million tons (218 Mtonnes) per annum.

In some communities the garbage collector has become obsolete. In one Swedish residential area, comprising 140 units, refuse collection has been replaced by a pneumatic system that consists of refuse chutes and an underground tunnel extending for 1.5 miles (2.4 km). Air is drawn through the tunnel by turbo-exhausters, and the resulting vacuum causes valve plates on the chutes to open and air to be drawn in from the storage areas at the tops of the chutes whenever their hatches open. Refuse is drawn into the underground tunnel and carried at speeds of up to 50 mph (80 km/h) to a silo. The refuse is dumped into the top of the silo, while the air is drawn off from the tunnel by the turbo-exhausters and filtered before being returned to the atmosphere.

▲ An electromagnet loads scrap ferrous metals, such as steel, into a basket. This basket will tip its contents into a furnace, where they will be melted to make mild steel.

Cutting back on trash

The increasing concern of environmentalists has raised the level of public consciousness of what happens to municipal solid waste once it has left the home. A number of approaches have been taken to reduce the amount of MSW produced.

One approach is to reduce the volume of trash. Devices for this task include combined electric shredders and wastebaskets that compact the bulk of paper ingested. Small-scale trash compacters are also available to consumers; some models are capable of reducing the volume of garbage by 90 percent and even of wrapping the compacted waste in a sealed plastic bag. These measures reduce the volume of trash produced, not the actual amount. In fact, where collectors charge by the number of trash cans emptied, such measures actually worsen the situation by reducing the incentive to produce less waste.

Waste-disposal units incorporated in kitchen sinks allow organic waste, such as food scraps, to be macerated and flushed into the sewerage system. This solution reduces the volume of refuse that reaches the garbage can and avoids the problem of organic waste rotting away in household trash cans. However, the use of waste-disposal units only transfers the final disposal problem from MSW disposal to the sewage works. A better solution for home gardeners is to dispose of their organic waste in small-scale composters.

The most effective way to reduce the volume of trash is to reduce it at its source. Manufacturers and packagers aim to reduce to a minimum the amount of material—usually packaging—that will become trash during the life cycle of the product. A good example can be found in the manufacture of beverage cans, whose necks have become progressively narrower over the years to reduce the area of the top end of the can, which is made of the thickest metal.

Measures such as these have helped put the brakes on the rate of increase of MSW, as can be seen in the EPA figures for the late 20th century. Whereas the average amount of municipal solid waste produced by a U.S. citizen rose from 2.7 lbs. (1.2 kg) in 1960 to 4.5 lbs. (2.0 kg) in 1990—an increase of 67 percent in three decades—the increase during the following decade was only 0.1 lbs. (0.05 kg), or 2 percent.

Efforts to promote recycling have also started to bear fruit: in the United States, the proportion of MSW that was recycled rose from 9.6 percent in 1980 to 16.2 percent in 1990 and then to 27.8 percent by 1999. The same pattern is repeated in many other countries, particularly where waste collectors promote segregation of waste in the household, a system that reduces the sorting at the refuse depot. Typical categories for segregation are glass, paper and card, and metal.

Composting

Composting has perhaps the longest history as an organized process of recycling, since it returns to the land the useful nutrients in refuse. The Romans are believed to have dealt with their organic wastes in this way. Early methods included methodical layering and turning of waste to aerate it and to assist biological activity.

Mechanical composting concentrates on ways to improve the rate of decay by creating optimal conditions for biological digestion. Careful control is exercised over particle size, homogeneity, concentrations of nutrients for microorganisms, moisture content, temperature, agitation, and aeration. Horizontal rotating drums have been tried, as have multideck plants in which material gradually turns to compost as it works its way down the decks, but the most effective plants use multideck silo digesters, which are enclosed so that greater control over conditions is possible.

Landfill

Material that is not recycled or composted must be disposed of by landfill. This process encloses waste matter in a plastic-sealed tomb, where it

SPECIAL AND HAZARDOUS WASTE

Certain types of waste require treatment or containment to render them harmless to humans and the environment. Nuclear waste is an example, and a whole industry has grown out of the need to deal with its various grades. Many other types of waste present potential biological, chemical, and ecological threats, and each type demands a specific form of processing.

Chemical waste. Industries that make or use chemicals also produce chemical waste. Those that manufacture chemicals are best equipped to deal with potential waste at source by recycling it into the manufacturing process or by using it as a raw material in another process.

Chemical waste that cannot be recycled must be disposed of according to its nature. Reactive wastes include those that are corrosive, flammable, or explosive. Corrosive agents—mostly acids and bases—are easily neutralized and diluted. The salt solutions that result are often innocuous and can be disposed of in the sewage stream. Most flammable wastes are safe to burn in incinerators provided there are adequate checks on the efficiency of combustion and flue gas treatment.

Reactive waste that explodes on contact with air, water, or any other chemical must first be treated to make it less reactive. The precise methods used depend on the chemistry of the waste. The products of the neutralization reaction are then treated as waste in their own right.

Toxic chemical waste is categorized as organic or inorganic toxic waste. One form of treatment for organic toxic waste, such as pesticide by-products, is incineration. Some cement manufacturers earn extra income by burning organic waste in their lime kilns, which operate at somewhat higher temperatures than those found in municipal incinerators. Strict monitoring of the flue gases ensures that no toxic materials are released to the environment.

Inorganic toxic waste differs from organic waste in that the toxicity usually stems from elements present in the waste—heavy metals, for example—rather than from the chemical groups that are present. Whereas incineration can destroy chemical groups, it cannot destroy elements, so it is not an option for inorganic waste. The best options are recycling or specialist landfill.

VOCs. Volatile organic compounds, or VOCs, are released by industries that use solvent-based substances, such as paints. They have the potential to cause a variety of problems—from strong odors to health damage—and many authorities impose strict limits on VOC releases.

Fortunately, VOCs are released mainly in drying ovens, where they can be drawn off in the hot air that circulates in the oven. Some ovens have afterburners that ignite the VOCs and use the heat produced to heat the oven. In other cases, VOCs are condensed in water baths that contain nutrient-fed microbes that convert them into harmless substances.

Hospital waste. Hospitals produce many different types of hazardous waste that require special treatment. Infectious waste, such as used dressings, can be made harmless by incineration but must be marked as biohazardous and handled with care. Sharp items, such as used scalpels, must be collected in rigid containers to reduce the risk of injury. Radioactive material, such as cobalt-60 cartridges from radiation therapy machines, must be handled like any other form of radioactive waste.

▶ This equipment processes the waste from an electroplating plant. The materials it handles include corrosive acids, poisonous cyanide salts, and plating solutions that contain mixtures of compounds. The plant recovers useful chemical reagents for recycling and chemically treats those that are beyond recovery so as to make them as innocuous as possible. The processed waste solutions are then evaporated to dryness to reduce the volume of waste to the minimum. The dry residues from evaporation are then pressed into cakes for disposal in troughs for hazardous waste.

gradually decays and collapses under the action of microbes on some of its components. Other components, such as plastic, remain intact.

A landfill site is started by placing an impermeable plastic lining in a pit that has been previously lined with compacted clay. These measures prevent waste products from contaminating the groundwater. Drains are placed at intervals to collect leachate—the product of rain falling on the landfill site and washing soluble matter from the refuse. The drainage pipes are buried in a porous layer of gravel that prevents their clogging. Once these structures are in place, earthmoving equipment spreads trash in layers, sandwiched between intermittent layers of soil, and compacts the layer structure. Compaction is necessary to make the most of the available area and also to help prevent subsidence once the landfill is complete.

When layering has finished, a network of perforated pipes is placed over the ground to collect the methane and other gases that will be generated by anaerobic microbial action for many years after the landfill has been sealed. An impermeable plastic layer is then spread over the landfill to prevent the ingress of water and reduce the quantity of leachate. This layer is then covered with a cap of soil, which weighs it down, and the soil is planted with grasses and shallow-rooted vegetation. These plants bind the soil together to reduce rain and wind erosion without posing the risk of their roots penetrating the plastic covering.

Landfill is often used to reclaim land, such as exhausted quarries. Many finished sites have been turned into parks or artificial ski slopes, and some have been used as bases for low-level construction. These activities help pay for the monitoring of leachate and gas emissions after the landfill has been sealed. Furthermore, landfill gas can be sold for use in factory furnaces and heating boilers.

Transfer stations

Where a landfill site is close to the city it serves, garbage may be dumped directly from the trucks that collect it from neighborhoods. In many cases, however, it is more efficient to dump from these trucks at waste transfer stations, which are usually multiactivity centers that undertake some sorting into recyclable material and nonrecyclable material. Many act as receiving centers for special wastes, such as old motor oil for reclamation, lead batteries for recycling, and CFC (chlorofluorocarbon) refrigerants for safe disposal.

The principal function of a waste transfer station is the preparation of MSW for dumping in landfills. In some cases, the station simply collects waste for loading into high-capacity trucks for delivery to the landfill. In others, at least some of the waste is dispatched for some form of processing to reduce its volume and improve the efficiency of the landfill. One type of processing is incineration, as described elsewhere in this article. The other technique is pulverization.

Pulverization is a mechanical means whereby garbage is crushed, screened, and shredded to decrease its volume. The chief methods are wet and dry pulverization. Wet pulverization uses the power of water jets, thereby reducing the need for more expensive sources of energy, but its use is more or less limited to on-site dumping because of weight considerations and the problems of transferring wet waste. A wet pulverizer consists of horizontal rotating drums. Water is sprayed into the drum as waste enters, and pulverization occurs because of the pounding effect of deflector plates, baffles, and rotation. Inner and outer drums are often used, with a separating screen so that the pulverized waste in one drum is forced through the screen into the other drum.

Dry pulverizers use shredders, hammers, and rotors to reduce the volume of refuse. In one model, refuse enters at the top, is drawn downward by counterrotating rotors, and is shredded by teeth at the base of the mill. Most are of the hammer-mill type with a closed casing, hammers (attached to disks or fitted directly to rotor shafts), and shredding teeth or a grid. Refuse enters the machine at the opposite end from the rotor; upward-swinging hammers hurl uncrushable material up into a hopper. Unlike wet models, dry pulverizers crush glass to a powder, and greater control of particle size is possible. Some machines spin at more than 2,000 rpm and can pulverize 70 tons (63 tonnes) of refuse per hour.

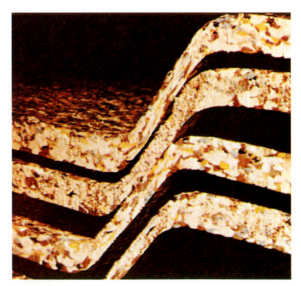

◀ These pallets, molded from plastic waste, are products of recycling.

SEE ALSO:	Fluidized bed • Pollution monitoring and control • Recycling • Wastewater treatment

Wastewater Treatment

In developed countries where water is plentiful and cheap, people often waste it, using much more than they need. It is used for drinking, bathing, and washing clothes and automobiles and for many industrial purposes. After it has been used, it is disposed of down the toilet or to a waste pipe or drain. In industrialized countries, each person on average uses between 50 and 100 gallons (227–455 l) of water per day, and it is critically important that the waste is cleaned before it enters rivers, lakes, estuaries, or bathing waters.

The need for wastewater or sewage as it is generally called, to be cleaned became apparent around the time of the Industrial Revolution. Initially the ability of organisms normally present in soil to remove or stabilize polluting matter was used extensively. For example, organic matter of animal origin contains nitrogen, often tied up in a complex form, but the soil organisms are able to break down the complexes and incorporate the nitrogen into the soil itself. So, by irrigating land with sewage effluent, a certain degree of purification could be effected. However, continuous fertilizing will upset the balance of the soil unless suitable crops are grown as part of the cycle—so the term *sewage farm* became part of the language.

Roughly at least 100 acres (40.1 ha) of land were required under this simple system for every million gallons (4.5 million l) per day of sewage to be dealt with (which would be the sewage from a population of about 20,000).

When limited amounts of sewage are discharged into running water, natural biological processes oxidize the organic matter and act to reduce bacterial contamination to give a reasonably clean water flow within a relatively short distance downstream of the discharge. With larger sewage flows, the oxygen dissolved in the water is insufficient to clear the organic matter, and pollution rapidly builds up. A measure of the strength of sewage is given by its biochemical oxygen demand (BOD) or chemical oxygen demand (COD), which are determined by standard laboratory procedures. The major aims of sewage treatment include reducing BOD and COD, suspended solids, and pathenogenic bacteria in the final discharge to an acceptable level (normally set by regulatory authorities).

Sewage itself consists of dirty water containing not only impurities in solution but also in the colloidal state, in the form of fine sediment and as bulky solid matter, originating as it does from

▲ Giant tanks are used at wastewater treatment plants to digest sludge anaerobically. Bacteria in the sludge change its consistency by breaking down any remaining fatty material and organic matter so that it is suitable for use as a fertilizer or in composting.

▲ The activated sludge process is used at many large secondary treatment plants. It helps bacteria naturally present in the sewage to break it down into simpler molecules by providing them with a continuous source of oxygen. Air is pumped into the tanks through ceramic diffusers fitted on the bottom. As it bubbles up through the wastewater it agitates the sewage into a suspension, where the bacteria can work on the sewage particles more easily.

washbasins, toilets, bathrooms, kitchens, and a whole range of industrial processes. There are three levels of treatment: primary, secondary, and tertiary. In primary treatment, about 60 percent of total suspended solids and 35 percent of BOD are removed. With secondary treatment, 85 percent of suspended solids and BOD are removed, and if tertiary treatment is added, it can remove over 99 percent of all the impurities in wastewater.

Treatment works

In a typical modern treatment works, the raw sewage is first passed through bar screens to take out the large objects that sometimes get into the flow. It is then passed through finer 2 in. (5 cm) screens to remove smaller solids and rags. The detritus from these screens is generally scraped onto conveyor belts that remove the waste to collection trucks, from where it is either disposed of to landfill or incinerated. The next step is to remove grit, which might otherwise damage pumps and other equipment, by passing the sewage through constant-velocity channels. These channels are of parabolic cross section, which reduces the speed of the flow to a constant rate of around 1 ft. per sec. (0.3 m/s). At this speed the grit settles out and can be removed for land disposal, while organic matter is carried on in the flow. Next fats are separated out by skimming the surface of the flow as it is aerated to ensure the maximum amount of fat floats to the surface.

The sewage is then passed through primary settlement tanks, in which the remaining finer sediment separates out and settles as sludge. This sludge is scraped from the bottom of the tanks by a slowly rotating bar, which pushes the sludge down the sloped tank base to a central exit point, from where it is piped to be thickened slightly in consolidation tanks before being pumped to a mechanical dewatering plant. There the sludge is conditioned with chemicals and pressed to form a partly dried cake, which can then go for further digestion and thickening or be injected as a fertilizer into farmland or forests at this consistency.

If further treatment is required, the sludge undergoes heated, anaerobic (in the absence of free oxygen) digestion in large digesters, where the anaerobic bacteria break down the remaining soluble fatty matter and some organic material, thus changing the sludge's consistency and constituent elements. The heating process kills off bacteria and parasites, allowing the sludge to be used more freely on land as a fertilizer. A by-product of digestion is a gas rich in methane, which is collected and used for heating and power production—it is often used to heat the digesters where it was produced, and treatment works now sometimes convert the spare gas into electricity that can be sold back to the electricity grid. Where sludge disposal is a problem, it may be dried further and then incinerated or sent to landfill.

Sludge dryers take sludge that already has a high solids content and pass it through heated beds that remove the remaining moisture. The resulting product can be in the form of dried granules or pellets, depending on the proprietary process. These pellets are completely sterilized by the heating process and are odorless and safe to handle. Sludge in this form is sold in bags as a fertilizer, sometimes to the public as well as farms.

Back in the main process, the settled sewage effluent passing over the weirs of the primary settlement tanks is subjected to what is known as secondary treatment. The most common process is a simple mechanical one, though there is a faster method of achieving further treatment called the activated sludge process, which is described below. In either case, the impurities in solution are oxidized and stabilized, and the effluent then passes through final settlement tanks to remove any extra sediment that may have been formed during the secondary treatment process. This sediment, which is rich in the organisms that break down sewage, is returned to the secondary settlement tanks to keep the biological processes going. At this stage, the effluent is often fit to be discharged to the receiving waters, depending on the treatment levels specified by legislation for the particular treatment works. These levels will depend on two factors: the vulnerability of the waters into which the effluent is to be discharged and the individual effluent standard set for the treatment works in question.

Biological filters

The most common type of biological filter is the percolating, or "trickle," filter, which consists of a circular or rectangular basin with side walls between 5 and 6 ft. (1.5–1.8 m) deep and a slightly sloping floor to permit free drainage. The basin is filled with some durable material, preferably with a rough or porous surface to give a large surface area per unit volume (clinker, hard coke, rough stone, and blast-furnace slag are all used). Settled sewage is sprayed evenly onto the surface of this medium through long bars pierced with holes at intervals of 1 ft. (30 cm) to provide the necessary even spread as they travel across the filter bed.

Spraying the sewage onto the filter leads to the establishment of a slime film on the medium. This film contains colonies of the necessary biological organisms, for instance, aerobic bacteria and larvae, which digest the organic matter in the sewage and form more stable substances. For example, carbonaceous matter is oxidized to carbon dioxide, and nitrogen first to nitrite and finally nitrate. The filter creates an environment in which the organisms can live, do their job, and propagate, and once established, a filter bed will continue to function indefinitely unless it suffers physical breakdown or damage from external causes.

In addition to the bacterial organisms in the slime, percolating filters tend to grow algae and other plant growths, which can be carried out of the filter. The flow is accordingly passed through sedimentation or humus tanks to collect this material before the water is discharged.

Activated sludge

In the activated sludge process, sewage that has undergone primary treatment is mixed with activated sludge—a suspension of coagulated matter in which live the organisms necessary for the biological purification of the sewage. These, as mentioned earlier, are found in the sediment from the final settlement tanks, a portion of which is returned to the secondary treatment process.

▼ When sewage enters a large wastewater treatment, it undergoes a series of processes to remove suspended solids, chemical pollutants, and pathogenic organisms. First, it is screened to remove grit, large objects, and rags. It is then held in large tanks, and the sludge is allowed to settle out while the liquid portion enters a secondary biological treatment stage, such as a trickling filter or the activated sludge process. The wastewater is again allowed to settle out, some of the sludge being returned to the secondary stage to seed the next batch. The sludge is fermented in a digestion tank before being taken away for land disposal. The cleaned water then passes through a series of polishing and disinfection processes before it is returned to a river or lake.

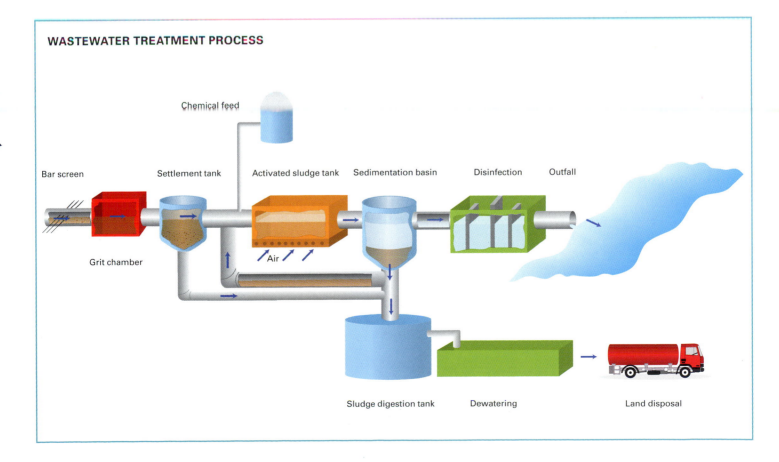

WASTEWATER TREATMENT PROCESS

Chemical feed

Bar screen — Settlement tank — Activated sludge tank — Sedimentation basin — Disinfection — Outfall

Grit chamber

Air

Sludge digestion tank — Dewatering — Land disposal

This mixture (known as mixed liquor) is passed through specially designed tanks in which air is supplied, either by blowing compressed air through fine diffusers or by mechanical means, using rotors that cause air to be taken in from the atmosphere. The sewage and organisms are kept in these tanks for about nine or ten hours, a period known as the retention time. During this time, the bacteria digest and stabilize the organic matter in much the same way as the bacteria in a percolating filter, though the activated sludge process is both faster (because the extra oxygen supplied in the air enables a far greater number of bacteria to grow and undertake the digestion process) and takes up less space in a treatment works. The activated sludge is allowed to settle out in tanks, and the cleaned effluent passes forward to be discharged or for further treatment.

A refinement of this type of treatment is the moving-bed bioreactor (MBR). In these systems, plastic media are added to an aerated basin, and the aerobic bacteria that digest organic matter form within the small plastic pieces. As the bacteria have a considerable surface area to colonize, this method is considered to provide more effective treatment in a shorter time.

Tertiary treatment

Where secondary treatment is not sufficient to comply with the regulations for discharge of effluent to a particular water body, for example, a water system that is eutrophic—vulnerable to nutrient input—further treatment may be

◀ An activated sludge tank that has been drained for cleaning. On the bottom are rows of ceramic diffusers that bubble air up through the wastewater to provide oxygen for the aerobic bacteria in the tank.

▼ Rotating scraper blades are used periodically to clean the floor of final sedimentation tanks. A build-up of sludge can upset the balance of aerobic and anaerobic organisms, which would affect the wastewater quality.

◀ After spending a number of hours in the activated sludge process, the effluent is passed to a series of sedimentation basins, where the sludge settles on the bottom of the tank and the treated wastewater is either discharged to the receiving water or sent for polishing in a tertiary treatment process.

◀ Many industrial processes, such as chemicals, textiles, paper making, and food processing, generate large quantities of effluent. Often, these wastes are very dilute and can be disposed to the sewerage system for treatment at the local wastewater plant. However, some are highly concentrated or polluted with substances that would be toxic to the bacteria in the treatment plant and have to be dealt with on site. This company has its own treatment plant where the effluent can be analyzed before being sent through a sequence of flocculation tanks, sedimentation basins, and clarifiers. Valuable chemicals can often be recycled in this way and harmful pollutants are prevented from contaminating the environment.

required either to remove nutrients or to remove more of the organic matter. A number of systems are used to achieve further cleaning, including ultraviolet (UV) light, membrane filters, micro-filters, and polishing sand filters.

UV treatment uses the capability of ultraviolet light at a particular wavelength to kill off bacteria and viruses. Secondary-treated effluent is passed through a channel in which UV lamps or tubes are suspended, and this simple process can produce crystal-clear effluent free from bacteria.

Membrane filters have tiny pores, as small as two microns (µm), through which the effluent has to be filtered. The effluent is circulated in a tank containing membrane units and is pulled through the membrane's pores by exerting a low pressure, or flux. There are various types of membrane systems, all using slightly different processes to achieve this goal—some membranes take the form of a series of flat plates, while others are compacted into banks of spirals or rods in order to save space if it is at a premium.

Also used in tertiary treatment are micros-trainers—filters made of a very fine steel mesh (though with holes relatively much larger than those found in membrane systems).

Beds of fine sand are also sometimes used to achieve a final polishing for effluent, to filter out any fine particles that may remain suspended following secondary treatment. In areas where the ground consists of peat, a similar effect is sometimes achieved by discharging secondary-treated effluent directly onto the ground.

Nutrient removal

At some treatment works, there may also be a requirement for nutrients such as phosphorus and nitrogen to be removed, because nutrients may cause algae to grow excessively in the receiving waters and harm aquatic life. Phosphorus is usually removed using chemical precipitation, though it increases the amount of sludge produced by a works. Nitrogen is removed using a two-stage biological process known as nitrification and denitrification, which takes place in a series of aerobic and anaerobic tanks. The nitrogen, in the form of ammonia, is first digested by bacteria to form nitrate. Next another type of bacteria further digests the nitrate to form harmless nitrogen gas.

Ammonia stripping is also used to remove nitrogen. In this process, chemicals are added to convert the ammonium ions to ammonia gas. As sewage is trickled through a columnar filter, ammonia gas is released from solution.

Other systems

One of the simplest forms of sewage disposal, used mainly in remote rural areas, is the cesspool. This is a tank or pit, watertight to prevent leakage

◀ Biological filter beds are used for treating wastewater. The beds are filled with clinker, or rough stone, which supports colonies of bacteria on its surface. The water is trickled over the surface by rotating arms. As it percolates down through the filter, the bacteria use nutrients in the sewage for food and break them down into harmless products. The clean water can then be discharged into a natural watercourse.

FACT FILE

- The year 1858 was known as the year of the great stink in London, because of the foul condition of the sewage-polluted Thames River. Deaths from cholera at this time exceeded 20,000 per annum and were chiefly attributable to a lack of an adequate waste-disposal system.

- The Chicago Tunnels and Reservoirs plan was designed to deal with a pollution problem that turned the Chicago River and Lake Michigan into virtual cesspits. Chicago produces more than 1.5 billion gallons of sewage per day in dry weather and can reach 60 billion gallons per day during severe storms. When it rained, the effluent had to be diverted straight into the lake to avoiding swamping the wastewater treatment plant. Now the sewage is held in huge underground caverns until the treatment plant can deal with the extra flow.

- Remotely controlled sewer-pipe crawlers are used to monitor the internal condition of many sewer pipes. The crawlers, which are in fact cylindrical cameras mounted on runners, relay pictures of pipe internal surfaces back to a control unit such as a specially equipped van for detailed examination.

into watercourses, into which sewage is drained. It is emptied two or three times per month, and the effluent is used as manure, often after chemical deodorization and the addition of lime or bleach to kill dangerous pathogens.

A more effective method for handling the sewage from domestic sources is the septic tank. The sewage takes about 16 to 24 hours to pass through the tank, where it is decomposed by anaerobic bacteria. The sludge settles at the bottom of the tank, which is emptied when it is a third to a half full of sludge; about two-thirds of the sludge is removed, and the rest is left to maintain the bacterial activity in the tank.

Another type of treatment system often used for smaller populations is the rotating biological contactor. It consists of a series of plastic disks on a horizontal shaft that are partly submerged in the effluent. As the disks are exposed to the air, aerobic bacteria grow on them and digest the organic matter in the effluent.

In coastal areas, sewage was at one time frequently discharged directly to the sea without treatment, but increasingly regulations forbid this. In Europe, the Urban Waste Water Treatment Directive covers towns with populations of over 3,000 and requires a minimum of secondary treatment. In the United States, the Clean Water Act similarly requires permits and treatment for point source discharges into any of the country's waters.

SEE ALSO: Biofuel • Drainage • Fertilizer • Pollution monitoring and control • Waste disposal • Water • Water supply

Watch, Electronic

The first watches to use electric power instead of a coiled spring were produced during the 1950s. They were made possible by the introduction of small batteries (similar to the type used in hearing aids), which can last upward of a year in operation. By the end of the 1960s, electronic watches of various types were being produced in very large numbers and at prices much lower than high-grade mechanical watches.

The elementary electric watch uses a balance wheel and balance spring as a motor. Instead of the balance being driven by the mainspring through the escapement, as in a conventional watch, the motive power comes from an electric coil mounted on the balance wheel. For a short period during each vibration of the balance, this coil becomes energized and repels the balance from a small permanent magnet mounted nearby. The current is switched on and off by a light spring contactor, which engages with a pin mounted near the axis of the balance wheel. The hands of the watch are driven through an adapted lever escapement.

Later versions of this design replaced the contactor with an electronic switching system. The coil on the balance passes over a permanent magnet and induces a small current in the coil that is used to trigger a transistor. The circuit containing the transistor operates a switch, sending pulses of current to impulse the balance wheel.

◀ Accurate quartz watches with liquid crystal displays are produced at a fraction of the cost of mechanical watches of similar accuracy. These watches are sports models and are water resistant. They also incorporate a stopwatch facility as well as ordinary date and time functions.

▶ Testing the frequency of quartz oscillators before installing them in electronic watches.

Tuning-fork watches

The best accuracy that can be attained by a conventional wristwatch, using a balance wheel, is of the order of three or four seconds per day (the highest Swiss chronometer rating is an average daily variation of four seconds). In an effort to find an alternative to the balance wheel, watch designers began experiments with tuning forks in the 1950s, and the first successful tuning-fork watch came onto the market in the early 1960s.

The advantage of the tuning fork is that it vibrates at a very precise frequency: the problem in using it as a time standard is to keep it vibrating and to use its very small amplitude to drive the hands of a watch. To maintain the vibration of the tuning fork, an electromagnetic impulsing system is used, controlled by a transistor switch similar to the type used in the electronic balance-wheel watches described above.

At the end of each tine of the fork is mounted a cone-shaped magnet; these magnets are free to vibrate in and out of coils mounted in a stationary position. A small section of one of the coils is used as a phase-sensing coil. During each cycle of the fork, the magnet comes close to the phase-sensing coil, inducing a small voltage in it that is used to trigger the transistor switching circuit. This circuit sends a pulse of current to the main drive coils, which repel the magnets on the tuning fork, pushing the tines inward and thus giving the impulse to maintain the vibrations of the fork. This cycle takes place in the first tuning-fork watches 360 times per second. Higher-frequency tuning forks were used in later watches.

The hands of the watch are driven by reduction gears from an index wheel, which is a small wheel with 300 teeth cut into its outer rim and is

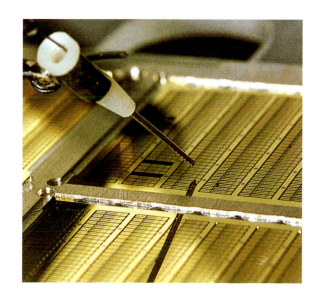

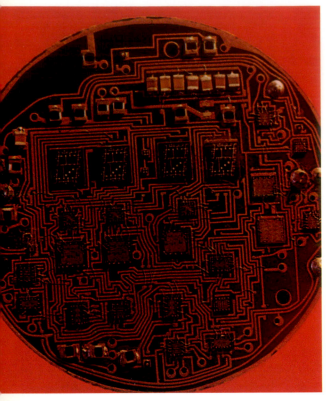

◀ The integrated circuit of an electronic wristwatch. The watch contains no moving parts and is accurate to within a few minutes each year.

mounted close to the tuning fork. A straight spring tipped with a tiny jewel is attached to one tine of the fork. This jewel engages with the teeth of the index wheel, and advances the wheel one tooth for each complete oscillation of the tuning fork. The index wheel therefore makes a complete revolution in a little under one second. The tuning-fork watch has an accuracy of within two seconds per day.

Quartz watches

During the 1970s, developments in the field of microelectronics made the production of quartz watches possible. They work in essentially the same way as the earlier quartz clocks. Two main types were developed.

The first quartz watches had analog displays and used the quartz oscillator to provide an alternating current that drives a small motor, which drives the hands of the watch through reduction gears. Later quartz watches had a digital display with no moving parts. Initially, these digital watches had red light-emitting diode (LED) displays. The LED display produces its own light, but it has a comparatively high power consumption. LED watches were provided with a button on the case that illuminated the figure for a short period and left the display screen blank at other times. By the late 1970s, watches with a liquid crystal display (LCD) became more popular. The LCD uses reflected light and therefore cannot be seen in the dark, but it has the advantage of a very low power consumption. By the mid-1980s,

▼ Omega's 1355 watch is thinner than a match and has no apparent works. The minute hand is printed on a transparent disk, and the hour hand behind it on a gold disk. Both disks are driven at their concealed, cogged edges. The integrated circuit has 1,000 transistors. (1) battery, (2) oscillator, (3) base plate, (4) adjustment control, (5) integrated circuit, (6) stepping motor, (7) gold hour disk, (8) crystal minute disk, (9) gear train.

quartz watches with traditional analog displays had become popular once again with consumers.

Quartz watches using solar energy were first developed in the United States. Two small solar cells are mounted on the upper face of the watch and collect light to charge the power cells. They keep the watch running for at least six months in total darkness, once fully charged. An LCD face shows the hours, minutes, and seconds and also the day and month. The calendar is programmed to allow for the varying lengths of the months and for leap years.

Because the watch does not use ordinary power cells, which have to be changed periodically, the movement can be sealed in a waterproof case, which is filled with a shock-absorbing gel. The time-setting controls are operated by magnets mounted outside the movement capsule that activate switches embedded inside the capsule.

Modern quartz watches

Digital quartz watches can display much more than simply the time and date. Modern quartz watches have a low-energy integrated circuit inside, with chips containing 100,000 or more components. Models on the market today have calculator, alarm, laptimer, and stopwatch features, and some models may also indicate pulse rate, temperature, numerical data, and even short messages. They can be purchased very cheaply.

The Japanese watchmaker Seiko introduced a TV watch in 1983. It has an LCD video display and can receive UHF and VHR TV signals and FM radio. The first radio-controlled watches, which synchronize automatically to radio signals based on atomic time standards, were introduced in the early 1990s.

SEE ALSO: CLOCK • INTEGRATED CIRCUIT • LIQUID CRYSTAL • TIME • WATCH, MECHANICAL

Watch, Mechanical

◄ The mechanism of the Tudor Oyster comprises more than 200 separate compartments. The waterproof case is carved from steel.

The spring-wound watch has a history of some 500 years. Over this period it has become a nearly perfect mechanical device, and its accuracy has only been superseded by the quartz clock and watch and finally by the atomic clock. No other mechanical device must work for 24 hours a day, 365 days a year for years on end; furthermore, if its error rate is 20 seconds a day, it is an error of only 0.023 percent. Such accuracies are normally found only in scientific instruments, which do not suffer the rough treatment received by the wristwatch.

Components

The mechanical watch is made up of several main sections. The source of motive power for the watch is its mainspring, a coiled steel spring contained in the spring barrel. The power is transmitted by a train (series) of gear wheels to the escapement, the device that checks the forward motion of the gear wheels and uses this energy to give the impulses that drive the balance wheel, the controller, or governor, of the watch. The escapement connects to a balance that turns in alternate directions at a fixed rate. The balance therefore controls the release of the

▼ The mechanism of a tuning-fork watch; the fork is pulsed by electromagnets and vibrates 360 times per second.

escapement and thus the timekeeping of the watch in the same way as the pendulum controls the timekeeping of a clock.

Development

The coiled spring was first used as a source of power in portable clocks in the late 15th century, probably in Nüremberg, Germany. By the early 16th century, the size of these timepieces had been reduced, and the introduction of the hog's bristle made the first truly portable watches possible. These early watches used the verge escapement, which consisted of a notched wheel, the appearance of which resembled a crown, driven by a pendulum or a weight and checked by a pair of metal leaves. A simple balance wheel replaced the foliot balance used in clocks of the period. The hog's bristle, which was a crude form of balance spring, consisted of one or two lengths of stiff bristle arranged to act as buffers for the balance at the limit of its arc of vibration (the extent of the to-and-fro rotational movement of the balance).

These early watches, often enclosed in fine pierced or gem-set cases, were really little more than expensive toys. The timekeeping errors must have been in the region of 15 minutes per day; in fact, only an hour hand was used in this era. The minute hand did not appear on watches until the late 17th century, when accuracy of timekeeping had greatly improved.

The period from 1675 to 1800 saw a revolution in the design of watches as well as clocks; from the primitive verge watch to fine chronometers that had an accuracy of better than two seconds per day (strictly, the term *chronometer* applied at this time only to the very accurate timepieces used for navigation at sea, but pocket versions were produced). The first step in the improvement of the verge watch was the introduction of the balance spring (sometimes called the hairspring): it was first devised by the English scientist Robert Hooke in 1658 and was developed later in the century by the Dutch physicist Christiaan Huygens into the form of a fine spiral steel spring of five to ten coils. The center of the spring is secured to the balance wheel, and the out-

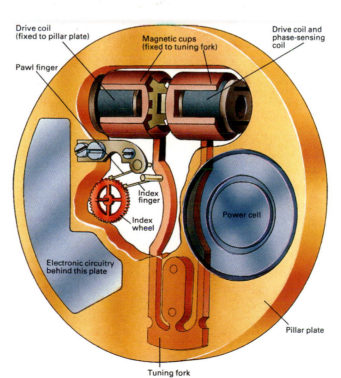

Drive coil (fixed to pillar plate)

Magnetic cups (fixed to tuning fork)

Drive coil and phase-sensing coil

Pawl finger

Index finger

Index wheel

Power cell

Electronic circuitry behind this plate

Pillar plate

Tuning fork

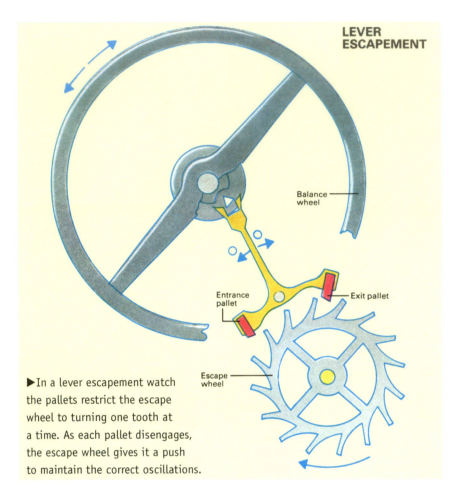

LEVER ESCAPEMENT

Balance wheel

Entrance pallet

Exit pallet

Escape wheel

▶In a lever escapement watch the pallets restrict the escape wheel to turning one tooth at a time. As each pallet disengages, the escape wheel gives it a push to maintain the correct oscillations.

side end is pinned to the balance cock (a removable bridge that holds the upper bearing of the balance wheel). The balance spring is alternately wound and unwound as the balance rotates, reversing its direction usually five times per second. The time taken by the balance to make each turn or vibration is controlled principally by the strength of the balance spring and the weight of the balance wheel.

It was soon realized that the improved balance could be a very accurate time controller if it were allowed to turn freely, with as little interference as possible from the escapement. The old verge escapement was discarded in favor of the cylinder escapement, which was perfected by the English clockmaker George Graham in about 1725 (earlier experiments were carried out in England by Thomas Tompion, Edward Booth, and William Houghton in the late 17th century). This escapement allowed the balance to turn much more freely than the verge, although a significant amount of friction was still involved; a well-made cylinder watch could be regulated to within two or three minutes per day.

An important breakthrough came with the invention around 1759 of the lever escapement by the British watchmaker Thomas Mudge. It allows the balance to turn without any interference except for a short period during each swing when

▲ The rate of oscillation of the lever escapement mechanisms of these watches can be adjusted by altering the tension of the internal spiral spring. If the rate is incorrect, the watch will either gain or lose time accordingly.

it receives its impulse. Another advantage is that this mechanism permits the watch to be wound without the watch stopping or losing time. The lever escapement, with a few minor improvements, is the one used in all modern high-grade jeweled lever watches.

Temperature compensation

A great problem that had to be overcome by the 18th-century watchmakers was temperature error. The trouble with the steel balance spring is that heat makes the spring lose its elasticity and cold temperatures cause the reverse to happen; the result is a change in the rate of the watch of about eight seconds a day per degree Fahrenheit. A solution to this problem was urgently needed in order to produce accurate timepieces for marine navigation; each year many ships were lost because no accurate means were available to determine longitude.

During the 18th century, the English horologist John Harrison produced a series of marine timekeepers (now at the Greenwich Maritime Museum in London) that would stand the rigors of a long sea voyage and still maintain a high accuracy. His solution to the temperature problem was the compensation curb. This was essentially a bimetallic strip of steel and brass fused together; the brass expands at a faster rate than the steel and causes the strip to bend at different rates according to the temperature. This device was used to shorten and lengthen the balance spring, thus compensating for changes in temperature. In modern watches, the balance spring is made of alloys of nickel, steel, manganese, chromium and other elements that are not affected by temperature changes.

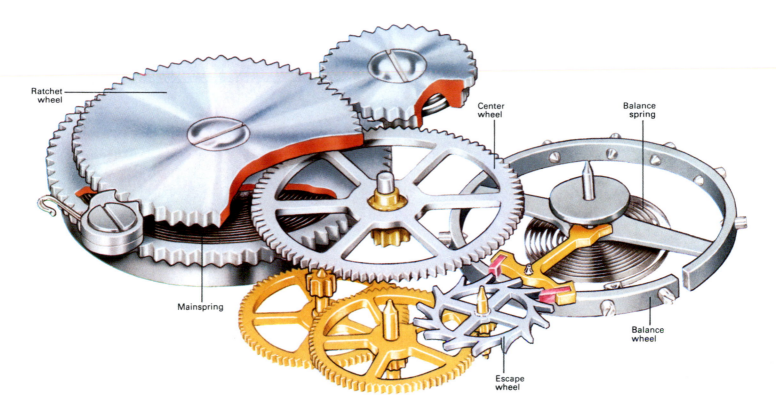

Ratchet wheel

Mainspring

Center wheel

Balance spring

Balance wheel

Escape wheel

Another source of errors in timekeeping occurs as a result of gravity on the escapement when the watch is moved through different positions. A solution to this problem was found in 1798 by the Swiss watchmaker Abraham-Louis Breguet, who invented a complex mechanism called the tourbillon in which the escapement is mounted on a carriage that revolves at a fixed rate. This constant rotation compensates for the movement of the watch by the wearer.

Other developments

Jewels in watches have been used since the early 18th century, as bearings, made originally from natural rubies, but synthetic rubies have been used since about 1900. Before methods of drilling rubies were discovered, brass bearings had to be used; they were subject to a high rate of wear. It soon became general practice to use jewel bearings for the balance wheel, escapement, and train wheels. The modern fully jeweled watch has upward of 17 jewels, which give protection against wear at all important points of friction.

The first documented use of a watch specifically made for use on the wrist is a watch made by Breguet in 1810 for the Queen of Naples. Wrist-worn watches were to eventually supplant pocket watches, and today the majority of watches manufactured are wristwatches.

After World War I, mass-production techniques, developed largely in Switzerland, revolutionized the watch market, and it became possible to produce accurate, reliable, small-sized watches comparatively cheaply. The fashion for wearing watches on the wrist also made the production of automatic watches a practical proposition. These watches are wound by wrist movement; an eccentric rotor pivoted behind the watch movement is free to swing to and fro with each motion of the wrist, and this energy is used to wind the watch through reduction gears.

The first patent for an automatic wristwatch was taken out by an Englishman, John Harwood, in 1924, although a similar principle had been used to produce self-winding pocket watches in the late 18th century by Abraham-Louis Perrelet, Breguet, and others. Apart from the obvious advantage of not having to wind the watch manually, the accuracy of the watch is improved by the mainspring being kept in a fully wound condition most of the time, the result being a much more even and consistent transmission of power to the escapement.

With the invention of the quartz watch in the 1960s, the mechanical watch became less popular, but during the 1980s a resurgence of interest began in the craftsmanship and mechanical ingenuity of spring-powered timepieces. Many of the more expensive watches produced today are spring powered, and watch makers display their skill by continuing to devise complex mechanisms to indicate not only hours and minutes but also, for example, the movements of the planets, eclipses of the Moon and Sun, and perpetual calendars that do not need adjusting for leap years.

▲ A watch movement incorporating a lever escapement mechanism. The escapement controls the speed at which the mainspring unwinds to drive the hands of the clock; the ratchet wheel stops the mainspring from unwinding without driving the mechanism. The hairspring controls the rate at which the spring oscillates.

SEE ALSO: CLOCK • LATITUDE AND LONGITUDE • SUNDIAL • TIME • TIMING DEVICE • WATCH, ELECTRONIC

Water

Water is by far the most abundant of terrestrial chemical compounds. Just over 97 percent of a total of almost 1.5×10^{15} tons (1.35×10^{15} tonnes) is present as saltwater in the oceans and inland seas that cover three-fifths of Earth's surface. The majority of the rest of the water, which is freshwater, is present in the polar ice caps. Rivers account for only one ten-thousandth of a percent of Earth's water resources, and the atmospheric moisture that forms clouds, fog, and rain only one-thousandth of a percent. Water is vital for animal and plant life, and it has played a major role in the industrialization of the developed nations, driving water mills, acting as the working fluid in steam engines, and performing as a coolant for countless industrial processes.

Structure and properties

Pure water is a colorless, odorless, tasteless liquid at room temperature. Its molecular formula, H_2O, indicates that each molecule consists of two hydrogen atoms attached to an oxygen atom. Each oxygen therefore participates in two O–H bonds and has two pairs of unbonded valence electrons (lone pairs) that occupy lobe-shaped orbitals. To visualize the shape of the water molecule, imagine the two bonds and the two lone pairs being directed toward the four points of an approximate tetrahedron centered on the oxygen atom; two of those points are occupied by hydrogen atoms.

Hydrogen bonding. Oxygen is much more electronegative than hydrogen, and so it pulls the electrons in O–H bonds toward itself and away from the hydrogen atoms. This reaction leaves a partial positive charge on the hydrogen atoms and a partial negative charge on the oxygen atom. At the same time, the lone pairs on each oxygen atom are accumulations of negative charge that exert an attractive force on the weakly positive hydrogen atoms of neighboring molecules. The resulting attraction is a hydrogen bond, which is weaker than a covalent bond but much stronger than the electrostatic attractions that occur between all polar molecules. In the extreme, a hydrogen atom can become detached from its own molecule and form a full covalent bond with the molecule to which it was hydrogen bonded:

$$H_2O + H_2O \rightarrow H_3O^+ + OH^-$$

This dissociation reaction is a source of conductivity in water, since the ions it produces can conduct electricity, whereas molecules cannot.

Hydrogen bonding can explain why the boiling point of water, 212°F, is much higher than that of other nonmetal hydrides of similar molecular sizes, such as ammonia, NH_3 (−28.17°F, −33.43°C); hydrogen sulfide, H_2S (−76.5°F, −60.3°C); and methane, CH_4 (−258°F, −161°C). Similarly, the latent heat of vaporization of water is high as a result of the unusually large amount of energy required to break hydrogen bonds.

Hydrogen bonding accounts for the relatively high viscosity and surface tension of water when compared with other liquids of low molecular weight. These effects are influenced by the additional attraction between molecules due to hydrogen bonding. The presence of hydrogen bonds also has an unusual effect on the density of water, which is just over half the value calculated for a similar size, weight, and shape of molecule without hydrogen bonding. This effect arises because the arrangement of molecules, which is strongly influenced by the hydrogen bonds, is less space efficient than the close-packed structure that would occur without hydrogen bonds.

In 1933, the British physicist John Bernal proposed a theory of the structure of water in which hydrogen-bonded rings of water molecules contain different numbers of molecules in an unsystematic arrangement. As temperature falls, the heat motion that opposes hydrogen bonding becomes less vigorous, and the spacing between adjacent oxygen nuclei decreases. X-ray diffraction measurements confirm this view by showing that the O–O spacing decreases from 3.05 Å (angstroms, or 0.305 nanometers, nm) at 185°F (85°C) to 2.90 Å (0.290 nm) at 59°F (15°C). Furthermore, below 39°F (4°C), the density of water suddenly falls as the ring structure becomes more systematic and open. In ice, the water molecules hydrogen-bond to form a more open cage structure of hexagonal rings.

The change to a more open structure on freezing is highly unusual and has some dramatic consequences. On freezing at atmospheric pressure, water expands by approximately one-twelfth of its volume, and its density diminishes accordingly, and thus ice floats in water. If water is trapped as it freezes, the processes that try to orientate water molecules into the less dense ice structure can exert pressures in excess of 30,000 psi (2,000 atmospheres). This effect causes pipes to burst and porous water-laden rocks to shatter in frosty weather.

There are at least nine structurally distinct forms of solid water, ice I through ice IX. Ice I is the form that freezes at atmospheric pressure, and it is the only form that is less dense than liquid water at its freezing point. Forms that freeze at higher pressures have denser structures.

Solvent power

Water has been called the universal solvent in reference to its ability to dissolve practically all substances to a greater or lesser extent. In many cases, the solvent power of water is attributable to its polarity—the charge separation caused by the drift of electrons toward oxygen in O–H bonds.

Hence, water molecules gather around positive ions or the positive regions of polar molecules, with their oxygen atoms closer to the positive charge. Conversely, negative ions and negatively polarized parts of molecules attract the positive hydrogen atoms. Furthermore, water molecules can act as both donors and receptors of the electron pairs used to form hydrogen bonds, which heightens the affinity between water and other substances that can form hydrogen bonds.

Heavy water

Around 0.0156 percent (by weight) of the hydrogen in natural water is deuterium (D)—an isotope of hydrogen that has a neutron as well as a proton in its nucleus, so its atomic mass is 2. Deuterium is present in the form of deuterium hydrogen oxide (HDO) and deuterium oxide (D_2O). Repeated electrolysis of water produces pure deuterium oxide (also called heavy water) because normal hydrogen is preferentially evolved at the electrodes. This process leaves an increasing proportion of heavy water in the electrolyte.

Heavy water has different physical properties than those of normal water. The boiling point and freezing point of heavy water are 214.55°F (101.42°C) and 38.88°F (3.82°C), respectively, compared with 212°F (100°C) and 32°F (0°C) for

◀ Each year, around 10^{17} gallons (4.6 x 10^{14} m³) of water evaporate into the atmosphere from oceans, lakes, and rivers. This moisture returns to Earth's surface as rain, snow, or dew, keeping constant the amount of water vapor in the atmosphere.

ordinary water. Also, heavy water has a maximum density of 1.1073 g/ml at 52.88°F (11.6°C), compared with a maximum density of 1.0000 g/ml at 39°F (4°C) for ordinary water.

Heavy water is used as a combined moderator and heat-exchange fluid in some types of nuclear fission reactors, since it is able to control the speed of neutrons and improve their chances of initiating fission. Heavy water is also important as a source of deuterium and other deuterium compounds, which are used to elucidate the mechanisms of chemical and biochemical reactions. Deuterium has a distinctive signature in nuclear magnetic resonance (NMR) experiments, and the positions of deuterium atoms in a reaction product indicate where hydrogen would end up in a normal reaction.

Drinking water

Water that comes from faucets in the home has been subjected to chemical processes to purify it. Natural water normally has impurities—both organic and inorganic. The inorganic impurities are in the form of salts that are, in general, harmless to humans. However, the organic impurities are potentially harmful—they may include bacteria or viruses, for example. Some of these impurities can be removed by flocculation, whereby a sulfate of aluminum or iron is added to the water and a gelatinous precipitate of the corresponding hydroxide forms, settling out of the water and dragging large particles of organic matter with it.

Subsequent disinfection using chlorine (Cl_2) or ozone (O_3) sterilizes any remaining organic matter. All but a trace of chlorine is subsequently removed by treatment with ammonia or by filtration through activated charcoal (carbon). In the ozone process, the sterilizing agent gradually decomposes to normal oxygen.

Hardness

Water is said to be hard if it contains significant concentrations of calcium and magnesium salts, which occur in natural water. Water hardness is not dangerous to health, but it does effect operations both in the home and in industry. Calcium and magnesium ions form insoluble scums with soaps, so additional quantities of soap are needed for washing in hard-water regions. Also, hard water forms precipitates of insoluble calcium and magnesium carbonates and other salts when it boils; they are responsible for the furring that clings to the elements of kettles. The same effect in the heating pipes of industrial boilers would cause blockages and reduce efficiency by insulating the heating pipes, so such boilers tend to use water that has been softened.

The hardness of water can be expressed as parts per million (ppm) of calcium carbonate ($CaCO_3$), which is equivalent to milligrams $CaCO_3$ per liter in the metric system. This classification does not ignore the magnesium content, rather it expresses it as an equivalent weight of calcium carbonate. Soft water has less than 50 ppm, moderately soft has 50 to 100 ppm, moderately hard has 100 to 200 ppm, hard has 200 to 300 ppm, and very hard has more than 300 ppm.

The two main ways of softening water are lime treatment and ion exchange. Lime—calcium oxide or calcium hydroxide—removes the bicarbonates (hydrogen carbonates) of calcium and magnesium by converting them into insoluble carbonates that precipitate out:

$$Ca(OH)_2 + Ca(HCO_3)_2 \rightarrow 2CaCO_3 + 2H_2O$$

The removal of bicarbonates is important, since these are the salts that release carbon dioxide and form insoluble carbonate fur when water is strongly heated, by the heating element of a washing machine or kettle, for example.

Ion exchange is performed using an anionic resin or zeolite to which sodium ions are attached. The water-hardening ions attach to the ion-exchange medium in place of the sodium ions, which enter the water (all salts of sodium are soluble, so they cause no hardness). Saturated resin or zeolite can be regenerated for reuse by treatment with concentrated sodium chloride solution.

Lime treatment is the cheaper but less effective method of softening water, and it is widely used in public water-supply preparation. In industrial and residential water-softening installations, the more expensive (and more effective) base-exchange method is usually used to remove the final traces of calcium carbonate.

▼ Using groundwater to irrigate deserts boosts crop yields, but such water supplies are not renewable, and their use causes drought and other problems.

SEE ALSO: CHEMICAL BONDING AND VALENCY • DESALINATION • DRAINAGE • IRRIGATION TECHNIQUES • RAIN AND RAINFALL • WATER SUPPLY

Water Mill

The earliest water mills, which appeared in the Roman Empire during the first century B.C.E., were of two types. In one, the wheel was set horizontally below the millstones and was driven by a jet of water directed onto its blades. The machines had no gearing, the axle of the wheel being extended and connected to the upper millstone. Partly because it could operate only in mountainous regions where there were perpetual fast-flowing streams and partly because of its low power output, usually no more than 1.5 horsepower (1.1 kW), this type of mill was not developed further and remains today as a relic in remote highland areas of Europe and Asia.

In the second type of water mill, the wheel was set vertically, and the water was directed below the paddles (undershot) or through a chute over the wheel (overshot), or fed into rim buckets rather more than halfway up the wheel (breast-wheel). The driving force thus often came not only from the pressure of the water emerging from the chute but also from the weight of the water in the buckets. It has been estimated that Roman mills, in which the wheel had a diameter of about 8 ft. (2.4 m), could develop from 3 to 6 horsepower (2–4.5 kW) turning at a speed of 30 to 45 rpm, which in turn would allow an output of some 650 lbs. (295 kg) of flour per hour.

Other uses develop

Although the water mill became widespread throughout Europe in the later years of the Roman Empire and subsequent migration period, it was not until the 11th century that it regularly began to be put to purposes other than grinding cereals. By the 12th century, however, mills had been adapted to grind oak bark for tanneries and mash for breweries. Furthermore, by replacing the gearing on the main shaft with a series of cams, the water mill could be made to drive hammers, bellows, stamps, and saws. Throughout the Middle Ages, more and more industries turned to the use of waterpower. The medieval iron industry could hardly have survived, let alone develop, without its water-driven furnaces and forges, and with the introduction of the cannon, the water mill was further adapted to bore out gun barrels.

Despite the increasing application of waterpower to industry, there was little development in the size or efficiency of the wheel. It was normally made of wood and worked through wooden gears. It has been estimated that a wheel of 12 ft. (3.7 m) in diameter could at the best deliver about 10 horsepower (7.5 kW) working at 30 rpm.

Houghton Mill in England last worked commercially in the 1930s. The waterwheel has been removed, but the machinery is preserved, and the mill race can be seen to the right of the mill.

Steam power replaces water

The use of waterpower tended to restrict industry to the river valleys, a fact that accounts for the siting of the earliest textile mills in the north of England, where there are more valleys than in the south of the country. It was not until the steam engine proved to be totally reliable—by the end of the 18th century—that industry moved nearer to its new source of power—the coalfields—and abandoned the water mill.

From the 19th century onward, the water mill survived in remote rural areas in its original form, as a means of grinding cereals. Today, the high cost of maintaining millponds, races, and sluices and the construction of the mill itself has rendered the water mill uneconomical.

Inside the mill, corn was ground between two huge stones, one of which rotated using the power from the waterwheel.

SEE ALSO: CAM • WATER • WIND POWER

Water Ram

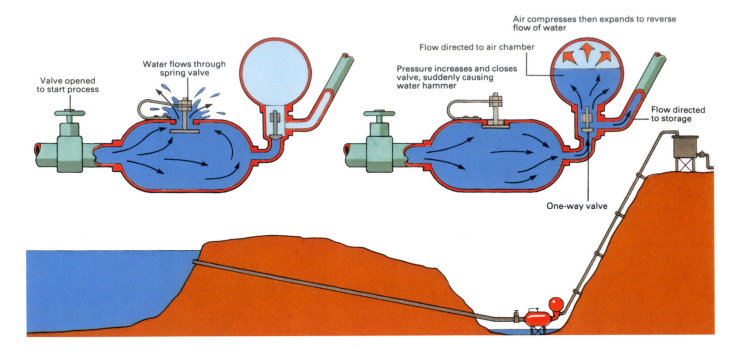

Valve opened to start process

Water flows through spring valve

Air compresses then expands to reverse flow of water

Flow directed to air chamber

Pressure increases and closes valve, suddenly causing water hammer

Flow directed to storage

One-way valve

The kinetic energy of flowing water can be converted into a useful form in some types of waterwheel and turbine. Another method of using the energy is the water ram (or hydraulic ram), in which the kinetic energy is applied to produce a direct pumping action that lifts some of the water well above the flow level, generally for irrigation purposes. Water rams were introduced toward the end of the 18th century and offered the advantages of simplicity and low running costs without the need for an external power source.

In operation, water from the source, such as a stream, is allowed to flow down through a pipe to an enclosed valve box. The one-way exhaust valve in the box is initially open to allow the water to flow through. Another one-way valve connects the valve box to an air chamber and the delivery pipe. The exhaust valve is designed so that the hydrodynamic forces generated by the water flow cause the valve to shut suddenly when the flow reaches a specific velocity. This sudden closure brings the water flow to an abrupt halt, and the kinetic energy of the moving water in the pipe is converted into a pressure surge. The sudden rise in pressure opens the second valve, allowing water to flow up through the supply pipe until the pressure has fallen to a value less than the required delivery head. Air in the chamber, compressed by the pressure surge, expands, forcing the valve to close and driving more water up the delivery pipe.

Reflection of the initial pressure surge results in a reduction of pressure in the valve box, and the exhaust valve reopens to allow water to flow freely again. As the flow velocity through the valve builds up, it reaches the critical velocity, and the valve closes again to repeat the cycle, so giving a continuous pumping action. The amount of water delivered depends on the precise design of the water ram. Usually around one-sixth of the original water flow can be lifted through a height of up to five times the original drop between the start of the inlet pipe and the exhaust valve.

A variation of this basic concept—employing interlinked flow and exhaust valves—can be used as an air compressor. Air is admitted through a separate valve before each flow cycle and forced into a reservoir by the subsequent pressure surge.

The pressure rise associated with a sudden reduction or stoppage of water flow can create serious problems in pipelines, where the effect is known as water hammer. In its simplest form, it can be heard as a knocking sound when a faucet is turned off very quickly. In some cases the hammer effect is strong enough to damage the faucet or the pipe, and with larger pipelines, special precautions have to be taken to prevent damage from the pressure shock. The penstocks (inflow pipes), for example, are often fitted with surge tanks to absorb pressure variations. Alternatively, the valve gear can be arranged to prevent rapid opening or closing actions, with a gradual valve operation allowing the water flow to slow down.

▲ The water ram works on the principle of a water hammer, which actuates a valve to vary the pressure of two internal chambers. Pressurized air in one chamber forces the water up an incline.

SEE ALSO: COMPRESSOR AND PUMP • HYDRAULICS • WATER SUPPLY

Water-Repellent Finish

Textiles are versatile materials: most are flexible yet durable, a combination of properties that makes them useful for making items such as clothes, upholstery covers, and tents. Many textiles are intrinsically vulnerable to water, however, a property that reduces their performance in wet weather and their resistance to stains, and also makes them prone to degradation by mold. A water-repellent finish is a coating that increases the resistance of textiles to water, thereby extending their scope of applications and durability.

The susceptibility of a fabric to water is measured in terms of two phenomena: penetration and absorption. Penetration is the passage of water through a fabric, which can cause discomfort for the wearer of a garment or cause damage to items within a tent, for example. Absorption is the ability of a fabric to soak up water or become waterlogged. Waterlogged garments become heavy and lose the thermal insulation provided by the tiny pockets of air trapped within a typical dry fabric. Absorption is also a problem for tents, which can become too heavy for their supporting frames and ropes if waterlogged.

Penetration depends to a large extent on the construction of the fabric, whereas absorption reflects the lack of ability of the constituent fibers to shed water. An open fabric will allow water to pass through its interstices—the spaces between its fibers—even if the water shedding by the fibers is good. On the other hand, a closely woven fabric will prevent penetration provided the water-shedding properties of the fibers are adequate. A closely woven fabric of absorbent fibers will resist penetration at first but will eventually allow water to seep through its sodden fibers.

Waterproofing

Complete waterproofing can be achieved by forming an impermeable barrier of water-resistant material on or within a fabric. In 1823 the British chemist Charles Macintosh developed such an approach by bonding two sheets of woolen material together using rubber dissolved in naphtha. The rubber formed an impermeable barrier, and this composite material became popular for making raincoats.

The same effect can be achieved by soaking a solution of a hydrophobic polymer, such as polychloroethene (polyvinyl chloride, PVC), into a textile and allowing the solvent to evaporate. The disadvantages of this type of treatment include a stiffening of the material, an increase in weight per unit area, and the loss of the soft surface feel associated with textiles made from natural fibers. For these reasons, totally water-resistant fabrics tend to be confined to applications where the absolute exclusion of water is more important than comfort or aesthetics. An example is the use of PVC-bonded materials in protective tarpaulins and side sheets for certain types of trucks.

Water-repellent fabric

Complete waterproofing is not the best option for fabrics for garments, because perspiration moisture accumulates in a waterproof garment—particularly during periods of exertion—causing discomfort and putting the wearer at risk of developing fungal skin infections. Hence, a good weatherproof garment allows moist air to escape and fresh, dry air to enter—a process called breathing—while preventing liquid water, such as rain, from reaching the lining layers.

The compromise between skin breathing and weatherproofing is achieved using woven fabrics whose pores are wide enough to allow breathing,

▼ This British marine models a reversible weatherproof jacket made of a combination of synthetic and natural fibers. The jacket provides warmth while keeping its wearer dry and allowing perspiration moisture to escape. The white side of the jacket provides camouflage in snowscapes.

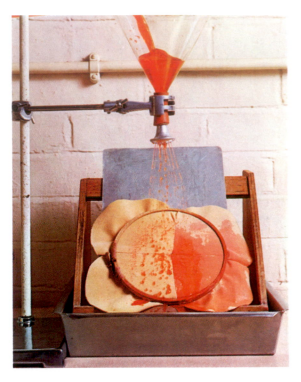

but whose fibers are so water repellent that droplets of water run off the fabric without wetting it. An acute contact angle between water and the fabric (contact angle is the angle between the surface of a water droplet and the surface of the fabric) is required to ensure that droplets retain their integrity and run off the fabric, rather than spreading out and wetting it.

Since contact angle is purely a surface phenomenon, any fabric can be made water repellent if it is evenly coated with a fine layer of a material that itself has a low contact angle with water—the lower the angle, the better the repellency.

Finishing agents

In nature, water shedding is achieved by means of oils (in the case of birds' feathers, for example) and waxes (in the case of leaves). The use of such materials on textiles would result in fabrics that are inflexible or unpleasantly greasy, however.

Early water-repellent finishes were achieved by treating a fabric with soap solution, then precipitating the soap with alum. It was found that mixing wax with soap improved the water resistance. Later, it was discovered that combinations of emulsified waxes with certain salts of aluminum (or, better still, zirconium) provided high levels of water resistance without altering the feel of the fabric or its ability to breathe. These products still form the basis for much of the treatment of woolen cloth, high-quality tent fabrics, and inexpensive polyester-cotton rainwear. Although extremely resistant to prolonged wet weather, these finishes possess no resistance to dry cleaning or repeated washing with detergents.

The resistance of wax finishes to detergents can be improved by chemically coupling wax molecules to melamine or pyridine groups. These groups form hydrogen bonds with cellulosic fabrics, such as cotton and linen. The resistance of these wax compounds to dry cleaning is limited, however, and they are unsuitable for artificial fibers. Some cotton rainwear and military combat clothing is treated with these products.

The demand for suitable finishes for artificial fibers led to the development of reactive silicone products based on methylsiloxane or dimethylsiloxane. These compounds are applied to textiles together with a catalyst and then heated to form a complex, insoluble polymer that stands up to repeated washing and dry cleaning. Silicone products are used on many lightweight nylon fabrics used for coats and camping equipment.

By far the best water-repellent finishes are those based on fluorocarbons, a group of fluorine-containing compounds related to nonstick Teflon coatings. Like silicones, they cross-link to form insoluble water-resistant polymers, but they also possess the property of resistance to oil and oil-borne stains.

Fluorocarbons are more expensive than silicones, but their stain-resistant property—as well as their water resistance and durability—have made them increasingly popular finishes for upholstery fabrics, fabrics for high-quality rainwear and ski wear, and lightweight nylon for foul-weather clothing. Cheaper wax-based products are sometimes blended with fluorocarbons to reduce the cost of the finishes without significantly reducing their performance.

SEE ALSO: Clothing manufacture • Cotton • Fiber, natural • Fiber, synthetic • Polytetrafluoroethylene (teflon) • Silicone

Water Supply

Humans have always depended on natural sources such as rivers, lakes, springs, and artesian basins for water supplies. As society has become more industrialized and urban populations have increased, the control of water supplies has naturally needed more careful supervision. Demand often exceeds supplies, so storage in the form of reservoirs or artificial lakes is necessary. In addition, pollutants, not only from industrial effluents but also agricultural sources such as fertilizers, have increased, necessitating the monitoring and purification of raw water supplies, although pollution of rivers is not wholly a 20th century phenomenon. Large quantities of water are used for industrial and agricultural purposes, while residential consumption in urban areas is in the order of 100 gallons (380 l) per day. Accordingly, most modern societies have had to develop extensive water supply systems to meet these varied demands.

Water sources

The main sources of water for supply systems are groundwater and surface water, although in some areas, desalination techniques are also used to obtain freshwater directly from the sea.

Groundwater consists of rain that has percolated through the ground surface and is trapped in layers of permeable rocks, where it gradually flows down to emerge, often after a significant time delay, as a spring. These water-bearing layers are known as aquifers and are exploited by means of wells or boreholes. In some cases, the groundwater is under considerable pressure and will be forced to the surface in an artesian well; otherwise the water is pumped up. Centrifugal pumps are normally used, with the pump being installed at the bottom of the well, or borehole.

Surface water consists of lakes and rivers, with rivers often being dammed to create reservoirs. The water from a reservoir may be supplied directly to where it is needed through a pipeline or aqueduct; high-quality water is generally obtained in this way. Often the reservoir is high enough for the flow to take place under the action of gravity, otherwise a pumped system is used. Water outlets from reservoirs normally have a series of openings at different levels to allow selection of the best water at any given time.

Alternatively the reservoir may be used to regulate the flow of the river, evening out the natural

▲ Rapid gravity filters work by pushing the water to be treated upwards through a base of graduated sand, gravel, and anthracite. The filtered water spills over a weir at the top, allowing the water to move on to another stage of treatment.

variations in level so that utilities farther downstream can take the water they need directly from the river. The return of much of the extracted water to the river after use and subsequent purification helps to maintain the flow for users still farther downstream. In some cases, canals are used to supply water to areas that are not situated on or by a natural river line.

Water quality

Municipal water supplies must be drinkable, and various simple tests are performed to monitor the quality. They include tests for taste, odor, color, turbidity (caused by suspended material, such as clay particles), dissolved solids, pH (acidity or alkalinity), and bacteriological and biological contaminants.

Taste and odor may be caused by the presence of hydrogen sulfide given off by decomposing organic matter, or algae, or even chemicals such as phenols, of which only a few parts per million in association with traces of chlorine used for purification are sufficient to produce noticeable

taints. Also, many serious diseases are waterborne—for example, typhoid, cholera, dysentery, and infectious hepatitis.

Waterworks aim to deliver neutral, or alkaline, water, that is, at pH 7, or at a slightly higher pH. Slight alkalinity is less harmful than acidity. Water sources, however, may be naturally acidic from containing dissolved carbon dioxide, which forms weak carbonic acid or sulfurous acid from dissolved sulfur dioxide, which is a common atmospheric pollutant in industrialized areas. Some purification processes may also cause the water to become acidic.

The test for assessing bacteriological quality is the coliform count. The name comes from *Escherichia coli*, bacteria present naturally in human intestines and excreted daily in the millions, and if present in a water sample, they would be an indication of other possible harmful bacterial contamination. The standard is simple: less than one coliform organism per 100 ml of water—that is, effectively none. There is also a biological or algal count that measures the amount of microscopic

▲ A water treatment works near Seville in Spain. Water is cleaned of algae and other small particles by passing it through filter beds. It is then sterilized by contacting it with chlorine or ozone before it is pumped into the main water supply.

plant and animal life found to be present in a given water sample other than bacteria.

Chemical analyses are carried out to determine the iron, manganese, lead, nitrogen (the presence of which indicates organic pollution), and calcium carbonate (which indicates water hardness) content of the water.

Contamination from radioactive fallout or waste may also need to be monitored regularly, and WHO (World Health Organization) gives maximum tolerances of one microcurie per liter of water for gamma emitters and 10 microcuries per liter for beta emitters where a population is likely to be exposed to this form of contamination for a prolonged period.

Treatment

A wide range of processes is available for water treatment, but those commonly employed are sedimentation, flocculation and coagulation, filtration, aeration, and sterilization.

Simply storing water in reservoirs assists purification by allowing the larger particles to set-

tle out, by buffering water quality, and by letting sunlight hasten the destruction of bacteria. One disadvantage, however, is that reservoirs have a tendency to develop algal blooms, a condition that has been exacerbated by the widespread use of nitrogen fertilizers. These are found in the runoff from rain falling on agricultural lands that has subsequently been washed into water sources. Copper sulfate is therefore sometimes added to reservoirs to kill off the algae.

The first stage in water treatment usually includes some form of coarse screening at water intakes to remove leaves, twigs, and so on. From then on, there may be variations; for example, chlorine may be added twice, as a pretreatment and a posttreatment.

A typical sequence is as follows: water enters the works via a takeoff tower that enables it to be drawn from selected levels, is passed through activated carbon to remove any taste and odor that may be present, and then receives its first dose of chlorine for bacteriological control. In the latest works, it will then pass to a microstrainer, which is

▼ The full-water purification process, which is necessary when water for residential and industrial use comes from unprotected sources, such as rivers and lakes. Water taken from underground aquifers or high mountain sources requires comparatively little purification.

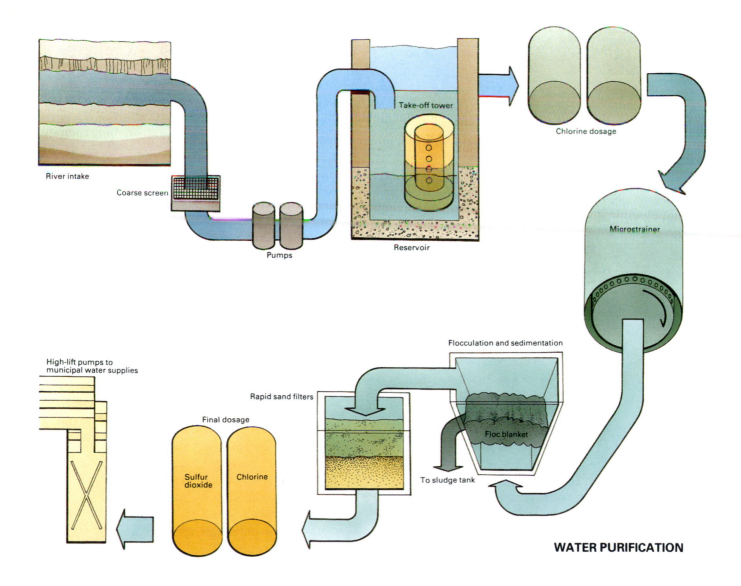

WATER PURIFICATION

A stainless steel microstrainer, which traps algae and other tiny particles that might be present in water abstracted from rivers.

a very fine stainless steel mesh cylinder capable of trapping algae and similar-sized material, before the water undergoes the processes of flocculation and coagulation, which involve adding chemicals.

Some particles present in water are so fine that they have to be trapped, or coagulated, by a sort of chemical blanket. Such particles include colloids, which cause turbidity and coloration, and bacteria. Chemicals commonly added as coagulants may be ferric sulfate, $Fe_2(SO_4)_3 \cdot H_2O$, aluminum sulfate, $Al_2(SO_4)_3 \cdot 14H_2O$, or ferric chloride, $FeCl_3 \cdot 6H_2O$. To assist with the coagulation process, starch is often added.

The chemicals form ions with strong positive charges, which attract the fine particles and some bacteria because they bear negative charges. For example, when aluminum sulfate is added to conical sedimentation tanks containing water that has been rendered alkaline, it reacts chemically with the alkali to form aluminum hydroxide, $Al(OH)_3$, a flocculant precipitate, which forms a distinct "blanket" layer about halfway down the tank; water entering the tank from below passes slowly through this blanket, which acts as a filter, bringing the positive and negative ions into close contact so that they coagulate.

The clear water passes to filters, which may be slow or rapid. One type of rapid gravity filter system employs three layers of filtration media: first, fine sand, followed by coarser sand and finally a layer of anthracite. The filter is cleaned by backwashing once a day (reversing and substantially increasing the flow of water to wash out trapped particles), though the filter always returns to its original series of layers because the differences in particle size mean that like-sized particles naturally group together. Other types of rapid filter may consist of a sand bed on top of a bed of gravel. Most systems are of the rapid gravity type. Slow filters, however, because of the time taken, offer the advantage of removing bacteria, algae, and inorganic substances. Cleaning is carried out about every eight weeks by scraping off the top layer of sand and replacing it with fresh material. Slow sand filters often have a layer of activated carbon granules added in order to remove taste, color, and odor impurities.

After filtration, the water may be passed through an aerator (either in the form of a fountain or water jets) to saturate it with oxygen before it is treated with chlorine. The chlorine dose depends on the flow rate, and the sterilized water then passes to a dechlorination unit, where sulfur dioxide is added. Some residual chlorine, however, may be desirable as a precaution against the possibility of subsequent slight contamination and to protect the water as it travels through the main network to its place of use.

Alternatively, sterilization may be effected by using ozone (a practice favored in Europe) but the cost of ozone production is high compared with chlorine and it is usually not economic for most countries. However, it is being used more and more frequently in treatment works that have high levels of organic contaminants, such as peat, in their source water. Such contaminants have been discovered to react with chlorine to form compounds known as trihalomethanes, which are known to have a negative effect on human health.

Ozone (O_3) also has the advantage that it needs no neutralization after sterilization. Sterilization is effected by passing water through tanks in which ozone is distributed through a system of nozzles, which evenly disperse the bubbles of ozone throughout the tank. The water is also usually stirred to ensure that every part of the

THE HYDROLOGICAL CYCLE

Water is continually recycled, passing through various physical states: rain, cloud, snow, ice, or fog. The energy released or absorbed, as it changes from one state to another, plays an important part in the general circulation of the atmosphere. Another important and unique property of water is that, on cooling, it expands (all other liquids decrease in volume). Water is in its densest state when the temperature reaches 39.18°F (3.99°C). This behavior, which is due to the peculiar molecular structure of water, is of vital importance, because ice will only form on top of water, and thus marine life is saved from being frozen to death. All air contains varying amounts of water vapor—the gaseous phase of water— depending on the temperature.

Water vapor is homogeneous, nothing like fog or mist, which are actually tiny droplets of water suspended in the air. Because water vapor is lighter than air, moist air is more buoyant than dry air and so rises, an important factor in the formation of clouds. The warmer the air, the more water vapor it can hold, up to a maximum at any temperature. For example, at 86°F (30°C) 2.2 lbs. (1 kg) of air can hold 0.98 oz. (28 g) of water vapor, whereas at −40°F (−40°C) it can hold only 0.004 oz. (0.12 g). The percentage relationship between actual and possible vapor content is called the relative humidity of the air. As long as relative humidity is less than 100 percent, the air will remain clear. If the water content of a body of air remains unaltered but the temperature rises, its humidity decreases. If, however, the temperature falls, the moisture-holding capacity of the air decreases and it eventually reaches saturation, or dew point. Should cooling continue beyond this point, the water vapor spills out of the air as liquid. If the dew point happens to be below 32°F (0°C), the spillage or precipitation forms ice crystals.

The process is reversible and, as the temperature rises again, the air absorbs water vapor. The dew point temperature is the temperature at which cooling must proceed for the air to become saturated; meteorologists use it to forecast fog and cloud.

If the relative humidity is high, water may not evaporate quickly, and the result is an oppressively clammy atmosphere— but if the relative humidity is low, less than 50 percent, evaporation may take place very quickly, and the air will feel very much cooler.

Although dew will form readily when the temperature falls below the dew point, droplets of water in air need small particles of dust or salt on which to condense. All clouds form by the process of water condensing out in rising air. The process of cloud formation is very complicated, but basically it depends on warm moist air rising high into the atmosphere. Here, the air pressure is lower than at ground level, and the warm air expands. As it expands, the temperature drops, and the air reaches saturation point. If the air continues to rise, the cooling process is accompanied by condensation of water droplet, which come together to form a cloud.

Most clouds rise to a height where the temperature is well below 32°F, and yet the water droplets rarely freeze. The droplets can even be supercooled, down to −4°F (−20°C), and still remain liquid.

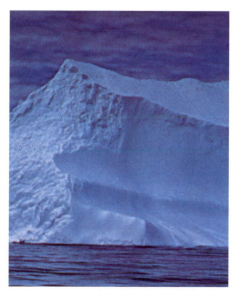

▼ Water, in the form of ice, occurs in Earth's polar regions and on the tops of mountains. Less than 1 percent of Earth's supply of fresh water is liquid—most of which is locked up in glaciers and icebergs far away from the areas where it is needed.

They have to cool to about −40°F (−40°C) before they freeze. This strange phenomenon is due to the latent heat of fusion, released when the droplets freeze. Unless temperatures are very low, there is nowhere this heat can be absorbed.

Water droplets in clouds range in size from 0.002 to 0.03 mm. They are too small to overcome air resistance, so they remain literally floating on air. To fall to ground as either drizzle (0.05–0.5 mm) or as rain (1–5 mm), they must coalesce. However, even this leaves out the smallest droplets. The most important process in rain formation is due to another strange property of water. When no more water can evaporate into the air, the air is saturated, and the water evaporates and condenses at an equal rate. If ice should be present at the same time, there will be a difference in the rate water condenses and evaporates on the ice particles relative to the water droplets. The vapor is supersaturated relative to the ice. At saturation point, with respect to water, the ice crystals will begin to grow. The resulting reduced humidity causes more evaporation from the water droplets. Soon after, the large ice crystals will begin to fall. At the warmer, lower levels, they melt, finally falling to Earth as rain.

The water cycle consists of evaporation, condensation, precipitation, and flow. Of the total moisture in the atmosphere, over 80 percent evaporates from the oceans. The rest comes from moist land surfaces and from transpiration by plants. Transpiration is the process whereby water is drawn up out of the soil by the roots and released into the atmosphere from the leaves. A large tree can draw up to 400 gallons (1,514 l) of water a day from the soil. Once in the air, the water vapor condenses and is precipitated out as rain, snow, dew, or fog.

The air contains only about one part in ten thousand of the total water supply. The rate of recycling of atmospheric water is on average once every ten days—that is, it is completely rained out and replaced. This means that it would take a million years for the total content of the oceans to pass through the atmosphere.

water to be disinfected comes into contact with the ozone. The water flow is designed in such a way that each part of the water remains within the ozone tank for a designated amount of time (known as the contact time); this method ensures that the water achieves full sterilization.

Ultraviolet light (UV) is also occasionally used to sterilize water, and this type of system is becoming more common in the United States. Again, UV has the advantage of not producing any disinfection by-products. Treated water is simply passed under a set of UV lights, which destroy any remaining bacteria or organic matter.

Membranes, which have pores as fine as 2 microns (μm), are also used in water treatment, although, as the process is expensive, it is as yet uncommon. In such a system, water will be passed through fine filters until it is sufficiently clean to pass through the membrane system. Membranes vary in construction—some are flat plates and others spirally wound to give greater surface area. They sit within the water to be treated, and a negative pressure, or flux, is applied to enable water to pass through the pores. The pores are too small for bacteria to pass through, so the water is effectively mechanically disinfected.

The final process in many countries is fluoridation, a practice that has increased in the United States since the early experiments in Michigan in 1945. Fluoride helps to prevent dental decay, although an excess of fluoride can cause a condition known as dental fluorosis, in which teeth become mottled. During the process, laboratory testing is used to check that the water being produced by the works is of the correct quality and does not contain any polluting substances.

Softening

Natural water supplies frequently exhibit a property called water hardness, a measure of the presence of dissolved calcium and magnesium salts. These salts react with soap to give insoluble precipitates, which make washing difficult, the result being the formation of a scum rather than a lather. In addition, hard water can cause serious problems in industries, where boilers and pipework can be damaged by scaling owing to the formation of insoluble carbonates on boiling the water. Accordingly, hard water is often put through a further softening process, one method being the addition of lime during treatment to precipitate the calcium ions as calcium carbonate and the magnesium as a hydroxide.

Another modern softening process that is occasionally found is the pellet reactor, which uses small grains of sand as a nucleus around which the positively charged calcium and magnesium ions coalesce out of solution. After the other treatment processes have been undertaken, the hard water enters a tank in which the sand particles are kept in constant motion. The water is retained there for a precalculated time to ensure that enough material has precipitated to make the water acceptably soft. Not many of these reactors are currently in use, because they are relatively expensive compared with lime treatment.

◄ A worker replacing a module at a reverse-osmosis water treatment plant. Membrane units are used for desalination of salty water supplies and for producing the ultrapure water required by some industrial processes.

Distribution

Cleaned and purified water from the treatment plants is distributed to consumers by a pipeline system. The main transmission pipes, or feeder mains, are generally of cast iron, steel, or reinforced concrete with a diameter of 12 in. (30 cm) or more, depending on the area to be served and the water demand. A grid system is normally used in which the prime supply is connected by lateral supplies, which are run underground along the streets. Valves connected to the supplies allow the isolation of leaking or damaged sections. Connection to individual houses is by small iron or, more common nowadays, plastic pipes running from the supply main to the premises.

The demand for water varies during the day, and most supply systems incorporate distribution reservoirs to meet the peak demands and even out the demand on the treatment plants. Both ground reservoirs and water towers are used, depending on local conditions, such as the general topography and relative height of the reservoir compared

▲ The Kariba Dam on the Zambezi River between Zambia and Zimbabwe in Africa. The 420 ft. (128 m) high concrete structure was completed in 1959. It was designed to even out the seasonal and year-to-year flow of the river and to provide a rapid flow of water for generating electricity.

with the users' location. Both types of storage systems are enclosed to avoid contamination of the water. Where the storage reservoirs are located above the distribution network, they can also provide the necessary distribution pressure. Otherwise pumps are employed, with typical service pressures being around 40 psi (3 bar).

Complex computer controls are used to ensure that sufficient water is put into the system to meet demand. A central command unit, or SCADA, can receive data via telemetry on the amount of water in the mains and the amount produced at each water treatment works, as well as process information, such as whether pumps and valves are working. This system can also feed instructions to treatment works to instruct them to increase or decrease abstraction and treatment rates so that the correct amount of water is always available for the main distribution network.

FACT FILE

■ Toward the end of the 19th century, ships sometimes towed small icebergs from the coastal region of southern Chile to drier northern parts of the country. The farthest north an iceberg was towed was to Callao in Peru, 12 degrees south of the Equator. Towards the end of the 20th century, scientists suggested that it might be possible to tow huge icebergs from the Antarctic ice cap as far as the drought-ridden Middle East.

■ From the 17th century onward, many large houses in Europe incorporated an icehouse to provide cold water for the table. Ice was cut into blocks in winter and stored underground in insulating jackets of straw. Alternatively, the blocks were stacked in pyramids on the stone floors of domed icehouses; supplies would last throughout the summer and even into the next cold season.

■ It is estimated that beneath the Sahara Desert lie at least 150,000 cu. miles (625,000 km³) of freshwater, spread over more than 2.5 million sq. miles (650 million ha). About half of the planet's 2 million cu. miles (8.3 million km³) of underground freshwater is within half a mile of Earth's surface.

▶ Water hydrants, which by a series of valves, discharge water from the city supply. Hoses can quickly be connected to them when needed to control fire.

SEE ALSO: COMPRESSOR AND PUMP • DAM • DESALINATION • PLUMBING • WASTEWATER TREATMENT • WATER

Waveguide

A waveguide is a hollow tube designed to carry high-frequency (microwave) electromagnetic waves. Waveguides are similar to conductors in that both can be used to transmit power or a signal, but they differ in that waves are transmitted inside a waveguide, while electric currents travel down a conductor. Also, for electric conduction, a return wire is necessary to complete the electric circuit, but no return conductor is required for a waveguide. A basic definition of a waveguide is any system in the form of a metal tube, dielectric rod or tube, or single wire designed for the purpose of transmitting electromagnetic energy by a wave.

There is a difference between the wave transmitted inside a waveguide and that radiated from a radio antenna. The latter is a transverse electromagnetic (TEM) wave, whereas the former is not. The reason for the difference is that the walls of the waveguide (which form a boundary) affect the characteristics of the wave.

In electronic apparatus concerned with the production, amplification, and transmission of electric energy at frequencies below about 1 GHz,

the energy is transferred from one component of the system to another by connecting wires carrying alternating currents (AC) in much the same way, and obeying all the same fundamental laws, as in the very simple DC (direct current) circuit.

Where energy is required to be transferred from one part of an electric circuit to another at frequencies in excess of 1 GHz, the traditional concept of conduction by wires requires significant modification. At these very high frequencies, the physical properties of a connecting wire or cable, for example, its physical dimensions, electric conduction, physical environment, and so on, are such that the efficiency of the energy-transfer process is very low. Usually this efficiency is so low that the use of a connecting wire or cable is totally impracticable.

As a result of the work of James Clerk Maxwell, J. J. Thomson, Sir Oliver Lodge, Lord Rayleigh, and many other scientists, it was shown, by about 1900, that electric energy could be transmitted by waves constrained within a guiding structure, or waveguide. By 1936, this work

▼ A tropospheric scatter station, showing curved tubular waveguides terminating at the antenna foci. Microwave transmissions rely on tropospheric scatter to reach a receiver. Range is restricted to around 300 miles (483 km).

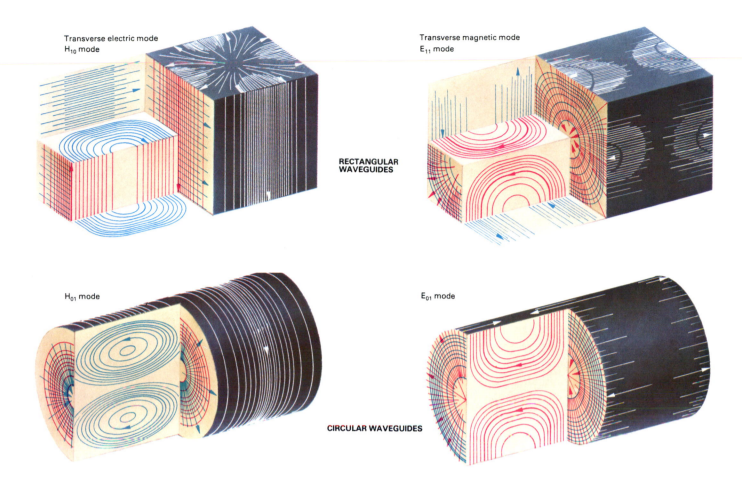

Transverse electric mode
H_{10} mode

Transverse magnetic mode
E_{11} mode

RECTANGULAR WAVEGUIDES

H_{01} mode

E_{01} mode

CIRCULAR WAVEGUIDES

had advanced to the stage where, in spite of the imperfections in the conducting or dielectric materials used in the construction of waveguides, their transmission efficiency had greatly exceeded any other cable type. Since that time, with further research and the rapid development of manufacturing techniques, the use of the waveguide has become extensive in electric apparatus that is concerned with the generation or transfer of energy at high frequencies. The design of most if not all microwave equipment is possible only by the use of waveguides as a means of transferring energy from one component to another.

The physics of waveguides

The transmission of energy by waveguide is achieved by radiating the energy, in the form of electromagnetic waves, into the inside of the pipelike structure by means of a transmitter antenna or coupling probe. Assuming that the waveguide structure does not introduce any loss into the operation, then this same energy is extracted from the waveguide by the use of a similar receiver antenna or coupling probe. This condition is similar to that when a radio transmitting antenna radiates energy into the atmosphere, some of which is absorbed by a receiver antenna.

In the simple radio, however, the wave that is radiated is known as a transverse electromagnetic wave, in which the electric and magnetic field vector components are at right angles to each other and act in directions at right angles (transverse) to the direction of propagation. For the efficient transmission of energy within the confines of a pipe or waveguide having walls made of perfectly conducting material (an ideal case), the transmitted wave is not of the TEM type. According to the basic laws of electromagnetism, the simple TEM wave cannot exist inside such a pipe because of the conducting boundary wall. Basically, a perfectly conducting boundary can only support an electric field (E) component acting normal (at right angles) to the boundary, while a magnetic field (H) component must be acting parallel to the boundary surface in order to satisfy the field equilibrium conditions associated with the conducting boundary.

Wave modes

The physical dimensions, particularly those of the inside, of a waveguide are so arranged that if an electromagnetic wave is radiated, or launched, into the enclosed volume, special field, or wave, modes are established and propagated. For the sake of simplicity, these modes and their attendant field configurations may be regarded as resulting from the combination of obliquely reflected TEM waves.

▲ Three-dimensional field configurations in rectangular and circular waveguides. The electric fields are colored red, magnetic fields blue, and currents in the waveguide walls white.

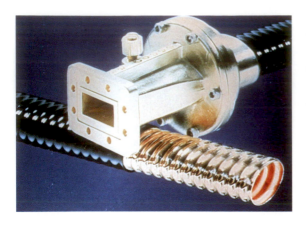

◀ Two pieces of waveguide and a connector used to link them to the antenna focus and to recording instruments in the observation house.

These modes, which are conveniently described as either transverse electric (TE, or H, modes) or transverse magnetic (TM, or E, modes) are unique to a particular waveguide cross section whether it is rectangular or circular.

In a given waveguide cross section there can be a multiplicity of modes, the simplest of which is the dominant, or fundamental, mode. The condition is very similar to the vibrations and waves in musical instruments. A simple nomenclature is used to describe the modes in a waveguide. Subscripts to the mode type nomenclature are given to indicate the number of half wavelengths (or half-period variations) at the particular frequency of transmission that can be accommodated in the width and depth of the waveguide. For example, the fundamental modes are written as E_1 or H_{10}.

In establishing a modal field structure there is an effective traveling wave structure transmitting energy along the length of the waveguide. Two

▼ A transverse electric, or H-mode, wave configuration formed from the combination of two transverse electromagnetic (TEM) waves.

distinctive features of the wave are that its velocity of propagation is less than that of light and its wavelength is greater than the free space value of a TEM wave having the same frequency.

With a traveling wave structure transmitting energy within a waveguide, there is a direct similarity to that which prevails in the radio-frequency transmission line. Indeed, there is a direct analogy between the E and H field intensity distributions, attenuation, standing wave ratios, and so on, along the length of a waveguide and the voltage and current distributions, standing wave ratios, and so on, along the length of a transmission line.

Construction

There are critical relationships between the inside physical dimensions of a waveguide and the field modal structures, and similar relationships relate to the attenuation, or energy loss, in the transmission process. Thus, the actual construction of a waveguide calls for high orders of accuracy in the principal dimensions, which must remain constant under all conditions of use.

With few exceptions, most waveguides are constructed of high-grade drawn brass and are drawn in convenient lengths or sections. There are certain special applications that require the inside wall surfaces to be gold- or silver-plated, but most sections are either cadmium- or nickel-plated to reduce oxidation to a minimum. There are other applications, for example, supplying energy to a movable microwave antenna structure, that require the construction of a flexible

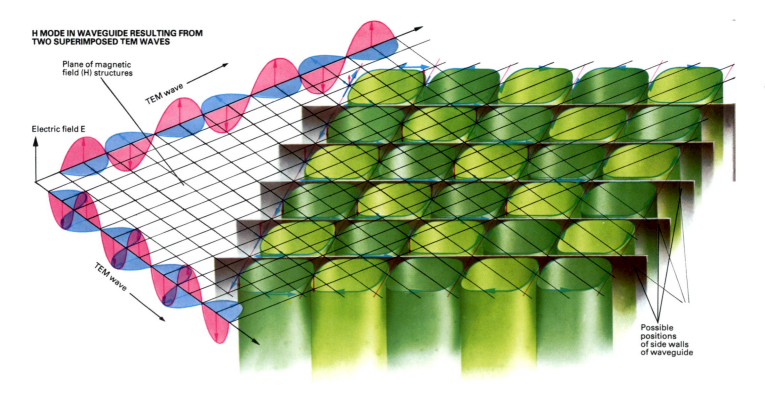

H MODE IN WAVEGUIDE RESULTING FROM TWO SUPERIMPOSED TEM WAVES

Plane of magnetic field (H) structures

TEM wave

Electric field E

TEM wave

Possible positions of side walls of waveguide

waveguide section. A very special type of flexible tube is required, constructed to the same close tolerances as the rigid section and usually very heavily bonded and protected by a rubber covering.

Waveguide sections, normally of exactly similar forms, are joined together by means of flanges attached to the ends of the sections. These flanges are of special design and, while providing a mechanically rigid joint, should not interfere in any way with the field structure within the waveguide. In addition to the simple flange joints, there is a wide range of special types of coupling devices that are used for coupling transmission circuits together rather than simply joining two sections of waveguide together. With these couplers, it is possible to cause a number of transmission circuits to interact, and energy may be directed as required.

All these devices, including the simple waveguide section, are extremely expensive to manufacture because of the high-precision engineering that is involved. This fact is particularly true of the more modern microwave equipment, which operates at frequencies in the region of 36 GHz (Q Band), where the preferred waveguide cross section dimensions are 0.28 by 0.14 in. (7 x 3.6 mm).

Applications

Some of the earliest applications of the waveguide were as simple antenna feeders. In early radar equipment, for example, they were used to transfer the very high power microwaves generated by magnetrons or klystrons to the antennas. In many cases, the same waveguides were used to transfer the very low power signals, received by the same antenna after reflection from a target, to a radar receiver.

Almost any technique requiring the use of energy at microwave frequencies will employ waveguides. They will be found in equipment used in microwave radio relay systems, radio telescopes, microwave ovens, radio meteorology (radio refractometer), mass spectrometry (spin resonance), surveying (tellurometer), material thickness gauges and monitors, and even burglar alarms. In all of these applications, the length of any waveguide run is usually very short and rarely exceeds 6 ft. (1.8 m).

There are other applications of the waveguide, of a specialized design. Recent research and technology have made it possible to construct relatively long waveguide runs of up to 1.2 miles (1.9 km) or more, of a low-loss type, that may ultimately replace the cables used in long-distance telephone trunk systems. Extremely compact and mechanically rigid, microwave antenna arrays frequently employ a single slotted waveguide section. A single narrow slot cut in either face of a waveguide radiates electromagnetic energy in much the same way as a simple dipole antenna. The excitation of the slot is derived from the currents circulating in the waveguide wall to satisfy the field boundary conditions. A number of slots in a single waveguide section form an antenna array, which produces a highly directional beam.

Optical fibers

Another form of waveguide is the optical fiber, used to transmit signals in the form of visible light and infrared. Analog or digital information is converted to an electromagnetic wave using an electro-optical transmitter. The electromagnetic wave travels along the optical fiber and is received at its destination by an optoelectric device that converts the wave back into an electric signal. Optical fibers are made of a core of glass fibers surrounded by a layer of transparent cladding, which is in turn surrounded by an outer opaque plastic layer that provides mechanical protection. The electromagnetic wave, produced by lasers or light-emitting diodes, reflects off the internal surface of the fiber, which has a higher refractive index than the cladding. The use of optical fibers permits the rapid transmission of large quantities of information and is used for sending telephone, television, and Internet signals.

◄ Waveguides, along which television signals travel from a signal substation (not shown) to an antenna, which transmits them.

SEE ALSO: ANTENNA • ELECTROMAGNETIC RADIATION • FIBER OPTICS • MICROWAVE OVEN • RADIO • WAVE MOTION

Wave Motion

◄ Water waves spreading radially from a central point of disturbance. As the waves spread out, they gradually lose energy and the amplitude of the waves decreases.

To most people the word *wave* conjures up the idea of ocean rollers or of ripples on a pond, but in physics, water waves are just one type of wave motion; others include sound, shock, and electromagnetic waves, such as light. According to the theory of quantum mechanics, even matter itself has wavelike properties.

A wave repeats itself in both space and time. The regular succession of ocean waves is evident to all, and the distance over which the wave repeats itself (the distance from one peak to the next) is known as the wavelength and represented by the Greek letter λ (lambda). At any particular place, an ocean wave repeats its regular rise and fall within a particular period (T), which is the time it takes a wave to reach from one maximum height to the next. However, instead of the period of a wave, it is common to talk in terms of the wave's frequency (f)—the number of times per second that it repeats itself at any particular place. The frequency may be calculated using the formula $f = 1/T$. Another important property of a wave is its velocity, the speed at which the wave crests move forward. It can be proved that velocity = wavelength x frequency ($v = f\lambda$) for any wave, so these three properties are, in fact, interrelated.

Although the shape of a wave moves forward with a certain velocity, the individual water molecules in the sea, for example, do not move forward. They merely oscillate up and down and convey this motion to the neighboring molecules so that the wave disturbance moves along without the molecules traveling with it. It might be thought that the back-and-forth motion of waves on the beach shows that the molecules are not just moving up and down, but these motions are not really waves, as they are not transmitting the disturbance farther along. After an ocean wave has broken on the beach, a physicist or mathematician would no longer regard it as a wave in motion.

All physical waves, such as water waves and shock waves, have this property of being a disturbance moving through a medium without the medium itself moving, and this is in fact a good definition of this kind of wave. The medium in which sound waves move is air, and an illustration of how waves convey energy through a stationary medium is the transmission of the sound energy of an orchestra or band to a listener's ears through the still air of a concert hall. Sound waves differ from water waves in one very important aspect— they are longitudinal waves, where the particles (air molecules) oscillate back and forth in the same direction that the wave travels, rather than at right angles to the wave direction, as in the case of water molecules in a water wave (a transverse wave).

Diffraction

When a wave travels around an obstacle or through a gap that is not much larger than its wavelength, the wave is seen to spread out from the gap—a phenomenon known as diffraction. In the case of water waves, this phenomenon is easily visible and in sound waves explains how we can hear a conversation around a corner or through an open doorway though we cannot see the speakers. In light, however, because the wavelengths are so small, the gap must also be very small before diffraction becomes noticeable.

Interference

Both types of waves show the phenomenon of interference, which occurs when two wave trains of the same frequency are brought together. If the peaks of the wave trains are in step (in phase) with each other, the waves combine to give a wave of greater amplitude. On the other hand, if the peaks of one wave train fall in the troughs of the other (out of phase), the waves cancel each other, and if the amplitudes (the height of the waves) are of equal size, they leave no disturbance of the medium. It was with this phenomenon that the British physicist Thomas Young proved in 1801 that light moved with a wave motion. The light from two slits illuminated by the same lamp was allowed to fall on a screen, and because the phase difference between the waves from the two slits depends on the relative distances from the slits, a pattern of light and dark bands was observed on the screen: the bright regions, where the two waves were in phase (constructive interference), and the dark, where they were out of phase (destructive interference).

Another phenomenon of interference occurs in the case of two sound waves with slightly different frequencies. These waves interfere in such a way that they alternate between interfering constructively and destructively. This phenomenon will occur in regular cycles so that the listener hears the sound pulsing as it changes in intensity from loud to soft—an effect known as beats.

Light waves

Light is a transverse wave and is made of oscillating perpendicular magnetic and electric fields. This means that light waves traveling in the same direction can still be oscillating in different directions (all at right angles to the direction of propagation). This property is called polarization and has important applications in optics.

The medium in which light (and other electromagnetic radiation) travels was for a long time thought to be a mysterious all-pervading substance called the ether, but the theory of relativity showed that the ether was experimentally undetectable and hence was scientifically meaningless. Simultaneously, the quantum theory reconciled the evidence for particles of light with its wave

▼ Clouds forming wave patterns. The Kyrenia ridge, Cyprus, induces a wavelike undulation. Clouds occur at the crests of the waves, where the air is cooler, whereas the troughs are clear.

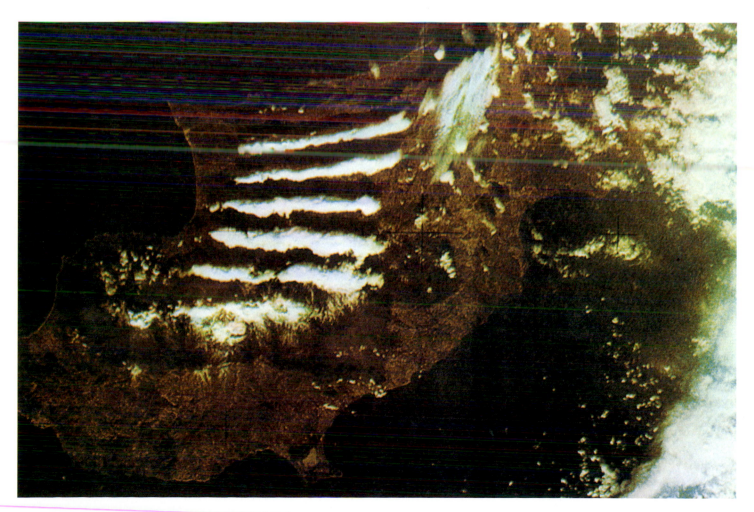

INTERFERENCE

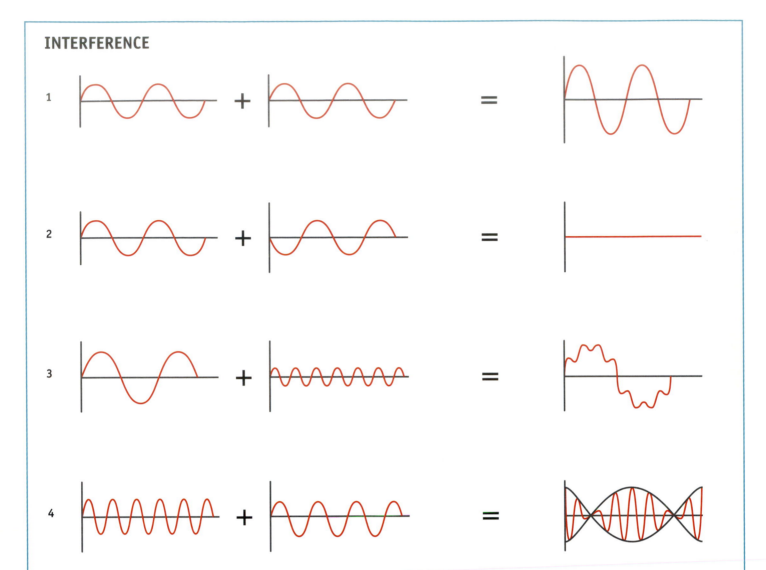

Wave motion effects simplified. (1) Adding two similar waves in phase gives increased amplitude; (2) if the waves are out of phase, they cancel each other, unless one is of greater amplitude. (3) Adding two waves of different frequencies gives a complicated waveform. The process of separating these waves is called Fourier analysis. (4) When two slightly different frequencies combine, they alternate between interfering constructively and destructively, and the result is a pulsing sound known as beats.

nature by showing that all particles of matter exhibit some wavelike properties. These waves do not occur in a material medium but represent the mathematical probability of finding the particle in a certain place at a particular time. Light waves are similar to these matter waves, and although they may seem to be unrelated to water waves and sound, the mathematical treatment of probability waves is identical. In particular, they show the same phenomena of interference and diffraction: a famous experiment carried out in 1927 demonstrated that electrons were diffracted by a crystal in the same way that X rays are diffracted, and this conclusion led the way to the development of the electron microscope.

A wave need not be of just one frequency like ocean rollers: the sound wave from an orchestra, for example, contains many different frequencies corresponding to the notes played by the various instruments. These vibrations of the air all add together (the principle of superposition of waves) to give a complex motion, which can be described by its waveform. It can be thought of as a graph either of how the intensity of a wave varies along its path or of how the intensity varies with time at one place. The ear can automatically separate the waveform of sound into its constituent frequencies; the mathematical process for doing so is known as harmonic analysis, or Fourier analysis. It finds wide application in all branches of science and technology, especially in electronics (where the wave is represented by the voltage in the circuit).

 SEE ALSO: DIFFRACTION • ELECTROMAGNETIC RADIATION • LIGHT AND OPTICS • POLARIZATION • QUANTUM THEORY • SEISMOLOGY • SOUND • WAVEGUIDE

Wave Power

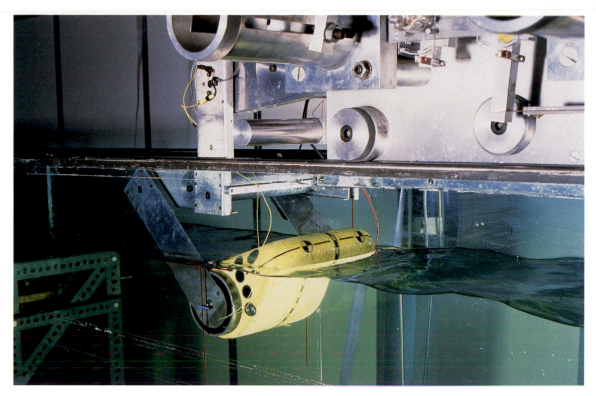

◀ A Salter's Duck undergoing tests in the laboratory. Waves generated from the right of the picture have their energy almost totally absorbed by the Duck, and the water calms behind it. The waves cause the leading edge of the device to bob up and down, rotating about the submerged axle. This oscillating motion is converted into electricity by a double-acting dynamo, with power being generated on both the up and down strokes.

Devices that generate electricity from the ceaseless motion of the sea have been around since the 1970s, but it is only in the late 1990s that serious interest has been shown in developing them for commercial use. A recent review by the British government showed that some wave power devices can now produce electricity for under $.10 per kWh (kilowatt-hour), which is the point at which making electricity becomes economically viable. Any country with a coastline, in theory, should be able to deploy these devices, so their potential could be considerable in the near future.

Waves are generated by friction between air and water and pressure changes in the wind. Friction develops as the wind blows across water, and waves are formed as energy is transferred between the two elements. A complex relationship exists between wind and waves: essentially, the height of a wave is governed by the strength of the wind and the distance over which it blows, and the speed of a wave depends on the depth of the water and the wavelength. The greater the height and speed of a wave, the greater the amount of energy it contains. The main type of energy found in waves is known as kinetic energy, energy an object or particle has as a result of its motion. Another type of energy—potential energy—is also utilized in some wave power devices. Potential energy is energy that is created by the relative positions of the elements of a system; the greater the height or depth of one part of

a device relative to another, the more potential energy it has. Translating these principles into mechanical or electrical energy is the methodology behind all wave power devices.

Types of devices

The most efficient of the current generation of wave energy devices, the Salter Duck, is able to produce electricity for under $.05 per kWh and can extract about 90 percent of the energy from a wave. The Duck was developed in 1973 by Professor Stephen Salter at the University of Edinburgh, and it generates electricity by bobbing up and down with passing waves. A Salter Duck system is made up of a chain of about 25 floats attached to a central spine. As a wave approaches, the outer shell of the duck rotates upward while the spine remains in place, with the shell returning to its normal position as the wave departs. The angular motion of the shell is used to drive a pump, which moves a liquid at high pressure through a hydraulic motor, thus generating electricity. The Duck is wing shaped in cross section and is stabilized using guys and anchor points.

The Clam is another device that, like the Duck, generates energy from sea swell. The Clam is a series of six airbags arranged around a hollow circular spine. As waves hit the structure, air is forced between the bags via the hollow spine, which houses a set of self-rectifying turbines. Even accounting for the cost of cabling to shore, calculations show that the Clam can produce electricity for around $.06 per kWh.

Another system is intended for use wherever there are suitable cliffs next to the sea. The oscillating water column (OWC) generators have their generators and cabling based on shore, making maintenance much cheaper. Incoming waves make the water level in the OWC's partially submerged main shell rise, forcing air up a funnel that houses a Well's counterrotating turbine. The retreating waves suck the air back down the funnel again, into the main chamber. The Well's turbine has been designed to spin in the same direction whichever way the air is flowing, so it generates electricity on both the upswell and the downswell to maximize efficiency. One such system, WaveGen's Limpet, has its water columns angled at 45 degrees rather than vertical, as has been shown in tank tests to be more efficient.

OWC devices are already in use at a number of sites, with test installations in both Japan and Norway. A commercial-scale 500 kW installation was commissioned on the Scottish island of Islay in September 2000. The Islay Limpet is the direct successor of an experimental 75 kW turbine built by researchers from the Queen's University of Belfast, which operated on the island between 1991 and 1999. Another trial-sized Limpet is in operation on the Azores.

One of the major problems with shoreline-based OWCs is their construction, which has to face the challenge of rocky shores exposed to wind and waves. In the case of the Islay OWC, a temporary dam was constructed on the shoreline to protect the unit. Limpet is a much larger system, with a lip 66 ft. (20 m) wide, so it was built a small distance back from the coastline, with the final sliver of ground removed after its construction.

Tapered channels

Another type of wave-power device was commissioned off Mu Ness, in the Shetland Islands. It is a form of TAPCHAN (tapered channel) system and uses the same machinery and principle as a low-pressure hydroelectric power station. A reservoir within the device is filled by waves trapped in a broad channel that reaches into the sea. As the waves move into the device, the channel is tapered and bent so that the water spills over its margin and into the reservoir. The water in the reservoir is above seawater level, and electricity is generated by dropping the water in the reservoir through a turbine and back into the sea.

The Shetland device uses a 395 ft. (120 m) steel barge anchored to the seabed, with remote sensors enabling its position to be changed to suit the wave and tidal direction. Incoming waves enter the barge via a ramp, spilling into a collecting basin and from there back into the ocean via low-power turbines. Computers regulate the height of the platform, adjusting its height via inlet valves and pumps, which add or remove water from the ballast tanks. If a storm is detected, the device's ballast tanks fill with water, so it is almost completely submerged, and thus the chances of damage are minimized. The Shetland unit is able to produce a maximum of 1.5 MW. Another trial-size sea power device is anchored off Gothenburg in Sweden, and a large TAPCHAN project, designed to generate 1.1 MW, is planned for the island of Java.

Unfortunately, TAPCHAN systems are not suited to all coasts. TAPCHANs need consistent waves, with a good average wave energy and a tidal range of less than 3 ft. (1 m), deep water close to shore, and a suitable location for the reservoir.

Other systems being developed include the Archimedes Wave Swing, a Dutch invention consisting of a 66 ft. (20 m) diameter cylindrical chamber, known as the "floater," that moves vertically with respect to the basement cylinder, which is fixed to the seabed. The floater is filled with air, which compresses as a wave passes over

▼ Waves crashing against the Limpet installation on the Scottish island of Islay. Limpet generates 500 kW of electricity, which is enough to power 300 homes. As the wave moves into the partly submerged hollow concrete chamber, the air trapped inside is forced out through a turbine. When the wave falls, air is sucked back through the turbine, which rotates in the opposite direction.

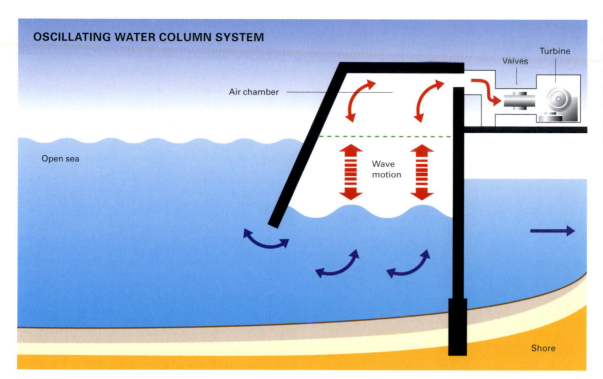

OSCILLATING WATER COLUMN SYSTEM

Turbine

Valves

Air chamber

Wave motion

Open sea

Wave motion

Shore

◄ Oscillating water columns (OWCs), such as the Limpet, work by the rise and fall of water inside a shore-based structure, which pushes and pulls air through a system of valves to drive a turbine.

the top so that the device sinks. A wave trough has the opposite effect, so the floater is in constant motion relative to the basement. This motion is translated into energy by a generator. In 2001, a 2 MW pilot project was being constructed in Romania for deployment near Portugal.

Another device, called Cockerell's raft, generates electricity by placing lines of rafts at right angles to the wave front. Between each of the rafts are sets of hydraulic motors or pumps, which utilize the energy of the wave to pump water at high pressure through the generating turbines.

The McCabe Wave Pump consists of three narrow rectangular steel pontoons, which are hinged together across their beam pointing into the incoming waves. The pontoons move relative to each other, and energy is extracted from this movement by linear hydraulic rams mounted between the pontoons near the hinges. A 120 ft. (40 m) long prototype of this device was deployed off the coast of Kilbaha in Ireland, and a commercial demonstration scheme has now been built.

The Pelamis is yet another wave power system, consisting of a number of cylindrical sections hinged together. The wave-induced motion of the cylinders is resisted at the joints by hydraulic rams that pump high-pressure oil through hydraulic motors via smoothing accumulators. The motors drive electrical generators.

Further research

Work is also under way at various British universities on other devices—Edinburgh University is refining the Salter Duck and developing a new device, the Sloped IPS Buoy, which is likely to

produce very cheap electricity. Lancaster University is developing a device called the PS Frog, and various universities are developing new versions of the floating oscillating water column.

In all, around 15 commercial wave-power devices are already in use around the world, off China, Denmark, India, Japan, Portugal, and Sri Lanka, with many more under construction. Plants are planned in Australia, Ireland, the Netherlands, and the United States.

However, both OWC systems and ocean-wave systems suffer from trying to harness violent forces. The first Norwegian OWC was ripped off the cliff face during a storm, and the Islay station is completely submerged under storm conditions. Many of the devices are also sited on the surface of the sea, in which case they may encounter damage from shipping, and—more important—they may cause damage to shipping.

Although in theory wave-generation devices could generate enough electricity to satisfy most of the global energy requirement, the costs and necessary maintenance mean the electricity produced is still expensive compared with fossil fuels. Also, removing the energy from waves has environmental implications—the resultant smaller waves may change natural erosion patterns and cause siltation, for instance. However, as fossil fuels are depleted and environmental considerations become more important, such devices may well become more popular choices.

SEE ALSO: ENERGY RESOURCES • HYDRAULICS • HYDROELECTRIC POWER • TIDAL POWER • TSUNAMI

Weed Control

The general definition of a weed is any plant growing where it is not wanted. It is difficult to precisely define which plants are weeds because, in some instances, even crop plants such as potatoes may be considered weeds. For example, if the small potatoes left after harvesting a potato crop survive the winter, they will produce potato plants in a field of some other crop. To the gardener, weeds are any wild species of plant growing among the shrubs and flowers. At the same time, however, these are plants that in another place, such as a wood, would be considered attractive and part of the country scene. Even trees may be weeds if they grow in a plantation of trees of another type.

There are many instances in which weeds need controlling. Weeds in a garden are untidy and restrict the growth of flowers and shrubs. Weeds growing on farms can drastically reduce the yield of crops by competing against the crop for essentials, such as nutrients, light, and water. Weeds growing along irrigation channels can, for example, use up twice as much water as crops.

Weeds can make the crop more difficult to harvest and can contaminate the produce. Seed heads may be gathered by machine along with beans and peas, or the seeds may get into grain that is to be used as seed for next year's crop, lowering its value and perpetuating the problem.

In some areas, wildflowers along the sides of roads may become a danger, as they restrict visibility around corners. In industrial areas, wild plants are sometimes regarded as unsightly and may actually be a nuisance to nearby workers who suffer from hay fever. Weeds that have accumulated on a derelict site may have to be cleared prior to building operations.

▲ Black plastic used as a mulch substitute to protect the roots of tomatoes being grown in a greenhouse.

▼ Thistles are a widespread problem in the United States. They can drastically reduce the yield of crops because they compete for nutrients, light, and water.

Mechanical weed control

The earliest methods of controlling weeds were mechanical; no chemicals were used. By hoeing the ground—loosening and disturbing the uppermost layer—any weed seedlings that are germinating will be cut off, uprooted, or covered with soil and thus prevented them from growing any further. Weeding can be done by hand or, more commonly, by machines drawn behind tractors.

Plowing, which cuts a furrow and turns the soil over, can uncover the growing weeds and kill them, particularly in cold weather. This system can be used only where there is no danger of subsequent soil erosion; otherwise, another system such as the stubble mulch method can be used: shallower furrows are made, and thus the weeds are cut off and deposited on the surface. This method conserves the water in the soil.

Other mechanical methods used to clear include dragging chains across the ground, flailing, and cutting. These methods are used for trimming verges, for example, but the timing of the operation is of great importance if the appearance of the roadside is not to be spoiled.

Many counties in the United States have introduced a two-tier system of weed control along roads, in which the immediate verge is trimmed closely by flail or cutters two or more times a year, but the areas farther back from the road are allowed to grow taller with less frequent cutting. In this way, weeds are kept under control, visibility around corners is preserved, and pedestrians have somewhere to walk, while the appearance of the roadside, with its wide variety of flowering plants, is not destroyed. Other non-chemical methods of weed control include

flooding fields for a period of weeks, burning, and the use of particular types of vegetation to prevent the growth of weeds under power lines. Low shrubbery will restrict the height of weed growth so that there is no danger of the weeds growing so tall that they interfere with power lines.

In some circumstances, it may be possible to introduce a foreign species of insect that will attack only one type of weed that has itself been introduced. One well-known example is the control of the prickly pear (*Opuntia* species), which infested wide areas of Australia at the beginning of the 20th century. A native of Brazil, it had no natural enemies. After research, it was decided to introduce the Argentine moth borer, which lays its eggs in the slablike leaves of the prickly pear. After their introduction in 1926, the moths caused spectacular destruction of the invasive weed within a short time.

Chemical weed control

A chemical used to control weeds is known as a herbicide. The first use of a herbicide was in 1896 in France, when a farmer, G. Bonnet, discovered that copper sulfate would kill charlock—wild mustard plants growing among cereals—without affecting the cereals unduly. Subsequently it was discovered that sulfuric acid and phenols could also be used. These materials became widely used, and although there is considerable risk in their use, are still employed today. Sulfuric acid, for example, is used as a herbicide for potatoes.

These chemicals were followed in the early 1940s by the discovery of the hormone group of weed killers known as the auxin group (from the Greek *auxein*, to grow). Auxins are chemicals that occur naturally in plants and affect their growth—for example, by increasing the elongation of individual cells. It is not fully understood why synthetic auxins are herbicides. One reason that has been suggested is that synthetic auxins can easily be absorbed by plant cells, where they build up to harmful concentrations.

The discovery of auxins transformed farming methods, and these materials, of which the best known is 2,4-D, are today very widely used, for example, in corn farming. The original auxin herbicides were particularly fatal to broad-leaved plants and were thus used to keep cereals free from weeds. Subsequent discoveries have produced a wide range of auxins with selective actions that affect only particular types of plant. Auxin-type herbicides are not generally poisonous to animals and do not remain in the soil for long.

There are many types of herbicide that select particular plants. In addition, there are nonselective herbicides—such as paraquat and sodium chlorate—which kill any vegetation they come into contact with. In some countries—for instance, Norway and Hungary—paraquat is considered too dangerous to use as a herbicide, but it is still available in the United States, where it is restricted to certified users.

In many cases, the precise way in which a particular herbicide works and why it is selective are not fully known. Some herbicides work on contact; they disrupt the actions of plant processes such as photosynthesis (the process by which a plant produces carbohydrates for growth using the energy from light). In other cases, the herbicides are absorbed by the surface and transported to centers of growth or to the roots (called translocation), where they cause a toxic reaction.

Common herbicides include 2,4-D (2,4-dichlorophenoxyacetic acid), MCPA (2-methyl-4-chlorophenoxypropionic acid), and the butyric acid derivatives of these, such as MCPB and Dalapon (2,2-dichloropropionic acid).

Selectivity and timing

Selectivity can depend on a wide range of plant properties, including the extent of the plant's waxy outer layers, the shape and position of the leaves, and the location of the growing point, where cell divisions occur. Grains, for example, grow at or just under ground level, but the buds and growing points of broad-leaved plants are on the shoots and leaves. So a spray that works by contact action will kill off broad-leaved weeds and leave grains unaffected.

The timing of herbicide application is of great importance, particularly where selectivity is needed. The germinating weeds can be killed off before the crop is planted or when the weeds have started to grow but the crop has not. The amount of moisture in the soil is critical, because a certain amount may be needed to activate the herbicide.

◄ Bundles of dried grass laid on the ground between the cultivated plants prevent weed growth on this traffic island in Nara, Japan. If allowed to grow, the weeds would obscure a driver's view of the highway and could be the cause of major traffic accidents.

WEED CONTROL METHODS

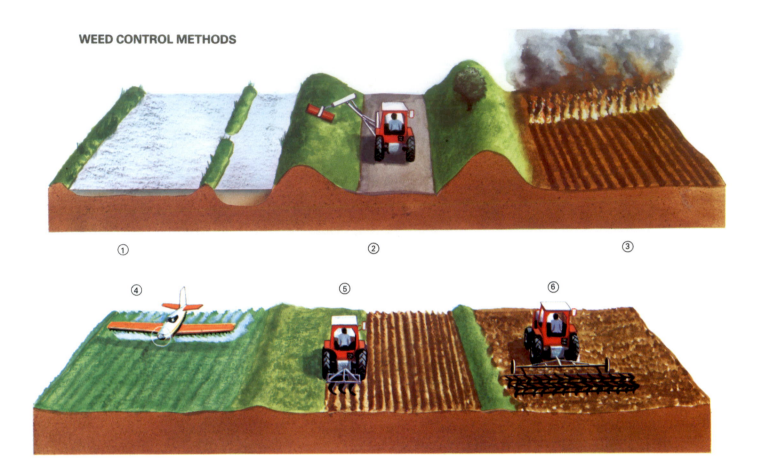

If there is too much rain, on the other hand, the chemicals may be washed down into the ground, where they could affect the crop or have no effect on the weeds at all.

Some herbicides stunt the growth of crops while killing weeds, so they must be applied to the weeds only. The concentration is also important: 2,4-D can kill any plant (especially germinating seeds) if its concentration is high enough.

Dangers

Herbicides are poisons, and no poison can be completely safe in use, but there is always a danger with any form of cultivation. Agriculture is abnormal—fields of wheat or potatoes never grow naturally. There is a school of thought that maintains that the traditional cultivation methods of plowing are destructive to the soil. Plowing disturbs the stratification, or layer structure, of the soil, which is important for drainage and for the populations of microorganisms that are essential to plant growth. Repeated plowing of the same layer can build up a plowing pan—a subsurface layer that is impervious to the downward flow of water and the upward flow of nutrients by capillary action in the soil.

As a result of the disruption to flow, it is possible that farmers in the future, particularly in regions of intensive cropping, such as the Midwest, might not plow at all but simply spray

▲ Methods used for controlling weeds differ widely. Flooding (1) is used in monsoon regions and part of the United States. Mowing with cutters or flails (2) keeps the edges of highways clear. Burning stubble (3) destroys pests as well as weeds and seeds. Spraying from the air (4) is a method used on large farms. Plowing (5) destroys weeds by cutting them off at the roots. Spraying herbicide from a tractor unit (6) may kill weeds or inhibit growth.

their fields with a herbicide that kills all vegetation, leaving a completely clear field for sowing. However, using herbicides in this way could produce further problems for farmers. If all weeds are eradicated from an area, local pests may attack the crops as the only available food source.

Because of these dangers, there has recently been interest in organic farming methods. Organic methods use biological and physical methods of weed and pest control rather than chemical. By building healthy soils, organic farmers aim to produce plants that are more able to resist weeds and pests. Another organic method for controlling weeds is mulching, in which the ground is covered by plastic sheeting or wood chips to prevent light from reaching the weeds, and thereby their growth is stunted.

Herbicide-tolerant crops

Many herbicides can control only certain types of weeds and may be quite difficult to use. For instance, the herbicide must be applied at particular times in the growth cycle of a plant and only on particular types of crop. Herbicide residues also remain in the soil for some time after they are used, so care has to be taken when planning suitable crops to plant in the future.

Herbicide-tolerant crops help to solve many of these problems, because they are genetically engineered to be resistant to particular herbicides. In this case, a nonselective herbicide that the crop is resistant to can be used to kill all the weeds while not causing any damage to the crop. If other crops are also resistant to the same herbicide, then the same herbicide can be used for several crops and in the same field for different crops in the future.

The first herbicide-tolerant soybeans were introduced in 1993 and could tolerate higher quantities of sulfonyurea, a herbicide that was already used very widely. Three years later, in 1996, Monsanto released the Roundup Ready soybean, which was completely tolerant of the herbicide glyphosate (Roundup). Adoption of this soybean has been extremely rapid—by 1999 around half of the soybean crop in the United States, totaling around 50 million acres (20 million ha), was glyphosate tolerant.

Glyphosate is an effective herbicide because it is nonselective, killing nearly all kinds of plants, and it breaks down very quickly in the soil. It therefore eases the future planting of crops in the same field and may reduce the environmental impact of the herbicide. More recently, other types of herbicide-tolerant crops have become available. Some examples of these include rice that is tolerant to glufinosate (Liberty) and other crops, such as cotton and wheat, that are also tolerant to glyphosate.

Herbicide-tolerant crops are an example of transgenic plants. The word *transgenic* is derived from the words *transfer* and *gene*, and means to transfer a gene from another unrelated plant or even from a completely unrelated species. Genes are hereditary features of plants and animals and are encoded in DNA. The Roundup Ready gene, which gives tolerance to glyphosate, was artificially created by combining genes from several different organisms.

Transgenic plants are often referred to as genetically modified, or GM, crops. This term is slightly misleading, since most crops have been genetically modified by breeding and selection for thousands of years.

Concerns

As with any newly emerging technology, there are always concerns about the possible dangers of introducing a product that is developed in a laboratory into the natural world. There is particular concern in the case of herbicide-tolerant crops.

A significant concern with herbicide-tolerant crops is that they may cross-pollinate weeds that are related to the crop and produce herbicide-tolerant weeds, often called superweeds. Cross-pollination is known to occur, for instance, with herbicide-tolerant wheat and the jointed goat

grass weed. There are proposals to prevent this unwanted effect from happening, but they require further genetic engineering, and for the moment, cross-pollination remains a real problem.

Other worries about transgenic crops include claims about their being a risk to health, damaging other organisms in the environment, and reducing the diversity of crops. There are also economic concerns—to protect the large cost of investment in research and development, many companies patent the transgenic plants, a step that could lead to more expensive prices and prevent developing countries from using these crops.

There are differences in the way in which governments around the world regulate transgenic plants. In the United States, many transgenic plants have been approved as crops, while in 1999, the European Union (EU) imposed a ban on approving new transgenic plants for sale in EU countries.

◄ The poppies growing alongside the crops in this field may look pretty, but they are weeds that have to be separated out at harvest.

SEE ALSO: AGRICULTURAL SCIENCE • BIOTECHNOLOGY • BOTANY • GENETIC ENGINEERING • HORTICULTURE • PEST CONTROL

Weigh Station

A weigh station is a weighing machine for weighing wheeled vehicles and has a weighing capacity in excess of 5 tons (4.5 tonnes).

In 1741, the most successful of many designs for a high-capacity weighing machine was devised by John Wyatt, an inventor from Thickbroom in England. Wyatt's cart weigh station used a compound lever system to support a flat weigh plate in such a way that a weight placed at any point on the plate would give the same weight indication. Wyatt's compound lever system is still the basis of all mechanical lever systems used today.

Road weigh stations

At the beginning of the 20th century, manufacturers were producing standard ranges of road weigh stations with platforms measuring up to 17 ft. by 8 ft. (5.2 x 2.4 m) and with capacities of up to 20 tons (18 tonnes). Current standard ranges include road weigh stations with platforms measuring 56 ft. by 7.5 ft. (17 x 2.3 m) and with capacities of 80 tons (72.6 tonnes). In addition, many special-purpose road weigh stations with platform lengths in excess of 81.5 ft. (24.8 m) and with weighing capacities in excess of 100 tons (90.7 tonnes) have been installed.

Rail weigh stations

From an early stage, railroads used weigh stations to weigh their freight cars for charges. The need to weigh cars of different lengths in a train without uncoupling them led to the development of

▲ The Salter Slimline electronic weighing system. An important component of any system is the load-sensing device, often a load cell. Load cells work on the electric principle whereby forces applied to a piezoelectric crystal produce voltages across the crystal. The voltages are measured and calibrated to give the force or weight of the load.

the combined weigh station, in which two or more independent weigh stations share the same weight indicator in such a way that the weight on any single weigh station or combination of weigh stations can be determined.

Electronic weigh stations

Since the introduction of the electronic road weigh station, the proportion of electronic to mechanical weigh stations has steadily increased. In general, the application of electronic weighing techniques to weigh stations has given greater flexibility both in siting a weigh station (because the weight indicator is no longer tied to it by a system of levers) and in the use of peripheral equipment such as microprocessors and other data-handling machinery.

Weighing in motion

The weighing of trains of railway cars, coupled and in motion, has been carried out in a crude form since rail weigh stations were first installed, by the operator estimating the steelyard or pointer swing. The method depended on the natural inertia of the indicator systems damping out the effect of the weight oscillations on the indicator and was at best an informed guess by a skilled operator. With the extremely fast response of the electronic weigh station, however, it is possible to determine true weight with a high degree of accuracy—by taking the average of a large number of individual weight readings in a very short time. Weighing-in-motion systems can also be employed for trucks.

Automation

To speed up the process of weighing trucks, a variety of automated systems are now being used. Hughes Transportation Management Systems (HTMS), for example, produces technology for the automatic identification of vehicles. A truck is weighed at the first station on its route, and information about the truck is stored in a transponder mounted inside the cabin. When the truck passes another weigh station, the transponder radios the information to the station's computer, which then determines whether the truck is allowed to pass or whether it must pull in. This information is then transmitted to the transponder, and the driver responds accordingly.

SEE ALSO: BALANCE • PIEZOELECTRIC MATERIAL • RAILROAD SYSTEM • TRUCK

Well

◄ A camel working the pulley mechanism of a well at Djerba, Tunisia. Problems of water pollution can occur where a large number of people bring their own buckets and dip them in the water, but the system shown here (a covered well and a single dipper) is much more hygienic. Shallow wells may need treatment by frequent chlorination.

A reliable water supply is perhaps the most important consideration for any human habitation. In many places, a river or stream can produce an adequate supply, and in others, the natural flow of water from the ground at a spring will suffice. Often, however, the collection of groundwater by means of a vertical shaft, a well, is the only means of providing a completely reliable source of water. Until 1930, for example, the city of Teheran (in Iran) was completely dependent on 12 wells for its water supply; in many desert regions human settlements are possible only because of this subterranean source of water.

The term *well* can also be used for a vertical shaft that produces other liquids—oil, sulfur that has been melted by hot water forced down the well into a sulfur deposit, and salt solution from water forced into a salt deposit.

Water wells depend on the fact that many rocks are water permeable. Rain falling onto rocks such as limestone, sandstone, basalt, gravel, and sand sinks through until it reaches the level at which the rocks are saturated with water. This level, the water table, varies in depth from over 100 ft. (30 m) in arid regions to ground level in others. At these places, water appears at the surface either as a flowing spring or a nonflowing seep. A vertical shaft sunk to below the depth of the water table will fill with water until its surface is at the level of the water table in that locality, because of seepage from the surrounding rocks. Traditional methods of drawing water from a well include the bucket and windlass for a moderately wide, 3 to 6 ft. (0.9–1.8 m), brick-lined well and the village pump, which abstracts water through a pipe a few inches in diameter. Many wells, however, have a water level that is only a few feet below ground level and can be reached by a short descending flight of steps.

The wells discussed so far are termed shallow wells, as opposed to deep artesian wells. All shallow wells are susceptible to contamination, particularly by sewage, as in the case of the pollution of a well in London, England, which caused the cholera epidemic of 1854. The risk is decreased by lining the well with impervious materials and making it as deep as possible so that water from a great depth seeps in. Greater depth also means that the well is less likely to run dry during a drought, when the level of the water table falls significantly. These wells were traditionally dug by hand with picks and shovels but are now usually dug using machinery, such as drills or earth augers, and lined with a metal or concrete pipe.

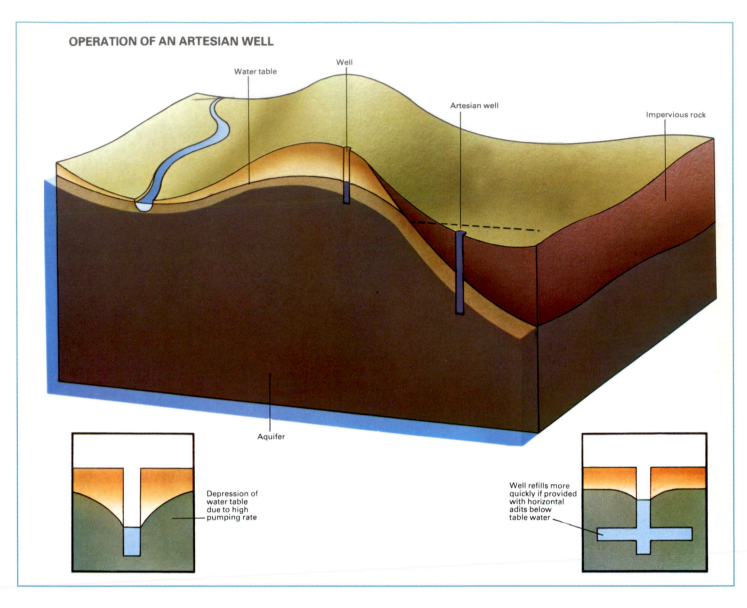

OPERATION OF AN ARTESIAN WELL

Water table

Well

Artesian well

Impervious rock

Aquifer

Depression of water table due to high pumping rate

Well refills more quickly if provided with horizontal adits below table water

The pipe lining is made to rise above the level of the ground to a height more than 1 ft. (30 cm). This lining prevents contamination of the well with floodwater from heavy rains, which could contain pesticide runoff or bacteria. New wells also need to be treated with chlorine to ensure that any harmful bacteria are destroyed before the water is used.

Artesian wells

In the London region of England, a stratum of chalk forms a saucer that rises at the edge in the Chiltern Hills and the North Downs and is covered in the center by the impervious London clay. Before the large-scale sinking of wells (up to 1,000 ft., or 305 m, deep) in the London region, rainfall on the hills produced a water table that was higher than the ground level in London, so a well sunk through the clay to the chalk would actually flow because of the pressure of water in the rock. Such artesian wells were a major source of water to the population of London for hundreds of years, but the advent of piped supplies

and the building of a new ring main has replaced the reliance on groundwater. An unforeseen consequence is that the water table has risen rapidly, flooding basements, and old wells are having to be reopened and pumped to lower the water table.

The word *artesian* derives from the French province of Artois, where artesian wells were in use as early as the 12th century; another artesian basin lies under Paris, but probably the largest is in Queensland in Australia. The Great Artesian Basin, as it is known there, covers an area of over 600,000 sq. miles (1,554,000 km^2), and some of the wells are 4,600 ft. (1,400 m) deep. At this depth, the temperature is near the boiling point of water, and it must be allowed to cool before it is given to cattle and other livestock. This supply has too high a mineral content for use in irrigation, which is the principal use of well water elsewhere in the world.

▲ Artesian wells occur where an aquifer, surrounded by rock or dense clay, slopes downward. The water in the aquifer is trapped under great pressure, so when a well is driven through the rock or clay, it spurts up forcefully.

SEE ALSO: COMPRESSOR AND PUMP • GEOLOGY • IRRIGATION TECHNIQUES • RAIN AND RAINFALL • WATER SUPPLY

Whaling

◄ A selection of harpoons used in the Icelandic whaling industry. When the harpoon hits the whale, the barbed point anchors in its body. The whale is then hauled into the catcher boat.

▶ A harpoon gun on the bow of a catcher boat. The harpoons are fired by detonating an explosive charge in the barrel of the gun, which has a range of about 160 ft. (49 m). Various types of harpoons are used: one type carries an explosive device that detonates seconds after impact. It may take several of these harpoons to kill a whale. Electric harpoons are much more effective.

stations for processing. In the 1760s, however, tryworks (brick ovens used to convert whale blubber to oil) appeared on American vessels, making possible voyages of four years and more.

The hand-thrown harpoon was developed and modified until, in 1864, a Norwegian, Swend Foyn, invented a gun to fire harpoons with explosive heads. A heavy line ran from the harpoon through a spring tackle to absorb shock and was controlled from a steam winch. Heavy guns mounted on the foredeck of faster, steam-powered boats made it possible to hunt the elusive fin, sei, and blue whales.

New techniques, and consequently larger catches, encouraged the development of massive shore stations where entire carcasses could be processed. Whale oil formed the base of soap, perfume, glycerin, and varnish. A substance called spermaceti, which comes from a cavity in the head of sperm whales, was widely used in the manufacture of candles. (The candle-power unit of illumination was based on the illuminating power of candles made from this material.)

The technology of whaling began with the Stone Age weapons of early polar people. Explorers discovered the North American Inuit to be proficient at killing whales and using the blubber and its oil for light, heat, and food. The Inuit hunted whales from small skin boats. When a whale was sighted as it came to the surface for air, the Inuit threw harpoons, attached to lines made of skin, into it. Then they were taken for a fast ride until the animal gradually tired and could be brought close enough to be killed with spears or lances. People of the Aleutian Islands and northern Japan were thought to have used poisoned spear tips, without a line. They waited for the wounded whale to die and float to the surface before securing it and bringing it back to shore.

The first whaling of commercial importance was done by the Basques in the Bay of Biscay around the 11th century. As more uses were found for whale oil, many countries began competing in the lucrative business, and by the 19th century, overfishing had already depleted stocks.

Because whale meat and blubber deteriorate very quickly, early whaling expeditions were hampered by the need to return catches to shore

Factory ships

At its peak in the 19th century, the whaling industry was highly competitive, and fishing rights and sovereignty encouraged the Norwegians to develop offshore floating factories. These in turn developed into totally independent factory ships.

In pelagic (open sea), or floating factory-ship whaling, a whaling expedition may consist of a factory ship (the processing station) complete with laboratory and hospital, a fleet of whale boats called catcher boats, buoy boats for towing the dead whales back to the factory ship, and even helicopters for sighting whales. Supplies and fuel are delivered to the fleet by a tanker, which also takes the factory-processed oil back to port.

Hunting

Finding a group, or pod, of whales can be extremely difficult. Conventional aircraft were tried at one time, but helicopters have been found to be more effective. Sonar has also been used, and other ultrasonic devices are sometimes employed to frighten whales into flight.

Catcher boats are approximately 200 ft. (61 m) long, capable of 18 knots, and designed for quick turning. A bow gun, mounted on the raised foredeck, fires 6 ft. (1.8 m) harpoons made of soft metal and weighing 120 lbs. (54 kg). The harpoons carry an explosive device that is fused to detonate seconds after impact. Several hits are often required to kill a whale in this way.

More humane electric harpoons (which stun or kill a whale immediately) have been developed. The dead whale is winched to the side of the boat and compressed air is forced into its stomach to keep it afloat; an identifying flag is attached. Radio-signal emitters are frequently attached as well to enable the buoy boat or the catcher boat to locate and round up the drifting whales. Catcher boats frequently cover more than 100 miles (160 km) in a day.

Processing

When the dead whales are towed to the factory ship, they are maneuvered to the whale slipway—a large hole through which the whale is pulled from the sea to the main deck by steel claws and winches. Because decomposition sets in quickly, all whales are processed within 36 hours. Giant factory ships are therefore equipped to handle as many as 12 whales a day. Blubber is flensed (stripped) lengthwise in sections, ground, and put in high-pressure steam cookers. The oil is then purified in a centrifuge. Lemmers (butchers) separate the flesh from bone. The bone is cut up and, because it is oily and porous, pressure cooked for

▼ Whalers are factory ships designed to process whales as quickly as possible. The size of a whale is such that it has to be cut into smaller pieces on the flensing deck before it can be processed. Below deck are separate grinding and boiling systems for the blubber, whale meat, and bones. Sometimes the meat is used for human consumption and is canned on board or is frozen. The processed oil is kept in tanks in the bottom of the ship for collection by a tanker.

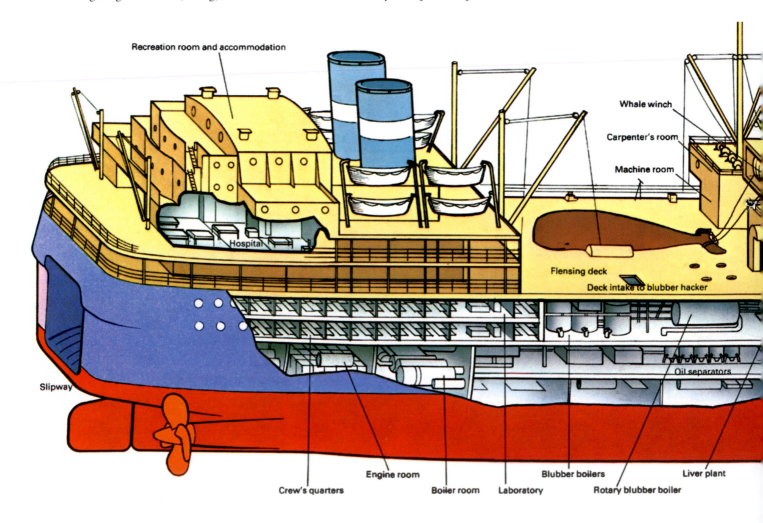

Recreation room and accommodation
Hospital
Whale winch
Carpenter's room
Machine room
Flensing deck
Deck intake to blubber hacker
Slipway
Oil separators
Crew's quarters
Engine room
Boiler room
Laboratory
Blubber boilers
Rotary blubber boiler
Liver plant

oil extraction; the residue is ground and bagged as bone meal. The flesh not used for human consumption is processed for oil, and the remaining solids are kiln dried and sold as animal food. In less than an hour, a 100-ton (91-tonne) blue whale can be fully processed.

Edible flesh is frozen, canned, or reduced to meat extract (whale meat is popular in Japan). Sometimes the fresh meat is transferred to freezer ships for faster distribution. The purified oil is held in the lower deck until collection by a tanker.

Today fleets rely on advanced equipment—including gyrocompasses, depth recorders, radio telephony, and radar—to locate whales. Most whaling ships have underwater rangefinders and bearing indicators that provide continuous information on a whale's position.

Despite the advance in technology of operations, however, a much smaller number of whales can be taken per fleet per day than were taken by comparatively primitive whaling operations in earlier times. The whale's gestation period is a year or more; thus, replenishment of depleted herds is difficult.

Protecting whales

The International Whaling Commission (IWC) was established in 1946 with the aim of exploitation without extermination. It acts in an advisory capacity on behalf of member nations, but not all whaling countries—Iceland, for example—belong.

By the end of the 1970s, stocks of whales had become dangerously depleted, and some species were on the verge of extinction. In 1982, the IWC banned all commercial whaling, effective since 1986. Catch limits were placed on subsistence whaling by aboriginal populations, such as Alaskan Inuit and Greenlanders. The IWC prohibits taking calves and all females with calves.

Two member nations, Norway and Japan openly flout the IWC's moratorium on whaling, and both are pushing to overturn the ban. Since 1987 Japan has hunted minke whales in the Antarctic under the guise of "scientific" research, even though the whale meat is openly sold on the market. In 2000, Japan expanded its whale hunt in the North Pacific, adding two new species—sperm and Bryde's whales—to its catch and further defying the IWC ban. Norway started

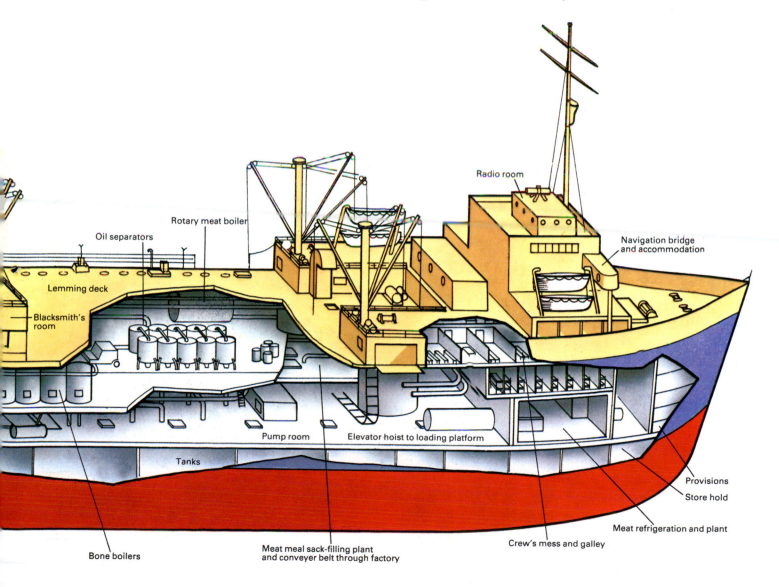

Oil separators

Rotary meat boiler

Radio room

Navigation bridge and accommodation

Lemming deck

Blacksmith's room

Pump room

Elevator hoist to loading platform

Tanks

Provisions

Store hold

Meat refrigeration and plant

Crew's mess and galley

Bone boilers

Meat meal sack-filling plant and conveyer belt through factory

◄ Hauling in a sperm whale for marking so that it can be identified later by the buoy boats and towed back to the factory ship.

FACT FILE

■ Native whalers of the Indonesian island of Lembata claim that their ancestors were brought to the region on the back of a sperm whale. They now hunt the sperm whale in wooden boats with palm-leaf sails. The harpoonist leaps onto the whale's back as he strikes it. Ecologists believe that the islanders may now suffer from the high levels of mercury found in sperm whale flesh.

■ In 1931, at the peak of commercial whaling, more than 2.5 million tons (2.3 million tonnes) of whales were caught in the Antarctic Ocean alone. Fifty years later, the catch for all waters was less than 200,000 tons (181,000 tonnes).

■ Basque whalers operating on the Labrador coast in the 16th century were sometimes paid in whale oil, from 30 barrels for a captain, down to five barrels for a seaman. As the average ship could carry a 50,000-gallon (190,000 l) cargo, most of the profits went to the owners of the ships.

commercial whaling of minke whales again in 1993, undermining the authority of the IWC.

Despite a long period of protection, several whale species remain highly endangered, threatened, or vulnerable. The endangered species include blue whales, fin whales, sei whales, and all three species of right whales. The population of the North Atlantic right whale is estimated at only 300, and the species is close to extinction.

◄ Whaling is still practiced in some countries, but stocks have become depleted, and some species have even been hunted to extinction.

SEE ALSO:	AQUACULTURE • FISHING INDUSTRY • SONAR

Winch and Windlass

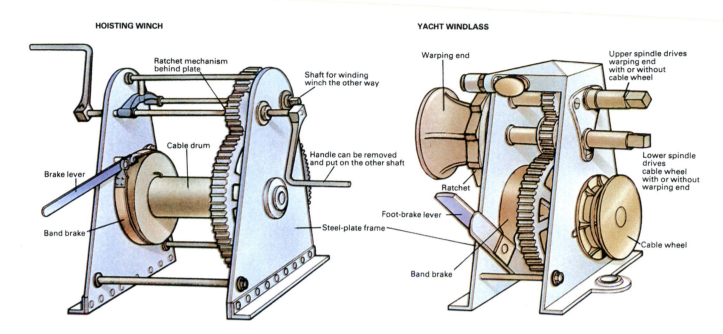

HOISTING WINCH

Ratchet mechanism
behind plate

Shaft for winding
winch the other way

Cable drum

Brake lever

Band brake

Handle can be removed
and put on the other shaft

Steel-plate frame

YACHT WINDLASS

Warping end

Upper spindle drives
warping end
with or without
cable wheel

Ratchet

Lower spindle
drives
cable wheel
with or without
warping end

Foot-brake lever

Band brake

Cable wheel

The origins of the windlass are probably as old as the wheel. Grindstones turned by a cranked handle were known in China as long ago as 2000 B.C.E., and in Europe by 400 C.E. Rotating shafts, as seen in a windlass, are probably equally as old. The development of the wheel in Europe and the Middle East started with the cartwheel. Not long before the beginning of the Christian era, this invention was followed by the waterwheel, revolving shaft, windlass, and pulley.

The windlass

The windlass is a form of wheel and axle used for hoisting or hauling. It consists of a drum or barrel supported in a vertical frame and turning on a horizontal axis. The drum is fitted with a crank and handle, and can be turned by hand directly or through a gear drive, or by motor. A rope that is attached to the drum transfers the applied force from the crank to the load in the same ratio as that of the length of the crank to the radius of the drum. This ratio is known as the mechanical advantage, and the applied force is magnified by it. The mechanical advantage also works in reverse.

The winch

The winch is a slightly more elaborate form of windlass, although the two words were originally synonymous. The term *winch* is now normally applied to a power machine having one or more drums onto which a rope is wound for lifting or hauling a heavy object. It is almost invariably driven through a gear train or worm drive such that the weight of the load will not turn the drum backward when the power source is removed.

The differential windlass and capstan

A more advanced type of machine is the differential windlass, also called a Chinese windlass. This type of windlass gives a greatly increased mechanical advantage by having two barrels of different diameters attached rigidly to each other on the horizontal axis. As in the simple windlass, a crank and handle are attached to one end of the barrels. The principle is that both ends of a rope are fastened to the barrels in such a way that as the handle is turned, the rope unwinds from one barrel and winds onto the other.

A pulley block positioned in the bight (loop) of the rope between the barrels carries the load. The rope is shortened by winding onto the larger barrel while being simultaneously lengthened by unwinding from the smaller one, and the load moves upward by half the difference. The nearer in size the two diameters are, the greater the mechanical advantage will be.

A capstan is a windlass that has the barrel mounted on a vertical axis. The original design had a series of radial holes around the top of the barrel, into which poles could be inserted and used to turn the barrel. The most common application for a capstan was, and still is, for hoisting the anchor of a ship. A few turns of the anchor warp (hauling rope) are taken around the barrel, and friction between the warp and barrel is sufficient to prevent slippage.

▲ A hoisting winch (left) and a yacht windlass (right). The hoisting winch has a ratchet to stop it from slipping backward and a brake to slow it when lowering heavy loads. The larger, double-purpose yacht windlass is used for hoisting large sails. The warping end is for light line, such as hemp, and the cable wheel is for heavier wire rope.

SEE ALSO: CABLE AND ROPE MANUFACTURE • CRANE • DYNAMICS • FISHING INDUSTRY • GEAR • PULLEY • SAILING • SEA RESCUE • SHIP • SUBMERSIBLE • WARSHIP

Wind Power

Winds are currents of air that originate from the differential solar heating of surface air at different latitudes on Earth's surface. Intense heating near Earth's equator causes air to become less dense and rise, whereas the much weaker solar heating near the poles allows air to cool down, so it becomes more dense. This effect causes air near Earth's surface to drift from the poles toward the equator. Wind directions are further influenced by factors such as Earth's spin and the presence of land masses and mountain ranges. On a more local scale, smoothly flowing winds can be made turbulent and gusty by hills and buildings and by small-scale weather systems, such as local storms.

In effect, wind is a manifestation of the transfer of heat energy from the Sun to Earth, and it can be made to play a part in producing other forms of energy, such as mechanical energy or electrical energy. Mechanical energy can be kinetic energy, such as that of a moving grindstone, or it can be the increased potential energy of water pumped from a well to a surface reservoir.

Wind has the disadvantage of being to some extent unpredictable, so devices that harness it must operate together with a storage system if a constant supply of power or pumped water is required. Nevertheless, wind power is completely renewable—it will be available as long as the Sun shines. Thus, it has gained the interest of energy suppliers faced by dwindling fossil-fuel reserves and increasing pressure to reduce emissions of carbon dioxide, a greenhouse gas, and various other pollutants, such as sulfur dioxide.

Early windmills

The Persians were probably the first people to use windmills, to mill grain and lift water, around the seventh century C.E. Persian mills had vertical

THE FUTURE OF WIND POWER

Wind is a clean and inexhaustible source of energy, and it can be produced cheaply once the initial equipment costs have been met. For these reasons, it is currently earning more attention than ever as a renewable energy source, and wind farms —collections of wind turbines linked to a distribution grid—are being built and run all over the developed world.

Electricity from wind turbines is no novelty: the first generating wind turbine was built in Denmark in 1890. Early wind turbines produced direct current power but at low voltage, so they could be used to charge batteries for low-power devices, such as household lamps, but were impractical for power-thirsty appliances, such as washing machines. This situation changed with the introduction of wind-powered alternators, whose alternating-current outputs could be transformed to distribution and supply voltages.

Electricity from wind regained interest when petroleum costs soared as a result of the worldwide oil crisis of the 1970s. By 2001, wind was the fastest-growing sector of the power-generating industry, with the main countries of growth being Germany, the United States, and Spain. Denmark has the greatest proportion of wind power of any country, its 2,300 MW of wind power provides 18 percent of the national demand. Denmark is an exception to the rule, however, since the global wind-power electrical generating capacity of 23,300 MW at the end of 2001 met the needs of only around 25 million people.

The potential for exploiting wind power is much greater, however. In the United States, it is estimated that the national power demand could be met by available wind power from just three states—North Dakota, Kansas, and Texas. In Europe, Scottish wind power would be enough to meet more than half the needs of the United Kingdom.

One of the factors that has slowed the development of wind power is, somewhat ironically, concern for the environment. The replacement of a typical fossil-fuel power station would require thousands of wind turbines, and some people fear that thoughtless siting of wind farms could wreck whole landscapes, particularly as good wind resources often coincide with areas of outstanding natural beauty.

One approach to reducing the visual impact of wind farms, followed by the Danes, is to build them out at sea. This idea has the added benefit that winds at sea tend to be more constant and therefore better for generating electricity. Another, being taken up in Britain, is to build wind farms on so-called brownfield sites, areas of dereliction left by heavy industry on closure. An example is the 47.5 MW wind farm planned for construction on Teesside, northeast England. Such projects have the potential to improve the environment by replacing spoil tips and contaminated wasteland with elegant wind turbines set in landscaped surroundings.

The other main hindrance for the development of wind power is economic: the operators of conventional power plants have little interest in spending money on wind power just to see their current plants lie idle. Measures to spur suppliers into action include the Renewables Obligation of the British government's Department of Trade and Industry, whereby electricity suppliers will be required to provide 10 percent of their output from renewable resources by 2010. Another impetus comes from the private sector: on February 14, 2002, the outdoor apparel manufacture Timberland announced its intention to sponsor the construction of wind farms that will provide more than twice the energy demands of its retail outlets.

▼ This wind farm at Altamont Pass, California, has 85 turbine generators rated at 330 kW, 10 at 60 kW, and 1 at 750 kW—a capacity of almost 30 MW. Typical coal-fired power stations produce around 2,000 MW.

A traditional wooden post mill with combined fantail and access stairs. The purpose of the fantail is to keep the sails facing into the wind—a manual task for the miller prior to their introduction.

shafts and sails that rotated in a horizontal plane within a building that channeled air over the sails. They were completely unlike the horizontal-shaft mills of four or more sails that became traditional in western Europe from around the 12th century, but they were adopted in China and are still in use for pumping irrigation water.

Numerous theories relate to the introduction of windmills in western Europe, the most popular being that they had been seen in the Near East by European crusaders who took the concept back to their homelands. The first reliable documentary evidence of windmills in Europe refers to an order from Abbot Samson to Dean Herbert in 1191, requiring him to demolish a windmill in his glebe lands at Bury St. Edmunds in Britain. It is strange that this first reference should be for the removal rather than the construction of what must have been a novel structure.

Post mills

All the earliest windmills were post mills. In this design, a heavy and rigid underframe of two balks of timber, set at right angles, rest on level ground or brick piers. Quarter bars, mortised into the underframe and set at an angle of about 30 degrees, support a central post, around which the entire mill could rotate. The mill would be turned into the wind by means of a tail pole pulled by the miller. Sometimes the tail pole was combined with the steps that led up into the mill building. Later mills were automated to turn toward the wind by the addition of a small wind wheel, called a fantail. When the windmill was facing directly into the wind, the fantail did not turn; if the wind shifted it would rotate. It was geared to wheels that, running on a circular track, would slowly move the mill back into the wind direction without work for the miller.

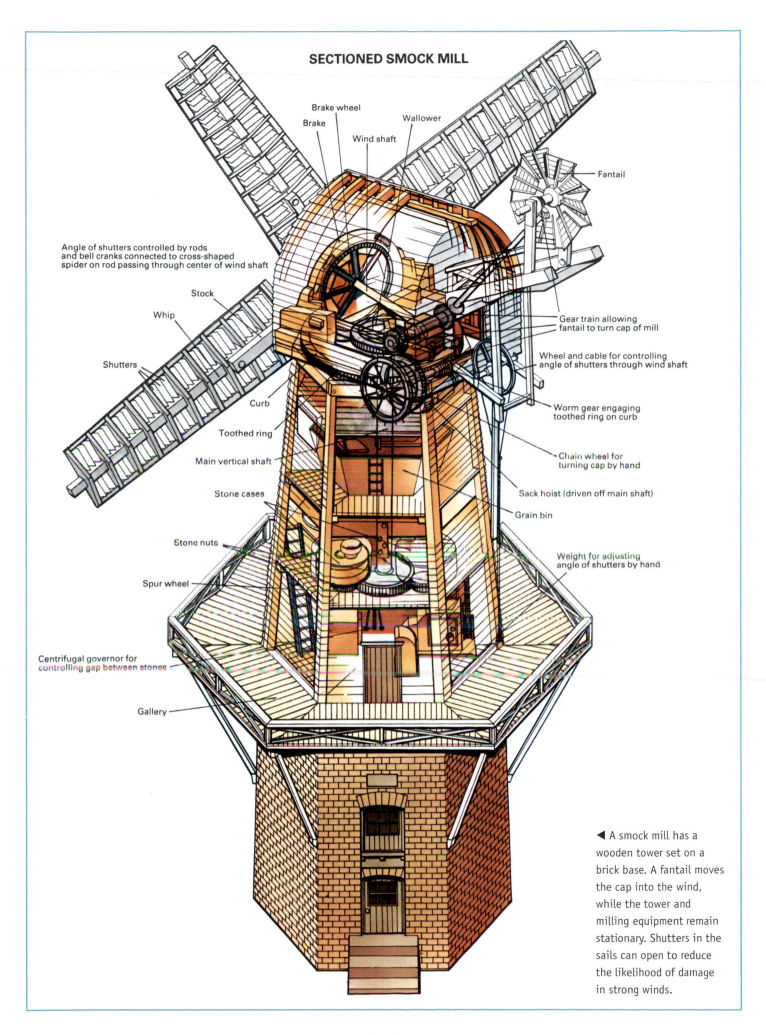

SECTIONED SMOCK MILL

Brake wheel

Brake

Wind shaft

Wallower

Fantail

Angle of shutters controlled by rods
and bell cranks connected to cross-shaped
spider on rod passing through center of wind shaft

Stock

Whip

Shutters

Curb

Toothed ring

Main vertical shaft

Stone cases

Stone nuts

Spur wheel

Centrifugal governor for
controlling gap between stones

Gallery

Gear train allowing
fantail to turn cap of mill

Wheel and cable for controlling
angle of shutters through wind shaft

Worm gear engaging
toothed ring on curb

Chain wheel for
turning cap by hand

Sack hoist (driven off main shaft)

Grain bin

Weight for adjusting
angle of shutters by hand

◀ A smock mill has a
wooden tower set on a
brick base. A fantail moves
the cap into the wind,
while the tower and
milling equipment remain
stationary. Shutters in the
sails can open to reduce
the likelihood of damage
in strong winds.

▲ A brick tower mill at Hecklington in Britain. The height of the tower improves exposure to the wind, while the gallery gives access for attaching sails to the sail frames.

to the top of the tower carried the cap on wheels, and a set of horizontal wheels located the cap in the correct position over the tower.

Sails

Typical British windmills had four sails, or sweeps, each comprising a relatively light wooden frame secured to the sail stock and a substantial wooden beam attached to the wind shaft. When the mill was required to work, the miller would spread canvas over the frames, much as a sailor sets the sails of a boat. It was a laborious and time-consuming task, because each sweep had to be turned by hand until the end was close to the ground and the miller could climb up to set the canvas.

In 1772, a British millwright, Andrew Meickle, invented the spring sail. The canvas was replaced by a series of hinged slats, not unlike those of a venetian blind. The slats were linked together and kept in the set position by hand gear and a strong spring. If the force of the wind suddenly increased, the slats would open to spill the wind and thus reduce the risk of damage.

When hollow cast-iron wind shafts replaced their solid wooden predecessors, it became possible to incorporate series of linkages that could adjust the angle of the slats while the mill was turning. At first, this was a manual operation; later, it was overtaken by a centrifugal governor that kept the mill turning at a constant speed.

Milling

The wind shaft, set at a slight angle to the horizontal, was supported by two journal bearings and a simple thrust bearing to carry the thrust of the wind on the sails. A gear wheel was attached to the wind shaft and drove a vertical shaft, usually set in the center of the building.

Generally, the rim of this wheel had a band brake around it, used to stop the mill, called the brake wheel. The wheel on the vertical shaft was called the wallower, a term borrowed from water mills, and the great spur wheel at the bottom drove stone nuts that would be engaged with the millstones as required for milling.

Sack hoists, dressing machines, and other equipment in the mill were also driven from the wind shaft. Individual millers developed ingenious methods to help perform heavy work. By adapting a mill to power other forms of equipment, millers could boost their income by amassing a stock of work to be done when there was little demand for milling grain. In this way, a given mill might be pressed into service to drive a gang saw (for cutting lumber) or an oil mill (for pressing oil from seeds) when grain was short and the wind was favorable for work.

The post mill, although popular in Britain, was a fragile structure that was likely to overturn in a severe gale, burn down, or become irreparably damaged by rot or neglect. The danger of rot to the underframe and quarter bars was reduced by building a round house, usually of brick, to protect the stationary base structure. The mill itself would still rotate about the post to face the wind, and the roundhouse also served as a store.

Tower mill

Tower mills evolved in western Europe well before the 17th century. The tower was usually built of brick, but it was sometimes of timber on a brick base, when it was called a smock mill. The great advantage of the tower mill was that rotation into the wind was confined to a top cap that carried the wind shaft and sails. Gears linked the wind shaft to a vertical shaft that transmitted power to machinery in the base regardless of the orientation of the top cap. An iron track secured

Land drainage

The use of windmills for land drainage started in the Netherlands centuries ago, as part of an effort by the Dutch to extend the area of land available for cultivation. Early designs featured scoop wheels. They were similar in appearance to water wheels, but their paddles lifted the water rather than being driven round by it. The brake wheel on the wind shaft drove a vertical shaft through angled gearing, and it in turn drove a horizontal shaft attached to the scoop wheel.

Some mills pumped water using Archimedes' screws. These devices, reputedly invented in the third century B.C.E. by the Greek mathematician Archimedes, consist of inclined shafts in which helical blades rotate. The lower end of an Archimedes' screw is submerged in water, and the shaft rests at a shallow angle so that the angle of inclination of the shaft to the horizontal is less than the pitch of the helical surface. In this way, water can be trapped between adjacent turns of the screw. As the screw turns in the appropriate sense, water flows up the shaft and is discharged at the top.

Water supply

The windmill for residential water supply is sometimes called a wind engine to differentiate it from a conventional windmill. First built toward

◀ This wind pump is set on a hill to catch the wind. It pumps water from underground to a barrel that acts as a reservoir.

the end of the 19th century, they were mainly of wooden construction and operated reciprocating pumps through a simple crank mechanism. Modern variants of the water engine continue to be used for household water supplies in regions where the sparse population makes a centralized piped water supply unfeasible, as is the case in some regions of the United States.

A basic design of water engine includes a wind wheel with some 20 pressed-steel blades secured to a wind shaft that turns on ball bearings. A typical wheel is 10 to 14 ft. (3.0–4.3 m) in diameter, and the windmill head is mounted on top of a lattice steel tower around 25 ft. (7.6 m) tall. The wind shaft drives a crank shaft through reduction gearing, and connecting rods work a crosshead to which pump rods are attached. The whole mechanism is contained in a cast-iron oil bath, and the complete head is free to rotate around a tube at the top of the tower through which the pump rods pass. A windmill of this type should run for a year without attention.

The actual water horsepower of a 14 ft. (4.3 m) windmill pump when driven by a 24 mph (39 km/h) wind is approximately 0.5 horsepower (0.38 kW). This value refers to the rate at which the potential energy of water can be increased by lifting it at a given rate through a given height; it is somewhat less than the power developed by the wind wheel at its shaft. With a shallow borehole giving a good yield or a surface supply, only limited amount of irrigation may be done using such a mill, but it is usually sufficient for backyard watering.

SEE ALSO: BEARING AND BUSHING • ELECTRICITY • ENERGY RESOURCES • LAND RECLAMATION • WATER SUPPLY

Wind Tunnel

A wind tunnel is a device used for the aerodynamic testing of full-size and model constructions under controlled conditions. The most important requirement of a wind tunnel is that it produce a flow of air that is uniform and smooth. To achieve this end, several different arrangements are required, depending among other things on the operating air speeds within the tunnel.

Originally, wind tunnels were used for testing airfoil designs for aircraft, but now they are also used extensively in the design of missiles and road and rail vehicles, as well as to predict wind loading and wind-excited oscillations of buildings, bridges, power lines, and radar scanners. Other applications include tests to ensure the safe disposal of flue gases from ships' funnels and industrial chimneys; to study local wind patterns in the precincts of tall buildings; and to examine snow drifting on landscape models featuring highways.

Modeling rules

The first powered flights by the Wright brothers on December 17, 1903, were the outcome of an intense program of research they completed in the preceding year. Disappointed with the slow progress of build-and-fly methods, they built a wind tunnel late in 1901 and, in about two months, tested over 200 airfoil models. Each airfoil had a different section shape and planiform, and they were tested at 13 angles of incidence to the wind from 0 to 45 degrees.

Knowing the forces on the model, they estimated the full-scale forces (for a full-size wing at true flying speed) from the ratio (full scale to test condition) of air density, square of linear size, and square of wind speed—exactly as is done today.

Experience has shown that accurate predictions of full-scale forces depend on certain modeling rules. Where the test features a curved model, the Reynolds number for the test should be near that of the full scale for the boundary layer to be reproduced correctly. The boundary layer is the layer of air adjacent to the surface of the body over which the air is flowing and where viscous forces predominate over inertial forces. This layer is likely to separate from the body. The Reynolds number is a nondimensional number that gives the ratio of inertial forces and is calculated by the expression (air speed) x (size of object) x (air density) ÷ (air viscosity). The Reynolds number for the test is nearly always smaller, if for no other reason than the model being less than full size. One way of increasing the Reynolds number for the test is by raising

▼ Wind tunnels were first used to test aircraft designs, but today they are also used in the design of automobiles, buildings, and bridges.

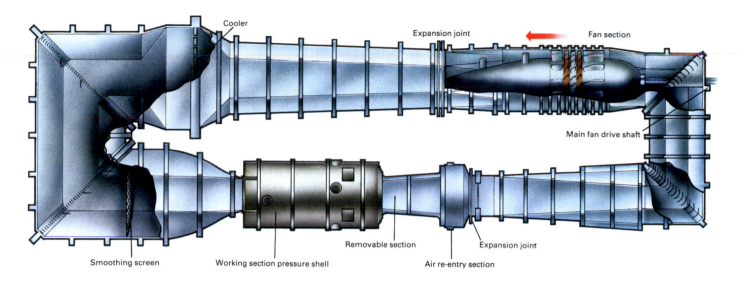

Cooler

Expansion joint   Fan section

Main fan drive shaft

Smoothing screen   Working section pressure shell   Removable section   Air re-entry section

Expansion joint

▲ A conventional closed wind tunnel design, showing the turbine (in the fan section) and smoothing screen, made of wire mesh.

the operating pressure, which increases the density but does not affect the viscosity.

Where tests involve compressible flow (that is, where air flows around a body at speeds sufficient to cause large changes in pressure and therefore in density), the full-scale Mach number must be employed. The Mach number is the ratio of air speed to the speed of sound in that medium, and it varies with the temperature. Where tests involve the rotation of propellers, helicopter rotors, or radar scanners, the advance ratio (rotor tip speed to forward wind speed) must be the same as the full-scale value.

Constructional features

Most continuous running wind tunnels use electrically driven fans or turbines, which impart angular momentum to the airstream, the result being swirl—an undesirable side effect. To offset this effect, prerotational vanes may be used, and any residual swirl can be further reduced by using straightener vanes after the turbine.

The power loss in each part of the wind tunnel increases as the cube of the local air speed. For this reason, wind tunnels are designed with local air speeds as low as possible except in the working section (the area where the model is tested). Diffusers—ducts with a slowly widening cross section—are used to reduce the air speed; in the process, the static air pressure increases according to Bernoulli's equation (this equation relates the kinetic and potential energy of a fluid in a system where energy is being conserved). Mitered corners are fitted with corner vanes to turn the air uniformly with minimum loss. Because all the power put into the turbine is eventually converted

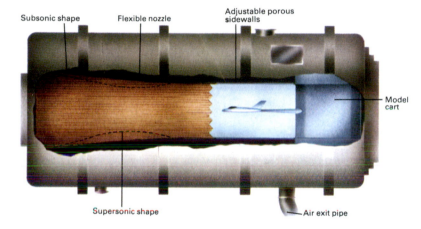

Subsonic shape   Flexible nozzle   Adjustable porous sidewalls

Model cart

Supersonic shape   Air exit pipe

into heat, banks of cooling tubes are needed in high-powered, continuous-running wind tunnels.

Next the air passes into a settling chamber. A honeycomb flow straightener often precedes wire mesh smoothing screens to produce a uniform smooth flow in this chamber. From here, the air is accelerated through a contraction or nozzle into the working section.

For intermittent running, it is possible to accumulate compressed air over a long period and then release it through an annular slot surrounding a circular duct. This system can produce a high-speed flow in the duct for a limited period. For wind tunnels providing hypersonic air flow (above Mach 5), high pressure ratios are required (this is the ratio of absolute pressure at the entrance and exit of the tunnel element). They can be most effectively achieved by connecting the evacuated sphere to the exit of the tunnel, so reducing the exit pressure.

Working sections

Most wind tunnels have a closed working section where the air flow is constrained within solid walls and in contact with them. When testing airfoils in a closed working section, the walls restrict the curvature of the streamlines past the model and, in

▲ Detail of the working section of a conventional closed wind tunnel. To generate supersonic speeds, a complicated duct shape is required. The flexible walls are adjusted to form the required shape.

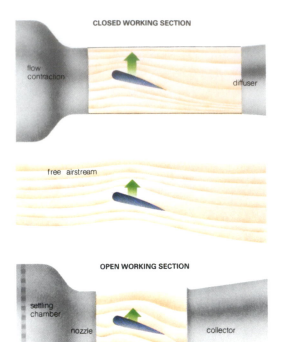

CLOSED WORKING SECTION

flow contraction

diffuser

free airstream

OPEN WORKING SECTION

settling chamber

nozzle

collector

◀ When testing airfoil designs, the type of working section is important because it affects the flow characteristics around the model.

Conventional closed working sections cannot be used near the speed of sound (Mach 1) because even the smallest models cause choking. In choking, a shock wave becomes attached to the model and dramatically destroys the uniformity of air flow. In open-jet wind tunnels, flow pulsations can develop at high speeds (in the transonic range—from Mach 0.9 to 1.2). Special techniques are required in these situations.

Supersonic wind tunnels

Supersonic testing is accomplished by using a convergent-divergent nozzle, which works by virtue of a peculiar consequence of the laws governing gas flow. Although the speed of a gas may be increased to the local speed of sound when forced through a contracting duct, further increase of speed is possible only if the duct area subsequently increases.

To maintain a constant mass flow of gas throughout the duct, this supersonic expansion is accompanied by a compensating reduction in gas density, which arises through a reduction in both static pressure and temperature. The fall in temperature as a gas expands is utilized in home refrigerators. Work has to be done to suddenly compress a gas (so that it becomes hot), whereas work is done by a gas during sudden expansion, and the energy for this change is extracted from the gas in the form of heat.

Not only does the actual speed of the gas increase on expansion but the accompanying fall in temperature decreases the local speed of sound—so the Mach number is increased on both counts. At high supersonic speeds (Mach 3 and over), the lowering of temperature, and thereby the local speed of sound, becomes the major factor in achieving the high Mach numbers.

As the applied pressure ratio is increased, a shock wave forms at the throat of the convergent-divergent nozzle when the local Mach number is unity. The wave gradually moves into the divergent region until the design pressure ratio is reached, whereupon the single shock wave is replaced by a more complex shock wave pattern

the process, slightly increase the measured lift. The lift measurement must subsequently be corrected to eliminate this error; these adjustments are known as boundary-constraint corrections.

Some wind tunnels have open-jet working sections, the model tested being in the free space between the convergent nozzle and a larger collector downstream. The absence of walls makes for easy access, especially with large models, but additional power is needed to overcome the turbulence losses at the edge of the jet. The curve of the streamlines around an airfoil situated in an open jet is slightly exaggerated and the measured lift consequently slightly too small. In this situation, constraint corrections of the opposite sign are necessary.

Slotted-wall working sections, with thin, parallel slots along the length of the enclosing walls, can eliminate the need for boundary-constraint corrections. They also serve to inhibit the formation of unwanted shock waves.

▼ For supersonic testing, it is necessary to use a convergent nozzle with a divergent duct in order to increase the Mach number.

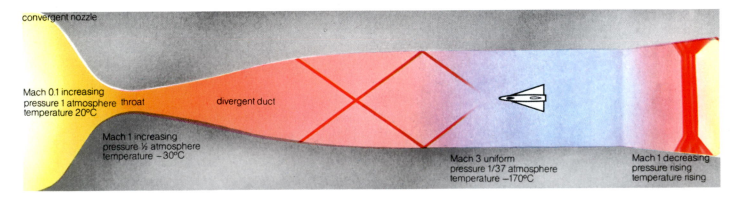

convergent nozzle

Mach 0.1 increasing
pressure 1 atmosphere
temperature 20°C

throat

divergent duct

Mach 1 increasing
pressure ½ atmosphere
temperature –30°C

Mach 3 uniform
pressure 1/37 atmosphere
temperature –170°C

Mach 1 decreasing
pressure rising
temperature rising

and followed by a uniform flow at the design Mach number, in the final parallel portion. At some convenient position well downstream, a further shock wave is formed through which the flow becomes subsonic again.

Transonic wind tunnels employ careful shaping of flexible walls upstream of perforated or slotted walls. Carefully controlled suction of part of the flow through the perforated wall provides stable uniform flow at each selected Mach number.

To cover a range of supersonic Mach numbers, it is necessary to use either interchangeable supersonic liners fitted in turn in the working section framework or a flexible-wall nozzle whose shape is changed for each Mach number.

Hypersonic wind tunnels must possess a means of preheating the air (or gas) to high temperatures to prevent liquefaction when the gas temperature falls on reaching hypersonic Mach numbers.

Visual aids

Apart from the measurements of forces on the model and local air pressures, the designer also needs information on the nature of the air flow, for example, its direction and whether it is turbulent or smooth. Several techniques are available to give this information visually. They include smoke filaments (streamers), wool tufts, and schlieren techniques.

To produce smoke streamers, a regular array of fine nozzles is placed upstream from the model in the working section. A thick white smoke is produced by heating some kerosene (the process is identical to that used in stage effects), which is then fed to the nozzles. This technique is widely used, and in some cases, helium-filled bubbles are used instead of smoke.

Wool tufts provide by far the simplest visual display. They are fixed to the model surface at regular intervals. They have a large drag-to-weight ratio, that is, they follow the air stream even at low air speeds. Their main drawback is that, in an air flow with a velocity gradient, they are drawn into the faster air stream, thus masking the true flow lines.

Automobile designers make extensive use of wind tunnels in their constant search for the lowest possible wind drag coefficients. The less drag produced by a car, racing or otherwise, the faster it will go and the less fuel it will use.

Flow measurements

Quantitative details of the flow may be obtained by the use of a variety of devices. Pitot tubes and hot-wire and laser anemometers are the most commonly used. Each of these devices can determine both the local velocity of the flow and its direction. Hot-wire and laser anemometers can also measure the velocity fluctuations associated with turbulence and vortex shedding.

A pitot tube is simply an open tube positioned facing directly into the flow so that it measures the local total pressure, from which the local velocity can be deduced if the static atmospheric pressure is also measured.

Hot-wire anemometers work on the principle that the heat loss from a hot section of wire placed in the air flow is a function of the speed of the flow across the wire. To obtain useful flow data, an electronic control box is required, and the whole system must be calibrated for a range of known flow conditions.

Laser anemometers are designed to take flow measurements nonintrusively—no physical objects are placed at the measurement point in the flow, so the flow itself is not distorted. A pair of correlated laser beams, derived by splitting a single laser beam, is directed onto the measurement point. This process establishes a stationary fringe system in the space surrounding the measurement point. Particles in the flow, whether occurring naturally or deliberately seeded, reflect light at varying amplitude as they pass through the alternate bright and dim bands of the fringe system. The flow velocity can then be deduced from a measurement of the frequency of the fluctuating light signal reflected by the particles and the geometric spacing of the fringes.

▼ A model of a proposed supersonic passenger airplane undergoing wind-tunnel tests. Wind tunnels enable designs to be extensively tested before the expensive business of building full-scale prototypes begins.

SEE ALSO: AERODYNAMICS • AIR • AIRCRAFT-CONTROL ENGINEERING • GAS LAWS • SCHLIEREN TECHNIQUES • SUPERSONIC FLIGHT

Winemaking

Wine is an alcoholic drink that has been made since the beginning of recorded history. Although it can be made from the juice of many plants and fruits, the term *wine* usually refers to the drink made from grapes that grow on the *Vitis vinifera* species of vine, of which there are many thousands of varieties.

Although Spain has the largest area under grape cultivation, Italy and France are the world's major wine-producing countries. Their annual production accounts for approximately 40 percent of the world's wine production and 50 percent of world wine exports.

Italy is the major producer of wine in the world with an output of 1.43 billion gallons (5.4 billion l) in 1998. However, the best wines come from France, which had an output of 1.39 billion gallons (5.3 billion l) in 1998 and is the second largest producer. Major wine-producing nations outside Europe include the United States, Chile, Argentina, South Africa, Australia, and New Zealand, and total annual world production is about 6.8 billion gallons (25.7 billion l).

Vines have been cultivated successfully in the United States since the 1700s, and about 550 million gallons (2.1 billion l) of wine are now pro-

▲ An old-fashioned wine press from the Beaujolais region of France. Although the basic winemaking methods remain unchanged, the whole process is often highly mechanized and technically sophisticated. The grapes may be picked by machine, for example, and before fermentation begins, the producer often removes the yeasts present on the skins and substitutes a more effective strain cultured in the laboratory. Bottling, corking, capsuling, and labeling are the final stages, usually done by machines in centralized bottling plants.

duced in the United States every year. Most U.S. wine is produced in California, and several Californian wines are recognized to be the equal of the finest produced in Europe.

Winemaking involves two processes: viticulture, which is the cultivation of the vines and grapes, and vinification, which is the processes involved in making the wine.

Viticulture

Much care and control has to be exercised all year round to produce a successful grape harvest. Methods of pruning are of particular importance. In some areas, vines are cut back very severely each winter because a small yield of grapes per vine tends to produce juice of high quality. The vines remain dormant during the winter months.

In the Northern Hemisphere, the flowering takes place during the first part of June, and warm, calm weather is most important. The vines must be regularly sprayed throughout the summer against insects, mildew, and oidium, a type of fungus that attacks young roots, leaves, and grapes. By about 100 days after the end of the flowering, the grapes are usually ripe, and the harvest can commence. It normally takes place toward the end of September or early October, but it may be considerably later in certain areas.

Vinification

Grape juice turns into wine by the natural and spontaneous action of fermentation, the process by which the sugar content of the grapes is converted by yeasts into alcohol and carbon dioxide gas. The yeasts come from the skin of the grape, although cultured yeasts are usually added, and fermentation starts as soon as the skin is pierced and the yeast has access to the pulp.

Fermentation normally continues until the sugar has been converted into alcohol or until the alcohol reaches a level of around 15 percent of the volume, at which point the yeasts cannot survive. It is, however, possible to arrest fermentation before all the sugar is used up and thus make a sweet wine. Fermentation may be stopped in several ways, one of which is to add alcohol.

The juice inside the grapes is more or less colorless, whether the grapes are black or white, and it is possible to make white wine from black grapes, as is the case with the majority of champagne wines, for instance. However, red wine is normally produced from black grapes, and white wine from white grapes. The color necessary for making red wine comes from the skins of the grapes, and hence techniques for making red wine differ in most cases from those for making white.

To make red wine, the grapes are fed through a machine that removes the stalks and slightly crushes the grapes. The crushed grapes are then pumped into a vat where they ferment with their skins. As the juice begins to turn into wine, more and more color becomes extracted from the skins. After sufficient color and tannin (a naturally occurring acid that gives the wine a characteristic taste) have been acquired, the must (juice) is run off from the skins. The skins are then pressed to extract more wine, which will be deeply colored and full of tannin. This wine is sometimes added to the other to provide more body.

The initial period of fermentation usually lasts about 10 to 14 days, after which the wine is racked and run off into wooden barrels. Racking is the process of separating the wine from the sediment that forms as a result of fermentation. Technological developments have enabled the production time to be greatly shortened. For example, in the carbon maceration of black grapes, the fruit is placed in a carbon dioxide atmosphere that kills plant material in the grape skins and enables the color to dissolve into the juice. This step shortens the red-wine vinification process, making the wine ready for racking in 48 hours instead of four weeks.

To make white wine, the grapes are also destalked and crushed, but they are then usually put into a horizontal press where two end plates gradually draw together and squeeze out the juice from the skins, which are left behind. Rosé (pink) wine is normally obtained from black grapes; the juice is allowed to remain in contact with the skins for just as long as is necessary for a sufficient amount of color to be extracted.

Fermentation

Fermentation vats can be made of wood, stainless steel, glass fiber, or concrete and are sometimes glass lined. It is most important that the right temperature is obtained, usually about 77°F

◀ Process diagram for how red, white, and rosé wines are made. (1) Red grape hopper, (2) white grape hopper, (3) crusher-stemmer, (4) horizontal press, (5) end plate, (6) screw, (7) trough, (8) fermenting vat, (9) sweet white wine, (10) sparkling white wine, (11) dry white wine, (12) crusher, (13) fermenting vat, (14) fermenting vat, (15) rosé wine, (16) running wine, (17) basket press, (18) descending plate, (19) vin de presse, (20) grape skins (marc).

(25°C), and most wineries today have efficient methods of temperature control. Once fermentation is underway, the skins float to the top of the vat, forming a cap. This cap prevents essential oxygen from reaching the must underneath, and so it is important to keep it broken up.

Although it is not normally necessary, sugar is often added to the must, particularly in vineyard areas where there is less sun and the grapes do not always ripen. The normal purpose of adding sugar is to increase the proportion of alcohol. The process is referred to as chaptalization.

A secondary, or malolactic, fermentation normally takes places in the spring following the vintage, although sometimes it can be induced immediately after the ordinary alcoholic fermentation. This malolactic fermentation is desirable to convert surplus malic acid, which would mar the quality of the wine, into lactic acid.

Maturation

The bordeaux method (named for the Bordeaux region in France), which is followed in many areas, is for red wine to be drawn off into barriques, or hogsheads, about the February following the vintage. Barriques are wooden barrels, usually made of oak or chestnut, in which the wine matures by breathing in a small amount of oxygen through the pores of the wood. As some of the wine evaporates during maturation, it is necessary to keep the barrels regularly topped up. This period of maturation may vary: 18 months to 2 years is normal, but some wines are aged for much longer in certain areas.

Before bottling the wine, it is normal to fine it with an albuminous substance such as egg white or gelatin. Fining renders the wine clear and bright. It is often desirable for wine to be matured still further in the bottle. The period of maturation for white wines is normally much shorter than for reds. In fact, it is normal to bottle whites in the spring following the vintage, if not even sooner. Generally, white wines are made to be drunk young while they retain their freshness. Indeed, many red wines are also vinified today in a way that makes them attractive to drink while they are young.

With the best red wines, it always takes time for the compounds of acids, sugars, tannins, esters, and aldehydes to resolve into an ultimately harmonious balance. Esters and aldehydes are by-products of the alcoholic fermentation that contribute to the bouquet, or aroma, of a wine. If a wine is left for too long, however, the color will fade and the wine will begin to taste lifeless and insipid as the fruit and acidity lose their strength. When maturing or storing a wine, it is important to have a place where the temperature remains fairly constant, preferably between 45 and 64°F (7–18°C).

Fortified wines

While ordinary wines have an average alcohol content of between 10 and 14 percent, fortified wines have a volume of alcohol between 16 and 24 percent. Such wines as port, sherry, and madeira are stronger than ordinary table wines because they are fortified by the addition of alcohol, usually grape brandy. This addition prevents further fermentation and thus leaves any residual sugar intact, so the wine remains sweet.

Port is made by mixing brandy with red wine that has only been half fermented and thus retains half of its high sugar content. The grapes are grown in the valley of the Upper Douro River in Portugal, but the wine is nearly always taken down to the port lodges near Oporto, where it may remain for between 2 and 50 years.

Vintage port is the product of a single year that was considered particularly good. It is bottled after only 2 years, but it is necessary to keep the wine in the bottle for 15 to 20 years longer before it reaches sufficient maturity. There are other varieties of port that can be consumed sooner, however. If kept in wood longer, the wine matures much faster and can be bottled when it is ready to drink.

Sherry, from the Jerez district of Spain, is also a fortified wine, although some dry fino sherry need not be fortified, because a high enough proportion of alcohol may be achieved naturally. The most distinctive feature of sherry production is the so-called *solera* system, whereby the wine is kept in butts, the older ones being topped up

◄ Vineyards near Meursault, France. This region—the Côte de Beaune—is famous for its distinctively flavored, dry white wines.

◄ A winery in California employing the latest technology and designed with hygiene and efficiency of operation in mind. In the foreground is a centrifuge, which is used to clarify wines quickly; the stainless-steel vats that can be seen to the left are used for the fermenting process.

from younger ones of the same style. Thus, by continuous careful blending, the same sort of wines can be produced consistently year after year. Sherry is produced in varying degrees of dryness or sweetness.

Madeira, from the volcanic island of the same name off the west coast of Portugal, is also produced by a *solera* system, though occasionally wines of a single vintage can be found. They are often none the worse even after 100 years or more. The wine is subjected to a prolonged period of up to four or five months in *estufas*, or stores, where the temperature is maintained at around 120°F (49°C), which helps give the wine its characteristic burned caramel flavor.

Sparkling wines

Champagne, from the Champagne region of France, and other sparkling wines made by the *méthode champenoise*, as it is called, are given a second fermentation in the bottle. The carbon dioxide gas produced is unable to escape and dissolves in the wine, thus producing the familiar sparkle. The second fermentation is carried out with the bottles upside down so that the sediment is deposited on the cork. The neck of the bottle is then frozen and the cork is drawn, along with the frozen sediment. A new cork is inserted and wired down. The wire and the special heavy bottle are required to withstand the gas pressure.

Some other sparkling wines are made by a system known as the *cuvé close* method. The principle is the same, but it takes place in a vat, or *cuvé*, rather than in the bottle. This method of production is clearly more economical, but the bubbles are likely to be less prolonged once the bottle is opened. A still cheaper method of producing sparkling wines is simply to inject carbon dioxide into the still wine.

Modern requirements

The wine industry has adopted new techniques as the requirements of the market change. For example, in California many new vineyards have been planted especially to accommodate mechanical pickers, so the grapes can be picked at optimum freshness, and production costs are reduced.

Plastic corks and metal screwtops lined with foam are now being used, even for top-quality wines. Although these stoppers suffer from an image problem with the public, they prevent wines from becoming "corked," which occurs when the cork becomes tainted with the chemical TCA (trichloroanisole). For this reason and the fact that they are cheaper to produce than natural cork, these stoppers are preferred by many winemakers.

SEE ALSO: ALCOHOL • DISTILLATION AND SUBLIMATION • FERMENTATION • SPIRIT • YEAST

Wiring System

A household wiring system brings electricity from the street to lighting fixtures and wall-mounted outlets, where it provides power for lamps and electrical appliances. Its insulation must be of a high enough standard to prevent shocks and short circuits, and its wiring must be of an adequate gauge to carry expected current loads without overheating and causing fires.

Supply characteristics

The principal characteristics of electrical supply—frequency and voltage—vary from country to country and sometimes from region to region within a country. Almost without exception, however, domestic supplies are in alternating current (AC), because the voltage of an alternating current can be transformed at will between high voltages that reduce power losses in the distribution network to lower voltages that are safer to use in the home and require less insulation. The frequency of alternation is either 50 Hz (used in Europe) or 60 Hz (used in the Americas).

The output from generators is generally in three phases, with each phase at 120 degrees to the other two. Thus, the second phase reaches its peak voltage one-third of a cycle after the first and is followed by the peak of the third phase after the same interval, and so on. The three phases pass through separate systems of wires in the local distribution network.

In many countries, household supplies can be tapped from the local distribution network at two different voltages: a higher voltage for devices rated at high-power consumption, such as air-conditioning systems, and a lower voltage for lighting circuits and low-power appliances. Higher voltages reduce the amount of current that flows—and the amount of energy lost by resistive heating—in cables that supply appliances with heavy power demands. As different types of plugs and outlets are used for the two voltages, equipment damage caused by connecting to the wrong voltage is avoided.

There are two ways of providing a bivoltage supply. In the United States, a single phase is used to drive a transformer with two sets of outputs. One output is in direct antiphase with the other, which means one line voltage reaches its positive peak at the same instant that the other line voltage reaches its negative peak. If each line is rated at 120 V, as is the case in the United States, the 120 V circuit connects between a live phase wire and a grounded neutral wire; the 240 V circuit connects between the phase and antiphase wires.

In an alternative system, the higher-voltage circuit connects between two of the original three phases from the generator. The 120-degree phase difference means that the positive peak of one wire never coincides with the negative peak of the other. The maximum voltage difference is √3 (1.73) times the line voltage, so a 127 V supply can be wired to produce a 220 V supply that alternates at the same frequency as the input lines.

At the house

The electricity supply to a house or apartment may be through an underground cable or through overhead power lines. Where the home supply is single phase at a single voltage, only two supply cables are strictly necessary: a live conductor and a neutral conductor. The neutral cable is at or near ground potential, but it carries the return current from devices connected to it within the house. In some cases, a third conductor provides a separate ground connection for safety.

Where the supply is dual voltage, the three supply cables comprise two live conductors at different phases but the same voltage and a single

▲ This meter measures the amount of power delivered to a house in kilowatts at any time, and sums that value over time to measure the total amount of energy consumed. The energy unit used is the kilowatt-hour (kWh). One kilowatt-hour is equal to 3.6 megajoules.

neutral conductor that carries the return current from both high-voltage and low-voltage equipment. A fourth ground conductor may also form part of the supply connection.

With both systems, the supply passes through a meter that records the quantity of electricity used and is the property of the electricity supply company. Many supply authorities also insist on there being a master fuse or circuit breaker rated to carry the complete load of the installation. If there is a major fault in the installation, the fuse will blow or the circuit breaker trip, so protecting the supply system and preventing the entire district from being blacked out. This fuse or circuit breaker is sealed and protected against tampering. If it blows or trips, it has to be replaced or reset by authorized representatives of the supplier once the fault has been identified and remedied.

From the meter onward, all wiring is the property of the householder. It is therefore the responsibility of the householder to ensure that wiring is installed and maintained to standards set by the appropriate regulatory authorities.

Ground connections

Proper grounding is essential for the safety of any electric installation. Any conducting component of equipment should be grounded to prevent it from becoming live if a stray power cable touches it, for example. In such an event, the short circuit activates fuses or circuit breakers before the short circuit can cause an electrical fire or shock.

In the case of equipment that connects to the circuit via a three-pin plug, the third pin connects the ground wire in the equipment cable to a ground conductor in the household circuit. This terminates at a metal contact attached electrically to a metal block buried under ground or to underground metal water pipes, if applicable. In the United States, this ground terminal connects to the neutral conductor, which can also act as a ground connection for two-pin appliances that have no separate ground conductor.

Service panel

After the meter, the next part of the wiring system is the service panel—a type of switchboard that splits the supply into separate circuits, each of which is protected against overloads by a fuse or circuit breaker. Appliances that can draw a lot of power—water heaters, ovens, air-conditioning units, and the like—generally have individual supply circuits, and these are at the higher voltage where there is a dual supply. There are a number of individual circuits for low-power appliances and lighting, and these circuits are typically at the lower voltage of a dual supply.

Where the supply panel is a fuse box, there is a master switch that controls the whole supply and a wire or cartridge fuse for each circuit. Both wire and cartridge fuses work on the same principle: they contain a wire that gets hot as current flows through it. Beyond the rated current strength, the temperature of the wire rises rapidly and the wire melts, breaking the circuit. In the most basic fuse systems, fuse wire is secured between two electrical contacts and is replaced when it blows. In one type of cartridge, the wire is suspended between metal caps at either end of a sealed, insulating cylinder. The caps fit into two metal clips that connect the fuse to the circuit, and the whole cartridge must be replaced if there is a failure.

In more modern circuit breaker systems, a master circuit breaker controls the overall supply, while subsidiary circuit breakers protect each circuit. Each circuit breaker is a switch that is turned on manually by forcing its lever against a spring until a catch engages. An electromechanical device releases the catch if a threshold current is exceeded, and the spring then disconnects the switch. A circuit breaker can be switched off to isolate a circuit before starting maintenance or installation work, and it can be manually reset if made to trip by a transient overload or when repair work on a fault is complete.

The advantages of circuit breakers include their ability to be reset without the need to replace parts, the accuracy of the trip current, and the speed with which they react to an overload. Some circuit breakers trip if the current exceeds precisely 1½ times the nominal rating; others trip

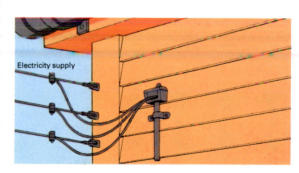
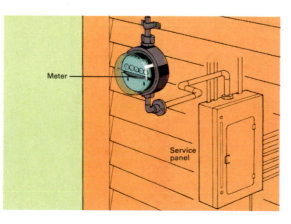

◀ In a dual-supply system, each house is fed by two live conductors and a neutral conductor. In some cases, these conductors are overhead wires from a tapping point or transformer on a telegraph pole (top). They pass through a meter to a service panel (bottom) that houses the fuses or circuit breakers for the whole house.

HOME WIRING

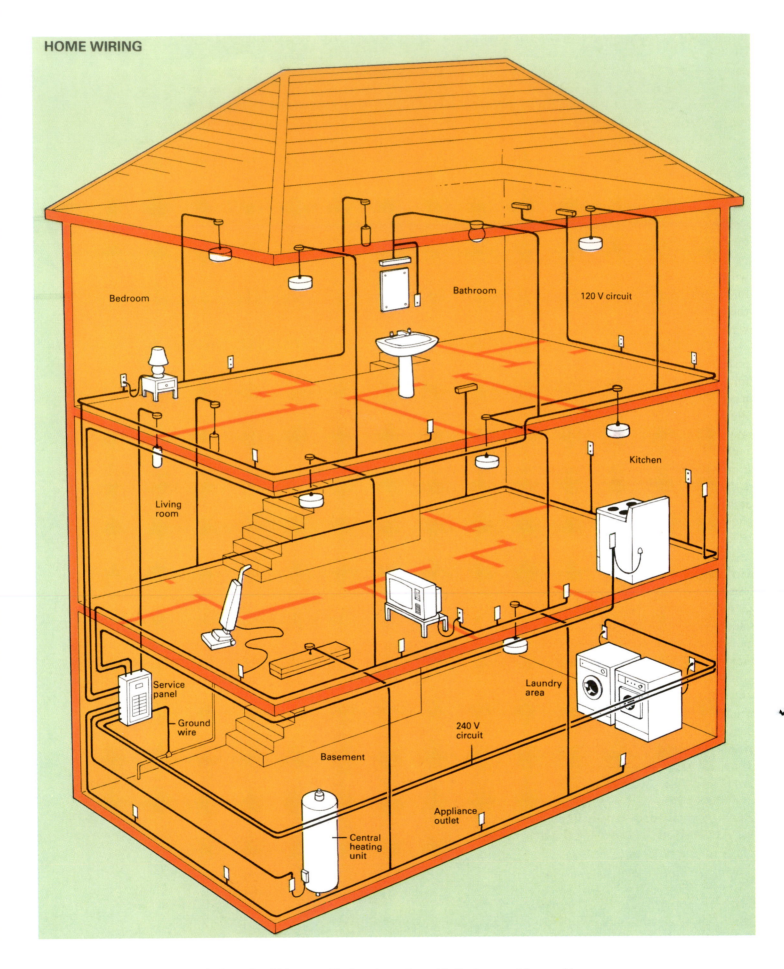

Bedroom

Bathroom

120 V circuit

Living room

Kitchen

Service panel

Ground wire

Basement

Laundry area

240 V circuit

Appliance outlet

Central heating unit

▲ This diagram shows the wiring of a house in which general supply circuits provide electricity at 120 V for both wall-mounted power outlets and lighting fixtures.

The laundry equipment in the basement is served by a 240 V circuit, and the cooker and electric central-heating unit receive power through dedicated radial spurs.

if there is more than 5 mA difference between the currents in the live and neutral conductors, indicating a short circuit or even that a person is receiving an electrical shock from faulty equipment. The latter type of device is called a grounding fault circuit interrupter (GFCI); the 5 mA threshold is chosen because it is below the current at which an electrical shock becomes painful and causes a shock victim to involuntarily tighten his or her grasp on the source of the shock and thereby increase the likely severity of the shock.

GFCIs must be used in conjunction with overload circuit breakers or fuses to provide complete protection. The overload device then protects wiring and equipment, while the GFCI protects humans (and animals) from electrocution, since the current required to trip an overload device would be potentially fatal.

Some houses have a separate main switch and fuse unit for each circuit—one for the stove, one for the lighting, one for the water heater, and perhaps a main switch and multiway fuse board for the sockets. This arrangement works in the same way as a service panel, but it is less compact and tends to be an untidy jumble of wires and boxes.

Lighting circuits

It is normal practice to have more than one lighting circuit in a house, so the whole building is not plunged into darkness if there is a fault in just one fixture. Lights can be wired into general supply circuits that also feed wall outlets, but it is more usual for them to be on separate lighting circuits.

With separate circuits it is possible to use a more lightweight cable than that required for power circuits, although heavier cable may still be needed where there is a need for extensive lighting with numerous lights on each circuit. With the loop-in wiring system, four-terminal ceiling fixtures are employed to give connections for live, neutral, ground, and switch wires. A twin-with-ground cable (twin conductors—live and neutral—and a ground wire) is run from the service panel to the live, neutral, and ground terminals of the first fixture in the circuit. From this outlet, the cable loops out to the next, then the next, and so on until all the ceiling fixtures are linked together and provided with an electricity supply. In the service panel, the live wire is connected to a suitable fuse or miniature circuit breaker, the return wire to the neutral connection block, and the ground wire to the grounding block.

A length of cable runs from each ceiling fixture to the appropriate switch to give a switch loop. If two-way switching is employed, a three-core and ground cable is run between the two switch positions. In the ceiling outlet, the switch cable is connected to the live, ground, and switch wire terminals; the three-core wire feeding the lamp socket connects to the neutral, switch wire, and ground. All metal lamp sockets, light fixtures, and switch plates throughout the installation are connected to ground to ensure safety.

Where cables are buried in the plaster of walls, they are either run in metal or plastic conduits or covered by a protective metal channel. Alternatively, a cable may be run from the service panel to a series of joint boxes instead of directly to the ceiling fixtures. There is usually a joint box

POWER-LINE NETWORKING

Many homes and offices have two or more computer devices that need to communicate from time to time. Examples of operations that require this type of computer "talk" include the transfer of data files between computers and the transmission of instructions from a computer to a printer. The most obvious way to provide for such communication is to use a dedicated cable network to which all related computers and peripheral devices connect. The disadvantages of this approach include the mass of cables that accumulates as the number of linked devices increases and the restricted numbers and locations of access points. Infrared (IR) networking removes the need for a physical connection to a cable network, but it is relatively slow and requires a clear line of sight between networked devices. Power-line networking is a technology that connects items of computer hardware through their power leads, thereby removing the need for network cables.

In one form of power-line networking, network cards fitted into the devices send and receive packets of digital information on 84 frequency channels between 4.3 MHz and 20.9 MHz. The power that runs through the network has a frequency of 50 to 60 Hz, so it does not interfere with the data signals. The data packets are encrypted so that they can be read only by other equipment on the same network, and frequency-shifting software avoids those channels that are subject to interference from electrical appliances or are in use by other power-line networks. Data transmission rates up to 14 Mbps (megabits per second) are possible, so power-line networks support real-time video and audio streaming applications.

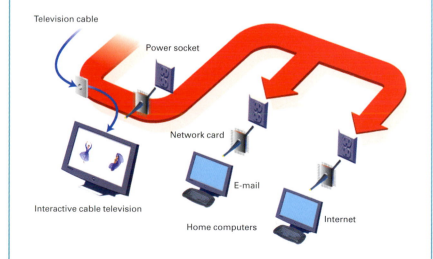

POWER-LINE NETWORKING IN THE HOME

for each lighting point. From each joint box there is a cable to the switch and another to the ceiling fixture or lighting point. Like the ceiling outlets, the molded joint boxes are generally circular and have four terminals: live, neutral, switch wire, and ground. The connections are made in the same way as those in the ceiling outlet of the loop-in system. When more than one light is controlled by a single switch—as would be the case for multiple uplighters, for example—a separate cable runs to each light from a single box.

Power circuits

Power circuits are those that feed appliances through wall sockets. They must cater for greater current flows than lighting circuits do, as can be appreciated by considering that a single appliance, such as an 800-watt vacuum cleaner, can draw the same amount of power as ten or more lamps (more than thirteen 60-watt lamps in this case).

There are two ways of wiring a power circuit: as a radial spur or as a ring circuit. In the case of a radial spur—the typical U.S. configuration—a single cable runs out from the service panel, supplying a series of power points along its length, and terminates in a power point at its end. In the case of a ring circuit, the cable runs in a loop starting from and returning to the service panel There may be several power points around the ring, and each can receive power through either arm of the loop. Hence, it is usually possible to use a lighter gauge of cable than for a spur.

A typical wire gauge, or thickness, for older copper circuits is AWG 14 (American wire gauge 14), which has a diameter of 0.064 in. (1.6 mm) and can safely carry a current of 15 A. The equivalent gauge for aluminum is AWG 12, which has a diameter of 0.081 in. (2.1 mm): the lower conductivity of aluminum calls for slightly thicker wires. In either case, the circuit must terminate at a suitably rated fuse or circuit breaker on the service unit. If connected to a higher rated fuse, it would be possible for the circuit wires to run hot without the fuse blowing and thus create the possibility of melting the cable insulation or even of starting a fire. More modern installations use AWG 10 copper wire, whose diameter of around 0.1 in. (2.6 mm) allows it to carry up to 40 A safely, corresponding to a total power capacity of 4.8 kW for a 120 V supply. The length of the circuit is limited to around 50 to 100 ft. (15–30 m) from the service panel. The cable is three core with insulated live and neutral conductors, together with a bare ground wire, all enclosed in an insulating plastic sheath. Protection against circuit overload is given by the circuit fuse in the service panel. At the middle-of-run outlets, the

live and neutral cables are connected to the fixture to provide power and then continued to the next outlet; the cable terminates in the end-of-run power outlet.

With ring circuits, such as those used in Britain, there is no limit to the number of socket outlets. The size of the ring circuit is limited by regulations that specify a maximum floor area (120 sq. yds., or 100 m²) that can be served by a single ring circuit. For larger houses, it is usual to provide more than one ring, with a typical arrangement using one ring for the living area, another for the bedrooms, and a third for the kitchen. The circuit is protected by a fuse at the fuse box, but further protection is given by the use of fused plugs, which act to isolate the rest of the circuit from a fault in a single appliance.

Other circuits

Electrical appliances that use electricity for heating—water heaters, stoves, and air-conditioning units, for example—often have sufficiently large power demands to warrant a dedicated radial spur from a fuse or circuit breaker in the service unit. Where there is a dual supply, it is not unusual for the high-demand components of an appliance to be supplied at high voltage, while the low-power components of the same appliance, such as timers, receive their power from the low-voltage circuit. If the appliance gets hot near the electrical supply cable, that part of the cable must be electrically insulated using butyl rubber, which has a good tolerance for high ambient temperatures.

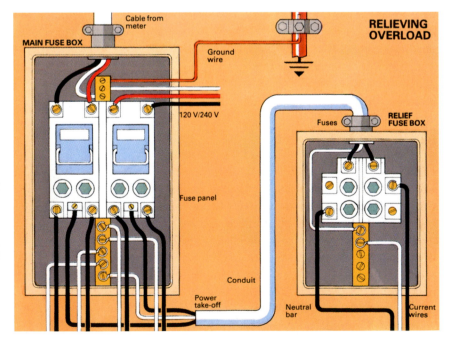

▼ When power demand exceeds the capacity of the existing fuse box, more capacity can be added by installing a relief fuse box. Such a box taps directly into the master fuses and distributes electric current to circuits through a separate set of fuses or circuit breakers.

SEE ALSO: CABLE, POWER • ELECTRICITY • FUSE AND CIRCUIT BREAKER • LIGHTBULB • POWER PLANT • POWER SUPPLY • SWITCH

Wood Composite

Plywood, chipboard (particleboard), and various kinds of fiberboard and insulation board are sheet materials manufactured from wood and offering a combination of properties that has resulted in their widespread use.

Plywood is constructed of several thin layers of wood, called veneers or plies, glued together with the grains at right angles to one another, with the result that plywood is difficult to split and has far more tensile strength, as well as resistance to changes in humidity and temperature, than solid timber. Poor grades of wood can be used for the interior plies or for all the plies in the case of plywood that is to be used where it will not be seen, as in subflooring. Alternatively, any kind of finishing-quality wood can be used for the outside ply; finished properly, sheets of such plywood make durable and attractive paneling. Despite its high strength, plywood can be worked with ordinary woodworking tools.

Chipboard makes use of waste material from timber processing and of forestry thinnings (undersized trees). This waste is chopped into small chips, which are coated with resin and pressed into sheets by machinery, using heat. Like plywood, the sheets can be used for paneling, shelving, and so forth, but without plywood's strength. The consistent characteristics of chipboard allow easy working, though its screw-holding properties are less than solid timbers. Special fitted parts have been developed for use in furniture manufacture to make solid joints in chipboard components that are assembled by the user into finished furniture.

Urea formaldehyde (UF) is the most common adhesive used for making plywood and chipboard, although many different formulas and additives are used to make these products more moisture-proof, flame resistant, and insect free.

Chipboard manufacture

Wood from thinnings and wastes from industrial timber processing are cut into small chips by a rotating disk with cutting edges around its face or by a cylindrical cutter block with knife blades set in it. The chips are crescent shaped. If the equipment has knife blades, they can be adjusted to make larger or smaller chips. The chips are then passed through a grading machine, which with a winnowing action, eliminates chips that are too big and particles of foreign matter. At this stage or later, magnets are used to extract any metal particles, which would ruin a saw blade if pressed into the board.

Regardless of source, chips contain a moisture content that must be reduced to 2 or 3 percent. The chips are dried by being tumbled in heated drums. They are then conveyed to the top of mixing cylinders through which they are allowed to fall; nozzles in the cylinder walls spray them with UF resin as they fall. They still feel dry because the resin content does not exceed 10 percent. The chips can also be sprayed while being tumbled in drums.

Next the chips are spread on a continuous band or a line of linked steel plates. The chips used to be spread by hand, but this method resulted in uneven distribution and subsequent weak places in the finished board. Some types of machinery can spread the chips so that they fall with the smaller chips on the top and bottom and the large chips in the middle; this arrangement makes a smoother finish and a more uniform density.

The layer of chips on the plate is called a mattress. At this point, the chips have a flow characteristic similar to that of coarse sawdust. To prevent loss on account of mechanical vibration or stray air currents, they go through a cold press, which exerts a relatively light pressure to consolidate them. They are also slightly dampened to replace moisture lost by evaporation and to compensate for losses during subsequent heat pressing. Then the units are loaded into heat presses. For ⅝ in. (15 mm) board the pressure is 150 lbs. per sq. in. (1 N/mm^2) and the temperature is 250°F (121°C); the application lasts ten minutes.

The boards are then stacked to cool and to allow localized inner stresses to become evenly distributed. This process takes several days. The boards are then trimmed and sanded by drum sanders on both sides.

◀ These wood chips will be reduced to a fiber and turned into pulp. They will then be pressed into hardboard or baked into insulating softboard.

An alternative process is extrusion, in which a reciprocating ram forces the chips horizontally through parallel heated metal plates, which are adjustable for thickness. Continuous lengths of thicker board can be produced this way, but the internal structure of the board is slightly different because of the longitudinal rather than vertical pressure on the chips. Extruded board has higher tensile but lower bending strength.

Chipboard is made in three densities. High-density board, weighing 40 to 50 lbs. per cu. ft. (640–800 kg/m³), is used for high strength and stability, as in flooring. Medium-density board, weighing 30 to 40 lbs. per cu. ft. (480–640 kg/m³), is used for such applications as paneling, partitions, shelving, and furniture manufacture. Lower-density board is used for roof decking, ceilings, and core material for composite paneling. Chipboard has sound-insulating properties that improve with lower density. Veneers and other surface finishes, such as laminates and plastic skins, are often applied to chipboard for applications such as furniture construction.

Plywood manufacture

For plywood manufacture, trees are chosen and inspected carefully before manufacture to ensure that they are used to best advantage. Wood is imported from all over the world; trees with long, cylindrical, clear trunks are necessary, and many of them grow in tropical areas.

First the logs are boiled or steamed in large vats. This step softens them, ensures that moisture is evenly distributed, and reduces the likelihood of splitting or tearing of the veneers during subsequent processing. Tropical hardwood especially requires this treatment; some species (such as birch and beech) can be peeled without it. In Finland, the practice is to leave the logs in the log pond for months while injecting steam into the pond to keep it from freezing.

The logs are then peeled of bark and cut to convenient lengths. The peeling of the veneers from the logs is carried out on a large lathe that rotates the logs against a knife blade running the full length of the log. Strict quality control begins at this point, for the veneers obtained must be of uniform thickness throughout. The rate of feed and the angle of the blade are adjustable for individual logs and species. Veneers are cut from about 0.03 to 0.16 in. (1–4 mm) thick. The veneer is then clipped to predetermined widths in such a way that defects are clipped off.

Next the veneers go through continuous tunnel driers to ensure that they are of uniform moisture content; otherwise the finished product will warp or twist. The permissible content varies

◀ A selection of sheet materials (1) double-veneered blockboard with a red cedar core and two gaboon veneers, which is lightweight and ideal for high-quality flush doors; (2) beech-face standard blockboard; (3) plastic laminate-faced blockboard, suitable for work surfaces; (4) double-veneered walnut-faced blockboard; (5) double-veneered mahogany-faced laminboard; (6) thick-core multiply with thin facing veneers; (7) exterior grade water and boil proof (WBP) birch multiply—one of the highest quality sheet materials available.

from 5 to 14 percent, depending on the adhesive to be employed. (There are also wet and semidry cementing processes, which do not require this careful drying; they give a cheaper but poorer grade of plywood.)

The dried veneers are then sorted and graded. Veneers for faces of the most expensive grades of plywood are often full width, but joins are permissible. To make the joins smooth and parallel, veneer guillotines or edge joiners are used. Materials used for core veneers may be edge joined using staples (which are removed later) to prevent core gaps, which would lower the strength of the finished board. Veneers for face joins are carefully selected for color and are joined by an automatic tapeless splicer, which draws the edges together and makes a join that is nearly invisible and as strong as the veneer itself.

Next the glue is applied for the sandwich construction. It must be evenly applied, for too much glue will result in a poor bond. An alternative method is the use of resin-impregnated paper that is cut to size and placed between the plies. The plies are arranged with the grain of each at a right angle to that of the plies on either side; nearly all plywood has an odd number of plies, but if the number is even, the center two plies can have the grain following the same direction.

The veneers are sometimes prepressed cold. The hot pressing is then carried out in hydraulic machinery between multiple heated platens. Temperature and pressure are adjusted to the type of construction under production. The finished boards are then stacked to allow stresses and uneven moisture content to work out, and finally they are trimmed and sanded.

Laminated wood is made from wood veneers, as plywood is, but with the grain running in the same direction in all layers, the composite being subjected to high temperatures and pressures during the pressing process. The result is a very dense material with high strength and abrasion resistance that is used for applications such as stair treads and handrails.

Fiberboard

Fiberboard is made by subjecting wood chips to high steam pressure and then suddenly releasing the pressure, which causes a fresh activation of the lignin, the natural plastic substance that binds wood fibers together. The chips, or pulp, are then rolled out and pressed into large thin sheets on heated presses. Fiberboard is used mostly for interior paneling and is available in a wide variety of finishes simulating, for example, troweled plaster or brickwork; a variety of simulated timber finishes are also available, together with plastic facings.

One of the most familiar uses of fiberboard is Peg-Board, a hardboard that has holes in it to accept wire attachments for hanging up tools or kitchen utensils, and for displaying goods in stores.

Insulating boards are made in a similar manner to hardboard, with the pulp being rolled to the required thickness and dried to give a spongy structure. Application of moderate pressure during manufacture results in a soft fiber board or softboard as used for bulletin boards.

Medium density fiberboard (MDF) is a form of fiberboard that has a wide range of applications. Strong, light, and with a smooth surface, this product is made into boards used in construction and furniture manufacture and is also formed into a variety of architectural moldings.

Health hazards

A variety of illnesses are associated with the manufacture and use of wood composites. They include skin disorders, asthma, a rare form of nasal cancer, and obstruction of the nasal passages. These illnesses occur as a consequence of high amounts of wood dust in the air. Manufacturers must therefore ensure that workers wear protective clothing or that the amount of wood dust is reduced to safe levels. An additional risk is that certain concentrations of wood dust suspended in air can burn explosively if ignited. Care must therefore be taken to avoid the build up of wood dust in the workplace.

▼ Wood composites are used widely in the construction industry owing to their strength and relatively low cost.

SEE ALSO: Adhesive and sealant • Boat building • Forestry • Lumber • Veneer • Woodworking

Woodwind Instrument

◀ The saxophonist Gerry Mulligan in action. Saxophones are mainly used in jazz and military bands for their loud, breathy tones, and appear only rarely in orchestral scores, such as Prokofiev's *Lieutenant Kijé* suite.

The feature shared by all wind instruments, including the pipe organ and brass instruments, is the enclosed column of air that is set in motion. The shape of the column and the material from which the instrument is manufactured will affect the timbre (tonal qualities), but the pitch remains in direct proportion to the length of the tube.

A pipe or tube of a given length will produce one pitch only, but it is possible by altering the breath pressure and embouchure (lip shape) to sound the higher harmonics, or partials, as well. The higher harmonics and the fundamental tone constitute the natural tones of the instrument. As soon as the lower end of the pipe is closed, its fundamental note becomes an octave lower, and only the odd-numbered partials will be obtainable. Modern woodwind instruments have been developed to play numerous pitches that lie between those of the natural series; changing pitch is done by temporarily shortening the length of the pipe by means of side holes in the wall of the instrument, which can be closed by the fingertips or by

keys. When all of the holes are closed, the instrument will sound its fundamental note, and as holes are opened, the acoustical length of the air column will be shortened, thus raising the pitch.

Inside the instrument, the enclosed column of air vibrates in a parallel direction to the length of the tube, and the molecules of air move in such a way that, at points along the column, the density swings regularly between the highest and lowest values and back again. In a pipe that is open at both ends, the ends of the column of air are among the points of lowest density, called antinodes; between these points are the nodes. The wavelength of the fundamental pitch of an open pipe is twice the length of the pipe. If, on the other hand, the pipe is stopped at one end, there will be a loop at the open end and a node at the closed end, the result being a wavelength four times the length of the pipe (and a fundamental note an octave lower), because the column of air doubles back upon itself. Much like a vibrating string, an air column vibrates not only as a whole but also in fractional parts along its length (½, ⅓, ¼, and so on), producing harmonics.

One other feature of particular interest in wind sounds is the incidence of audible difference, or beat notes, which occur where the frequency vibrations in the air column interfere with each other. The purer the sound of the instrument, the more audible the beat note produced will be.

Flutes

The flute player directs his or her breath toward the farther edge of a hole cut in the side of the tube close to the stopped end. This solid edge creates an eddy current both above and below the edge of the hole. The modern flute is side blown (transverse, Italian: *traverso*) with the player controlling the direction of the air toward the opposite edge by means of critical embouchure. Other types of flutes are played by blowing across the end of the tube, which is left open, as in the kaval, of Near Eastern origin.

The pitch of flutes depends on the length of the tube and on the speed of the air column, which, if increased sufficiently, will cause the instrument to overblow. Overblowing induces vibrations at half (or other fractional) lengths of the column, producing notes an octave, a twelfth, or a double octave higher than the fundamental.

Most types of flute have six or seven holes to allow for playing the diatonic scale. Further semitones can be added to these by the use of cross or forked fingerings, where a finger higher than the

◄ Three oboes from different periods and countries. From left to right they are a Dupuis oboe of 1710, an Indian shahnai, and a late-19th-century Millereau oboe with ring keys.

one in use is raised. Only three holes are actually necessary for playing an octave scale if the instrument can overblow at the third harmonic with notes beginning a fifth above the lowest. The three holes and the open tube produce the first four notes, and the third harmonics produce the subsequent four notes to make the eight-note scale.

Reeds

In reed instruments, the breath of the player causes a reed to vibrate so that a waveform is generated. Reeds can be employed either singly (as in the clarinet) or in pairs (oboe and bassoon).

The single reed was originally made by cutting a tongue capable of vibrating in the side of a strip of cane or elderwood closed at the tip. This method is still in use today by makers of some instruments. An alternative method is to have a separate single strand of cane tied over the opening at the end of the pipe, so forming a slit, one side of which (the reed) is able to vibrate.

Double reeds were traditionally made by pinching together one end of a freshly cut plant stem to produce a narrow aperture that widens and closes as the reed is blown. One of the oldest such instruments is the Greek aulos. Beginning with medieval double-reed instruments, the mounting section of the mouthpiece (the part holding the reed above the pipe) is a short metal tube known as the staple. The double reed itself is formed by folding a strip of cane over upon itself

► A rackett, which has up to seven interconnected tubes bored through the block and produces deep, harsh notes.

and then binding the ends that have come together onto the staple. The conical bore pipes (with which the double reeds are more commonly associated) give harmonics equivalent to the open flute and can readily be made to overblow to the second and third harmonics.

The saxophones are single-reed woodwind instruments having conical bores and made of brass. The available range of expression and resemblance to the human voice make the saxophone family especially popular in jazz and rock music.

History

It was not until the late 14th century that woodwind instruments began to appear in many guises. In earlier times, the serious form of music making in Europe had been in the church service, and the brash sound of the brass instruments had been preferred for filling the enormous cathedrals of that continent. The only woodwind instrument to leave any mark was the flute, which strongly influenced the popular music.

With the growing secularization of music came a courtly interest in dance, and in this new chamber music, the softer tones of the flute, recorder, and shawm found increasing favor. Although they can never be said to have presented any real threat to the viol family once it had been established, sources, such as the German composer of the 16th century Michael Praetorius, reveal that whole families were built of

▶ Sound waves passing through wind instruments. The pitch of the sound produced by the air within an instrument depends on the length of the instrument and the velocity of the air through it. Longer instruments produce lower sounds than those that are shorter. In some woodwind instruments, such as flutes, a greater air velocity is achieved by a technique called overblowing.

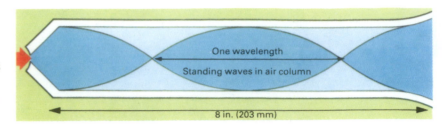

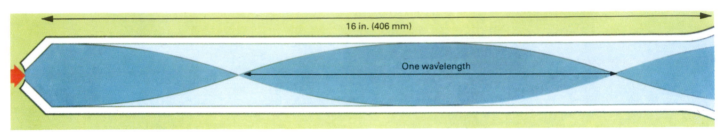

crumhorns, recorders, and shawms that could manage the chordal dances of composers like Susato and Simpson with delicacy and sonority.

The flute, keyless as it was then, and the recorder—famed by King Henry VIII of England's ownership of a large and expensive chest of recorders—were popular instruments at this time. The crumhorn (variously spelled) was a double-reed instrument with a cylindrical bore having a nasal, almost buzzing tone; the shawm (also known as the bombarde, pommern, pumhart, chalemie, and so on), having a double reed and made in many sizes, was an early ancestor of the oboe.

One interesting feature of the crumhorn was its mouthpiece, which consisted of a reed covered by a cap so that the player's lips were not in direct contact with the reed; the effect was to deny the player the facility of changing the sound, and thus, the crumhorn operates like an organ pipe. It also precludes overblowing. The sordune had a bore that ran up and down two or three times within the same piece of wood. Another curiosity

was the rackett (also variously spelled), which had a bore of around seven tubes connected in a series to produce notes amazingly low for its small size.

The baroque period, from 1550 to 1750, saw the establishment of a solo repertoire in which, because of the economics of publishing, many of the woodwind pieces were written to be played on a choice of different instruments; for example, sonatas were written to be played on the flute, hautbois (early French name for the oboe), or violin. During the classical era, an interesting development was that of so-called Harmoniemusik, which was music for a wind band usually including the then natural horn.

Keys

Simple key mechanisms were seen as early as the 14th century, when a lever key was added to the larger members of the shawm family in order to cover the lowest note hole. Not until the late 18th century was this simple mechanism, still used on the larger recorder sizes, developed into the sophisticated system in use today. Perhaps the

▶ The effective length of an instrument like the clarinet is reduced by opening holes to let air escape. The shorter the length of the tube, the higher the note produced.

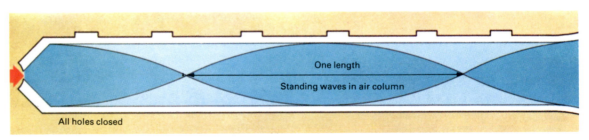

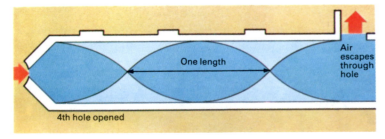

◀ The fundamental, second, and third harmonic waves set up by air blown into open and closed pipes. Notes higher than the fundamental are achieved by opening holes or blowing harder.

▶ Right: The Boehm system of clarinet fingering. It was patented in Paris, France, in 1844. Far right: The Boehm clarinet, which was invented in the early 18th century.

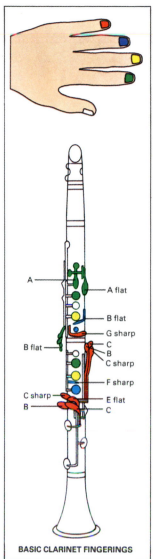

BASIC CLARINET FINGERINGS

Left hand

Right hand

most widely known name in this connection (though he was not actually its inventor) is Theobald Boehm, a flautist who adapted ring keys to his flute at the beginning of the 1830s. The principal advantage is that the Boehm system allows one or more fingers independently to turn an axle that actuates a key in the same movement as covering a hole itself. This more sophisticated movement not only opened up new potential in virtuoso playing but also allowed the instrument maker to increase the size of the holes, now covered by a comprehensive network of keys, thereby greatly increasing the possible volume of sound.

Orchestral woodwinds

In descending order as they appear in an orchestral score, the woodwind instruments of today are flute, piccolo, oboe, cor anglais (English horn), clarinet, bass clarinet, bassoon, and double bassoon.

Each pair consists of the main instrument and its bass version with the bass version coming second, for example, bassoon and double bassoon, except the flute, which has the higher-pitched version as a secondary instrument. The flute and piccolo are also exceptional in being the only ones without reeds. The clarinet and bass clarinet are the only reed instruments with cylindrical bores and single reeds; the remaining instruments all have double reeds. The clarinet, bass clarinet, piccolo, cor anglais, and double bassoon are all called transposing instruments, because the

note that they sound is not the note that the player reads in the music.

The ranges are piccolo: D a ninth above middle C up to C three octaves above; flute: middle C up to C three octaves above; oboe: B-flat below middle C up to G above the treble staff; cor anglais: E below middle C up to A above the treble staff; clarinet: E below middle C up to G above the treble staff; bass clarinet: E-flat an octave and a semitone below the clarinet up to G on the treble staff; bassoon: B-flat below the bass staff up to D on the treble staff; double bassoon: B-flat an octave below the bassoon up to E on the bass staff.

One of the clearest examples of the woodwind family playing together occurs in the third movement of Tchaikovsky's Fourth Symphony, where there is an antiphonal passage (alternating voices) for the different groups of instruments.

SEE ALSO: ACOUSTICS • BRASS INSTRUMENT • MUSICAL SCALE • ORGAN, MUSICAL • SOUND • STRINGED INSTRUMENT

Woodworking

◄ Cutting planks of wood with a band saw in a saw mill. Many industrial tools have been scaled down for domestic use by handymen and hobbyists.

Wood is the oldest and most useful of the materials from which consumer goods are made. For centuries, craftspeople have made furniture, interior woodwork, coachwork, and many other useful and decorative products from wood, and beautifully grained and finished woods have also been used by artists.

The earliest machine used to work wood was the lathe, which turns cylindrical parts, such as table legs. For centuries, the lathe required two operators—one to hold the chisel against the work and the other to turn the spindle by means of a crank—or else the turning of the spindle was intermittent, by means of a cord wrapped around the work and pulled back and forth by a treadle. A bent sapling was used at the other end of the cord as a spring, and this arrangement was called a pole lathe. The Italian artist and inventor Leonardo da Vinci is credited with inventing the lathe that was not intermittently turned and required only one operator. Da Vinci's lathe worked by combining the treadle and the crank.

Today wood lathes, like nearly all machine tools, are driven by electric motors. The first circular saw was built in the late 18th century, and now woodworking machines are widely available for the amateur at home who wants to do repairs or build furniture. Some woodworking machines are multipurpose, ingeniously designed to perform several functions by means of attachments. The highest-quality work, however, is done on

► Making joints to fit pieces of wood together is a key element of woodworking. Although these frequently used joints can be made with ordinary tools, such as saws and chisels, special implements like the mortiser, which makes square holes, are available.

specialized machines. The machines described here are also designed to large-scale specifications for fast, continuous production in the timber industry and in furniture manufacturing plants.

Saws

There are several different types of sawing machines of which the most common is the circular saw, or table saw. This device consists simply of a table below which is mounted an electric motor with an extended shaft forming an arbor on which is mounted a circular saw blade with teeth around its perimeter. The saw blade protrudes through a slot in the table and the work is pushed into and past it. The table is adjustable for height so that the blade can make cuts of various depths. On some models, the table or the blade can be tilted for making bevel or miter cuts, as when the ends of boards are sawn to a 45-degree angle so that they fit together at 90 degrees to each other without showing any end grain.

The most common type of table saw has a blade 8 in. (20 cm) in diameter; circular saw

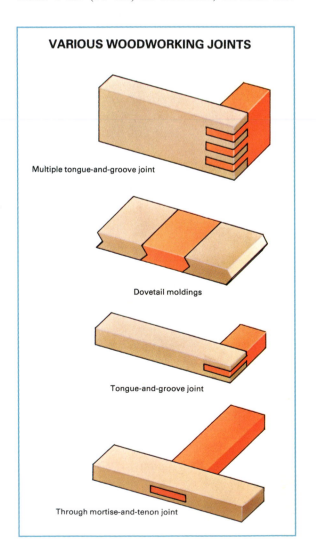

VARIOUS WOODWORKING JOINTS

Multiple tongue-and-groove joint

Dovetail moldings

Tongue-and-groove joint

Through mortise-and-tenon joint

blades used in the woodworking industries range up to 16 in. (40 cm) in size. The blades can be sharpened with a file; the person who does this in the timber industry is called the saw doctor.

The radial-arm saw is a versatile inverted version of the table saw in which the motor and blade are suspended from an arm over the table. The arm can be swung around in a full circle and clamped in any position; the motor and blade can also be turned in a circle or tilted in either direction. For many cuts, the work is held firmly on the table, and the radial arm is pushed away from or pulled toward the operator. For ripping (cutting with the grain), the arm is clamped tightly, and the lumber is pushed into the revolving blade, as on the ordinary table saw used in sawmills.

Both types of machines have fences that are adjustable laterally and are clamped to the table to guide the work past the blade in a straight line. Either type may also have provision for mounting two saw blades close to each other on the arbor for cutting grooves and slots. The larger models may have double arbors with a blade on each—when one is in use, the other is out of the way.

The band saw

The band saw has a blade that is a flexible continuous metal strip. It runs around two large wheels, located one above and one below the work table, and passes through a slot in the center of the table. The band saw can cut curves and patterns in any thickness of wood and can also be used to cut thin strips from the edges of boards. The wheels range in size from 14 in. (36 cm) for light work to more than 6.5 ft. (2 m) for use in sawmills. Band saws in sawmills can have teeth on both edges of the blade so that, when a log is passed back and forth, a board is cut from it in each direction. Such a blade may be 16 in. (40 cm) wide and 50 ft. (15 m) long. The band saw

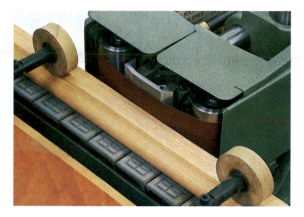

is also used in machine shops, with a blade having smaller, harder teeth and traveling at a slower speed for cutting metal.

The jigsaw (or saber saw) makes inside or outside irregular cuts for unusual patterns. The blade is driven in a reciprocating manner from beneath the table and is connected to an overhead support.

Circular saws and jigsaws are also available in portable models for the home user. In this case, the work table is the piece of wood itself supported by a pair of saw horses.

Planers

The planer is used to plane pieces of wood to a uniform thickness. It has a table adjustable for height across which projects a horizontal cylindrical cutter head holding three or more cutter blades. Models vary in size and can accommodate work between 1.6 and 4 ft. (0.5–1.2 m) wide. Industrial models can plane all four sides of a board at once.

Jointers

The jointer does much the same thing as the planer but has two separate tables—one is the front, or infeed, table, and the other is the back, or outfeed table. The work is pushed across the

◀ A belt-sanding unit for sanding straight veneer and solid wood edges. The sanding pad is designed to operate so as to prevent the rounding or perforation of workpiece ends and edges.

▼ These components for various items of furniture were shaped and sanded on an electrically powered woodworking machine.

◄ The electric motor of this profile disk sanding unit drives the disk at a maximum 1,500 rpm. The disk speed is infinitely adjustable downward by means of a frequency transformer.

Sanders

Sanding machines are often portable and consist of disks or belts with sandpaper attached. There are also machines with tables and projecting spindles to which sandpaper is attached. Orbital sanders, with a rectangular sanding plate oscillating in a small circle, are useful for finishing wood because the to-and-fro movement does not leave the unsightly swirl marks made by a rotary sander.

Adhesives

Wood adhesives are traditionally used with nails to strengthen joints, but some modern adhesives produce a bond that is stronger than wood and do not need the addition of nails. Adhesives are ideal for bonding softwoods and hardwoods, plywood, particleboard, and all hardboards.

Specific waterproof adhesive should be used for exteriors. Cascamite is a waterproof synthetic resin adhesive that is mixed with water to produce a glue for woodworking and is particularly useful for exterior building work and boatbuilding. Nonmix wood adhesives are PVA (polyvinyl acetate) emulsion based and specially developed for use on both softwoods and hardwoods. PVA is commonly used as the chemical additive in manufacturing water-based wood adhesives.

tables, and the adjustable height of the infeed table determines the size of the cut. The cutter knives range from 6 to 24 in. (15–61 cm) long.

Shapers and routers

The shaper is used to cut curved and ornate edges on table tops, picture frames, woodwork moldings, and so forth. It has a rotating spindle projecting through a table and carrying cutter blades shaped to cut the particular profile desired.

The router is an inverted shaper that has the spindle suspended over the table. It is used for shaping the inside of wood bowls, cut-out chair backs, and similar work. Portable routers are available.

Mortiser

A mortise is a slot with 90-degree corners, and a tenon is a projection with 90-degree corners that fits into a mortise to make a mortise-and-tenon joint. (A tongue-and-groove joint is similar, but the groove is open ended, and so it can be cut by a saw or a shaper.)

The mortiser is a hollow chisel with a square shape and a boring tool inside it. It bores a hole almost as large as the required shape; then the chisel removes the corners. The mortising device can be mounted horizontally or vertically. There are also tenoners for mass production.

Drilling machines

The portable electric drill is widely used for drilling holes in wood, but for mass production or greater accuracy in making doweled joints in furniture, the boring tool, or drill press, is used. Such a machine is similar to a drill press in a factory, consisting of a vertical spindle, a table with adjustable height, and provision for clamping the work firmly to the table. In mass production, boring tools can be automatically driven and may have several spindles.

▶ A rear view of the Arminius SH-1 belt-and-disk profile sander, showing the belt-drive mechanism. A wide range of profiles can be worked to various standards of finish.

SEE ALSO: Adhesive and sealant • Drill • Electric motor • Machine tool • Tool manufacture • Veneer • Wood composite

Word Processor

The development of the word processor was the single most significant advance in text handling. Before then, no matter how text was prepared—either by slate and stylus, pen and paper, or typewriter—the opportunities for correction and manipulation during or after writing were minimal.

Typewriters

Since its introduction more than 125 years ago, the typewriter has evolved from an essentially mechanical machine into a device using advanced electronic circuitry. The disadvantage of mechanical typewriters is that errors have to be corrected laboriously and are usually noticeable. If there is some change to be made, however small, the whole document has to be retyped, and if several people have to be sent a similar letter, the work becomes repetitive and boring.

The solution to these problems came in the form of automatic typewriters and their modern counterparts, the text editors. The first automatic typewriters were used primarily to solve the problem of repetitive typing by storing the information in coded form, usually on punched paper tape. If a mistake is made during recording, it is only necessary for the typist to operate a backspace key to step the tape back to record over the error. Thus, the typing may be done at a faster speed because any mistakes can be corrected instantly. The recorded tape may then be played back at a speed equivalent to 150 words per minute to provide a correct final copy any number of times that may be required.

The next development came in the form of using a magnetic oxide-coated card instead of tape. One card records each page, and each line is recorded along the length of the card in a succession of tracks. One of the main advantages of these systems is that each recorded track on the card is accessible, and so revisions can be made to any particular line without having to play out the whole text.

Text editors, while still using either magnetic tape or card, do not actually record anything until the text has been typed. These machines use a temporary storage, or buffer, in which the information is stored. The most advanced of these machines has a display on a cathode-ray tube (CRT) screen showing the characters stored in the buffer; the display enables the text to be monitored before it is actually recorded.

Computers

The key point about word processing is that the material being written is stored in computer memory and printed out—made into hard copy—

only after everything is correct. In addition, the information is stored, so it can be accessed and reprocessed many times.

Text is normally typed in at a typewriter-style (QWERTY) keyboard. The rest of the machine is a computer. Instead of appearing directly on paper, words appear on a screen (monitor). As the letters are typed, they are displayed at the cursor—usually a flashing square or line.

Early word processors were predominantly dedicated machines, functioning as word processors only. With the general acceptance of computers into the workplace, the balance between the dedicated machines and computers that are used for word processing shifted in favor of the latter. A computer can be used for many other tasks as well. In most cases, a computer is as good a machine to use for word processing as is a dedicated word processor.

The two types of machine use programs that are based on the same principles. Text is stored as bytes of information in computer RAM (random-access memory) and may be stored like computer programs on disk storage devices. All types of computers are suitable for use as word processors, provided suitable software—the set of instructions in computer language that tells the computer how to handle text—is available or can be written. As a computer application, word processing does not demand huge processing power, and most word processing today is done on desktop personal computers (PCs).

An increasing amount of word processing is carried out on portable battery-driven computers, or laptops. Executives can work on the move rather than wait until returning to the office. Journalists also use this kind of machine for writing articles, particularly when away from home.

Word processors need printers to generate their end product. The kind of printer that is used depends on what the printed material is to be used for. Dot-matrix printers are the cheapest but are noisy. Newer types of printers such as ink-jet and thermal ribbon transfer printers are much quieter and therefore more popular. The fastest, quietest—and most expensive—of all are laser printers, which produce the best quality.

Text manipulation

Most word processors offer broadly similar facilities. At the simplest level, they allow anyone to produce printed material free from typing mistakes. The cursor can be moved backward with a backspace key, but instead of merely typing over the letter as would be the case on most typewriters, the letter is removed from the computer's screen. Often word processors allow the operator

◀ A Canon word processor and printer. Information is typed and edited at the keyboard and then stored on floppy disks.

to put back the letters that have been removed by storing letters and words in a specially allocated part of the computer's memory.

Cursor control keys allow the user to delete and replace letters anywhere on the screen. If the document is longer than the screen allows, it can be scrolled up or down so that any part of it can be read and corrected if needed. In longer documents, sentences or entire paragraphs can be shifted elsewhere in a document. This type of editing normally entails highlighting the section of document that needs to be moved and moving the cursor to the new position. Pressing a button moves the text to the correct place.

Most word processors allow the user to set up headers and footers—text, such as titles, that need to appear on each page—and to number pages automatically. Others allow complex formatting, including positioning information in columns.

Many word processors have built-in spelling checkers. These dictionaries are equivalent in size to a single-volume printed dictionary and are stored on disk. The computer checks each of the words in the document against the dictionary. The next stage on from checking spelling is checking grammar, a task that is a standard feature on most word-processing computer software but not on dedicated word processors.

Desktop publishing

Desktop publishing, a logical progression from the well-established kinds of word processing, puts greater emphasis on the appearance of the finished document. The newest generation of laser printers are used for desktop publishing. They allow many different fonts (type styles) and produce results approaching the quality of typesetting. Page-layout and graphic-design software allow magazine-style layouts to be produced.

SEE ALSO: COMPUTER • COMPUTER PRINTER • DESKTOP PUBLISHING • TYPEWRITER

X-Ray Imaging

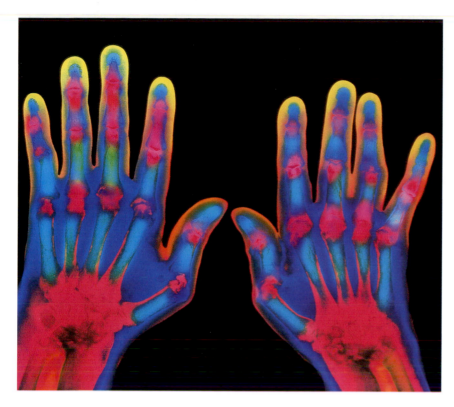

The penetrating radiation emitted when a beam of electrons (a cathode ray) strikes the glass wall of a discharge tube was discovered accidentally by the German physicist Wilhelm Röntgen in 1895. He named it X radiation because its nature was at that time completely unknown and its ability to pass through opaque objects was mystifying.

It is now recognized that X rays are electromagnetic radiation of wavelengths between 0.01 Å (angstroms) and 100 Å (0.001–10 nm). These wavelengths are significantly shorter than those of visible light, which are around 5,000 Å (500 nm). In terms of frequency, these wavelengths correspond to between 3×10^{16} Hz and 3×10^{20} Hz, compared with 6×10^{14} Hz for visible light. Since the energy of a photon is proportional to its frequency, the energy of each X-ray photon is from 50 to 500,000 times that of a photon of visible light.

The medical uses of X rays are probably their best-known application, but the penetrating power of X radiation is also important in industry for inspecting materials and welds for internal flaws. Further important applications occur in metallurgy and geochemistry, where X rays are used to analyze both the chemical composition and the crystalline structure of specimens.

Origins of X radiation

The mechanism that produces X rays is similar to the one that produces visible light: both involve the movement of an electron from a high-energy

▲ This colored X-ray image shows the effects of rheumatoid arthritis on the joints of a person's hands. Pink highlights inflamed and deformed joints.

state to a lower-energy state in an atom, its excess energy being cast off as a photon in the process. In the case of visible light emission, the electron moves from an excited state that is normally unoccupied to the ground state, which is the usual condition of the atom.

In the case of X rays, the transition occurs when an electron deep within an atom is knocked out of its orbit by a fast-moving electron in an electron beam, for example. One of the electrons in a higher energy level then falls into the vacancy, shedding a photon whose energy matches the energy difference between the two states. The difference is that the energy gap in this type of transition is many orders of magnitude greater than in the visible transition, so the frequency of radiation is much higher.

A second mechanism of X-ray production is responsible for *bremsstrahlung* (German for "braking radiation"). In this case, photons are shed to compensate for the drop in energy of electrons that decelerate in the electrical fields that surround atomic nuclei. Whereas the X-ray transitions that occur within atoms have precise energy values, bremsstrahlung can occur over a continuous range of frequencies. Hence, the X-ray spectrum of a target bombarded by electrons consists of sharp peaks (atomic transitions) set in a smooth hump (bremsstrahlung).

X-ray sources

The earliest X-ray sources were developed from Röntgen's discharge tube. It was difficult to keep a constant vacuum in such tubes, however, so they had only a short life span. In 1916, the U.S. physical chemist William Coolidge developed the prototype of the X-ray tube that is in general use today. A Coolidge tube has many features in common with a vacuum tube: it contains a hard vacuum in a sealed glass envelope, and thermionic electrons are produced at a cathode heated by a filament and held at high negative potential. The copper anode, or anticathode, is held at high positive potential, and X rays form when electrons, accelerated by the electrical field between the anode and cathode, strike a tungsten target set in the anode. The X rays escape through a window in the otherwise well-shielded tube. The process is highly inefficient—only around 1 percent of the energy of the electron beam is converted into X radiation. The remaining 99 percent of the beam's energy is converted to heat, so the copper anode must be water cooled as long as the tube is in operation.

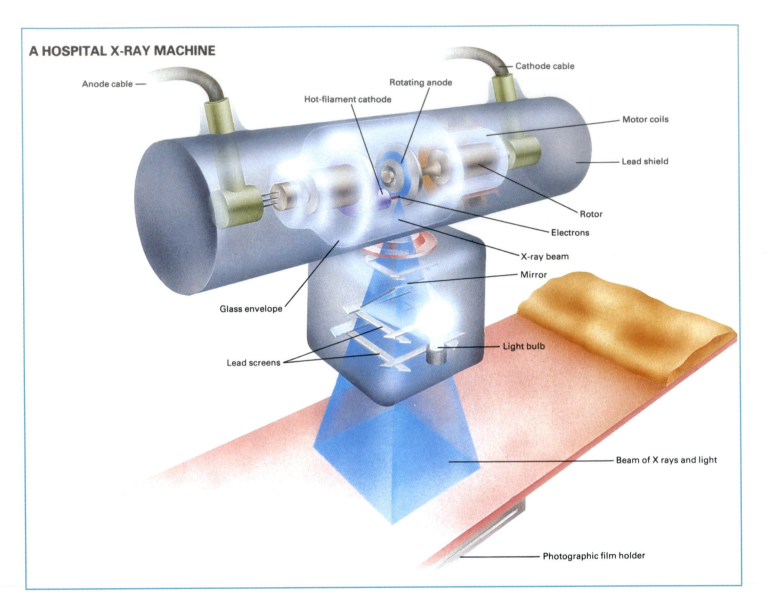

A HOSPITAL X-RAY MACHINE

Anode cable —

Cathode cable

Rotating anode

Hot-filament cathode

Motor coils

Lead shield

Rotor

Electrons

X-ray beam

Mirror

Glass envelope

Light bulb

Lead screens

Beam of X rays and light

Photographic film holder

▲ An X-ray machine of the type used in hospitals. The X rays are produced by a beam of electrons striking an anode. To prolong its life and prevent overheating, the anode is rotated at speeds of up to 10,000 rpm. Lead slats limit the area of the beam.

In the Coolidge X-ray tube, the intensity of X radiation is controlled by the current in the cathode filament, which governs the temperature of the cathode and, consequently, the rate of production of thermionic electrons. The wavelength of the radiation is controlled by the potential difference between cathode and anode: the greater the voltage, the higher the energy of the electrons in the beam when they hit the target, and thus the shorter the minimum wavelength.

In general, shorter-wavelength X rays are less easily absorbed than those of longer wavelengths and are therefore more penetrating. However, the shorter the wavelength, the greater is the energy of the X-ray photons and the greater their potential to damage tissue, for example. As a compromise between penetrating power and tissue damage, hospital X-ray machines usually operate at voltages less than 150,000 V, although standard Coolidge tubes can be used at many times that potential difference. Modified Coolidge tubes that incorporate several electrodes can operate at up to 2 MV, and even higher energies (and

shorter X-ray wavelengths) can be produced by using a particle accelerator to produce electron beams at exceptionally high energies.

Radiography

X rays are absorbed at different rates by different materials: for X rays of a particular wavelength, the absorption depends on the atomic number (equal to the number of electrons) of the atoms present and on the density. In radiography, the sample is placed between the X-ray source and a photographic plate; the more absorbent parts of the specimen throw shadows onto the plate, and they appear less dark when the plate is developed.

A radiograph of the human body shows the bones whiter than surrounding flesh because bones contain the element calcium, which has a relatively high atomic number. Any abnormalities, such as broken bones, arthritis, or foreign bodies in the stomach or lungs, are readily visible, and appropriate therapeutic action can be taken. Internal organs generally absorb X rays to about the same extent as the surrounding flesh, but they can be shown up on a radiograph by concentrating material of greater absorbing power into the organ. A meal of the insoluble salt barium sulfate shows up the stomach and intestinal tract, while iodine compounds injected into the bloodstream show where they accumulate in the thyroid gland.

Radiography also has important industrial uses in locating internal defects in materials and for inspecting welds. The movement of internal parts of machinery can be followed by motion-picture radiography; exposures of a hundredth to a thousandth of a second are obtained from an X-ray tube with a rotating target that lies within the electron beam for only this brief time. Another specialized type of radiography used in both industry and medicine is stereoscopy, where two radiographs are taken with the X-ray source displaced sideways through a distance that matches the gap between the human eyes. When the radiographs are viewed through a stereoscope, a three-dimensional image is seen.

An important technique for studying the three-dimensional structure of solids is tomography, originally developed to investigate brain tumors. The X-ray source, the patient, and the photographic plate are moved continuously during the exposure in such a way that the shadow of one particular plane through the brain is always in the same position on the plate, but the shadows of the rest of the brain are in continuous motion and are thus completely blurred out. The result is a radiograph showing a cross section through the brain. If several such cross sections are taken, they can be processed by a computer to produce a detailed three-dimensional picture of the subject for diagnostic purposes. This technique is called CAT (computed axial tomography) scanning.

Radiotherapy

Radiology is a branch of medicine that includes radiography and radiotherapy. Radiotherapy uses higher-energy X rays than those used in radiography to destroy cancerous growths and to knock out the immune system—and therefore the rejection mechanism—before certain organ-transplant operations. Great care must be exercised because the very high doses required can also damage healthy tissue and produce leukemia.

Fluoroscopy

Fluoroscopy is a technique for producing visible images from X-rays without using photography. Instead of the photographic film or plate used in conventional radiography, the X-ray shadow of the subject of a fluoroscopic investigation is cast on a fluorescent screen. This type of screen is coated with chemicals that emit visible photons

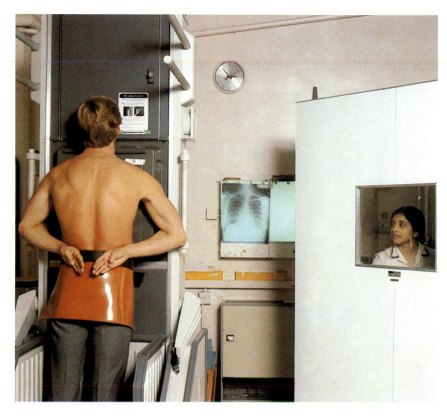

when struck by X-ray photons, so they produce a direct image of the subject. Fluoroscopy has two great advantages over radiography: it eliminates the expense and delay caused by photographic processing, and it shows movement inside the object rather than just a series of still images.

A variant of X-ray fluoroscopy, called X-ray television fluoroscopy, was originally developed for diagnostic use. It addresses the problematically high doses that would be necessary to produce a screen image of a human subject that is directly visible to the human eye. Television fluoroscopy uses lower-intensity radiation than used for direct fluoroscopy, and the faint screen images that result are intensified by viewing them with a sensitive television camera and increasing the brightness and contrast of the picture obtained. The television image can be magnified on a monitor screen, and it can be recorded on film or videotape for detailed examination.

The applications of television fluoroscopy include mass screening for early symptoms of tuberculosis (TB) and the diagnosis of defective body functions. For example, the detection of a slipped disk is facilitated by

▲ During a chest X ray, lead screens protect the subject and radiographer from unnecessary exposure to X radiation.

▼ This X-ray image shows a crossbow bolt embedded deep in the skull of a murder victim.

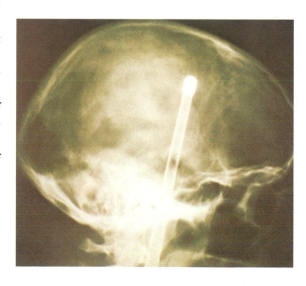

injecting a radiographically opaque dye in the suspect region of the spine. The flow of the dye is observed using X-ray television fluoroscopy while the patient is manipulated. The dye pinpoints the defective disk, enabling corrective surgery to be performed more effectively.

Nonmedical applications include automatic quality control during the manufacture or processing of metal products, such as electronic devices, and it is especially useful for checking the quality of welding. Television fluoroscopy is also the technique used for security screening of baggage at airports; low doses reveal the contents of baggage without damaging photographic film. The most diversified application of fluoroscopy is in the area of research and development. Direct observation of the moving interiors of engines, turbines, munitions, armaments, and so on has added a new dimension to operational studies. One important research application is in the observation of the flow characteristics of molten steel within sand molds.

XRF spectroscopy

X radiation can be used to perform a quick and accurate elemental analysis of a chemical sample. The technique uses a phenomenon called X-ray fluorescence, in which bombardment of a sample with high-energy X rays causes the emission of lower-energy X-ray photons that are characteristic of the elements in the sample. The mechanism is simple: the high-energy X-ray photon has enough energy to eject inner electrons from atoms, just as the electrons do in a high-energy electron beam. The emissions that characterize the elements present in the sample occur when electrons drop into the hole left by those electrons ejected by the incoming X radiation.

The elements present in a sample can be identified from the wavelengths of the emitted X rays, and the quantity of each element can be deduced from the relative intensities of the lines of the various elements. This technique can be a hundred times quicker than a conventional chemical analysis, and it requires only an extremely small sample. The results give no indication of the chemical bonding within the sample, however, since the electrons that participate are deep within the atom and shielded from any influence of neighboring atoms that could give a clue to bonding.

X-ray diffraction

All but the lowest-energy X-ray photons have shorter wavelengths than the spacings between atoms in compounds, and this makes X rays valuable in examining the structures of compounds. The result is not a direct image, however, but a

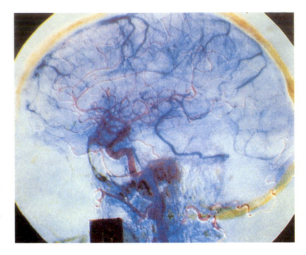

▲ A radiographic contrast agent, injected into the carotid artery, reveals the path of blood through the brain in this example of X-ray fluoroscopy. The yellow band is the outline of the subject's skull.

diffraction pattern produced by the X rays reflected off crystalline samples. It occurs because a crystal has several orientations of parallel planes in which the same type of atom occupies regularly spaced sites. If photographic film is placed in the field of reflection, it will show dots only at those points where all the photons reflected by two or more parallel planes are in phase—destructive interference prevents dots at all other positions. The positions of those dots can be used to calculate the spacings of each type of plane and hence the structure of the crystal.

Although the technique started with the analysis of the diffraction patterns produced by single crystals of simple materials, the application of complex mathematics and computer processing has allowed X-ray crystallography to elucidate the structures of synthetic polymers and even complex biological molecules, such as proteins. It revealed the double-helix structure of the hereditary material DNA (deoxyribonucleic acid), and the synthesis of penicillin would not have been possible without the information on its structure given by X-ray crystallography.

X-ray astronomy

For several decades, satellite-borne observatories have been examining X-ray emissions from the Universe. (Earth's atmosphere absorbs X rays before they reach the ground, so earthbound observatories are unable to detect them.) Natural sources of X rays include the Sun, especially around the dark sunspots, and certain double stars where matter from a giant star falls onto a dwarf star and is heated to a temperature of millions of degrees. At these high temperatures, X-ray bremsstrahlung occurs when electrons collide with atomic nuclei, and this radiation has been detected by satellites. Dwarf stars, also known as neutron stars or pulsars, emit large amounts of X rays that pulse as the small star spins. An X-ray satellite, *Uhuru*, launched in 1970, found a nonpulsing X-ray source in the Cygnus constellation. Astronomers concluded that the source, Cygnus X-1, is not a neutron star but a black hole.

SEE ALSO: BODY SCANNER • CRYSTALS AND CRYSTALLOGRAPHY • ELECTROMAGNETIC RADIATION • RADIOTHERAPY

Yeast

Yeasts are single-celled fungi whose cells are mostly spherical in shape (instead of being cylindrical and arranged end to end in long, branched filaments, as is more typical for fungi). Thousands of species of yeast are known, belonging to several widely different groups of fungi, but only a few are used industrially. Some fungi that are normally filaments produce yeast forms.

Although filamentous fungi are sometimes used in industrial fermentation, the use of yeasts is much more common. Because yeasts are single celled, they are more easily dispersed in the medium. Their globular shape gives the yeast cells a larger surface area-to-volume ratio than filamentous fungi. Thus, there is more surface area for the cell to come into contact with the medium in which it is growing, the result being a more vigorous fermentation.

Yeasts are found everywhere in large numbers: in the soil, in the air, in fresh and salt water, and coating the surface of living plants and prepared foodstuffs. In these situations, they are able to survive for long periods of time and even to grow and multiply slowly.

Very early in human history, people discovered that foods were altered by the action of these naturally occurring yeasts. Sometimes the food was spoiled, but in a few cases, there was a great improvement in the food's texture or flavor. It was only in 1866, however, that the French chemist Louis Pasteur discovered that fermentation is caused by living organisms. Pasteur did his original work on winemaking, and his classic paper "Studies on Wine" marks the beginning of scientifically applied fermentation.

Wine yeasts occur naturally in the soils of vineyards and find their way onto the skins of the grapes and so into the grape juice (must). In traditional winemaking, no other yeast was added to the must, but today there is an increasing tendency to add artificially cultured yeast.

Baking, brewing, and fermentation

The best-known yeast and the one most used in industry is brewer's, or baker's, yeast, *Saccharomyces cerevisiae* (*cerevisia* is Latin for beer). Strains of this yeast are used in bread and yeast cakes and in brewing ales and stout.

▲ An alcohol plant in the West Indies. During the fermentation process, yeast converts sugar into alcohol in the presence of oxygen, the process giving off carbon dioxide.

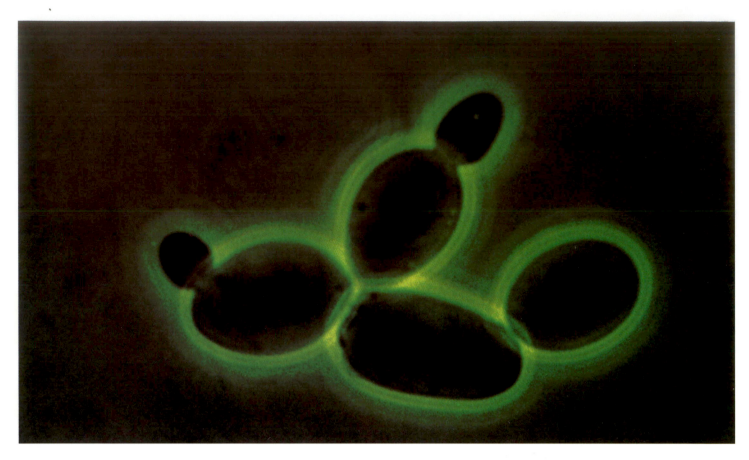

In Japan, the production of sake (rice wine) is a large industry in which the raw material, cooked rice, is first fermented by a fungus, *Aspergillus oryzae*, to break down the starch molecules into sugars. The resulting syrup is then fermented with the Japanese equivalent of brewer's yeast, *Saccharomyces sake*. This yeast is able to tolerate a high alcohol concentration, so the final product can be made as strong as European fortified wines without having to add distilled spirit.

Each yeast cell is egg shaped, about 0.00024 in. (0.006 mm) across, and is a complete organism capable of growth, reproduction, and of course, fermentation. The usual method of reproduction in brewer's yeast is by budding, where young cells bud and grow on the surface of the parent cell. Each young cell will have exactly the same characteristics as the parent because it receives a precise replica of its parent's nucleus. This feature is important for the fermentation industry because different strains of yeast have different characteristics and this method of reproduction ensures a particular strain remains the same for generation after generation.

When a yeast cell comes into contact with a suitable sugar, it absorbs and uses the sugar for growth and respiration, just as any other organism would. Oxygen is necessary for respiration, and carbon dioxide is given off as a result. If insufficient oxygen is supplied, as in a fermentation vat, the yeast simply converts part of the sugar into alcohol and oxygen. The oxygen is used for respiration, and the alcohol is excreted into the vat. When the concentration of alcohol becomes too great for the yeast to tolerate or when the available sugar is used up, fermentation ceases. In a fermentation vessel, the conditions are adjusted to obtain an adequate yield of alcohol while making sure the yeast grows fast enough to overcome any other microbes.

Food yeast

Yeast cells contain large quantities of protein, around 40 percent in dried yeast, and are particularly rich in vitamins of the B group. If properly

▲ Yeast cells undergoing division by budding. Each daughter cell receives a nucleus from the mother cell that is an exact replica of the parent and so maintains the purity of a particular strain of yeast.

◀ In yeast production, the yeast cells are kept in optimum conditions for them to multiply; they release alcohol and carbon dioxide as by-products.

prepared, they are excellent human and animal foodstuffs. Various fungi, yeasts, and bacteria are produced on a large scale for consumption and may be used as substitutes for conventional sources of protein.

When the aim is to produce yeast, rather than alcohol, air is forced into the vessel to ensure the yeast multiplies as rapidly as possible and a minimum of alcohol is produced. Baker's, or brewer's, yeasts can be dried to produce thin, flat flakes of inactive yeast cells for use in food. The flakes are sometimes milled to a beige-colored powder. The products in which dried food yeast is used include soups, condiments, flavorings, nutritional preparations, and snack foods.

Torula yeast, *Candida utilis*, has the advantage that it can be grown on waste products from other industrial processes—an example being wastewater from the sulfite process of making paper (where an acid bisulfite solution digests wood pulp). Once the sulfite has been removed, yeast can be grown in the sugary solution left over from the wood pulp. The solution is seeded with torula yeast and passed to a fermenter, into which compressed air is pumped. Liquid is then drawn off, and the crop of yeast cells is separated in a centrifuge. The waste now contains very little sugar and can be safely discharged without risk of pollution. The harvested yeast cells are killed and dried by mild heating. At one time, this yeast product was used in cattle feed, although now it is mainly used in human food.

Yeast extract is manufactured by adding an enzyme (a protein molecule that encourages chemical reactions) that causes the yeast cells to undergo autolysis—a process in which the cells break down and die. Extracts can then be modified in various ways to suit particular flavor applications, although most extracts sold to food manufacturers are nonmodified. Products that use yeast extracts include soups, gravies, and stock cubes.

Industrial uses of yeast

Many commercial processes are carried out with the aid of yeast. A large plant can produce 8,000 tons (7,200 tonnes) of yeast per year for making human food, animal feed, and vaccines; for fermenting alcohol or other chemicals; and for use in the biotechnology industry. Industrial yeasts are grown on a range of substances—for example, on the sugars in cane molasses or the waste products from the paper industry.

Industrial production of citric acid from strains of *Aspergillus niger* (not a yeast but a filamentous fungus) is highly successful and probably cheaper than extraction from citrus fruits. The method is complex, however, and precautions

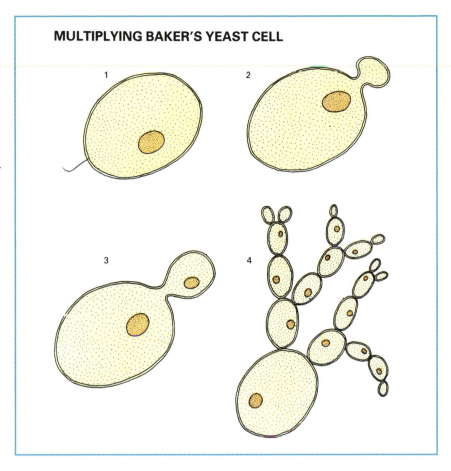

MULTIPLYING BAKER'S YEAST CELL

have to be taken to prevent the formation of oxalic acid, which is highly poisonous.

Yeast extracts make a good nutrient for growing other microbes—for example, bacteria and certain fungi. Being a good source of organic nitrogen, vitamins, and nutrients, yeast extracts are used in the production of antibiotics, enzymes, organic acids, vitamins, and cultures of bacteria for medicinal use.

Through genetic engineering, human insulin can be made from yeast or the bacterium *E. coli*, which are now the main sources of insulin used in medicine. Insulin is used for the treatment of diabetes, a medical disorder in which a person is unable to regulate the amount of sugar in his or her blood and needs injections of insulin.

Commercial yeasts with a high selenium content are sold through natural-food stores and sometimes added to vitamin and mineral supplements. Selenium is beneficial for the liver and can help to prevent liver cancer.

Yeast extracts are used to obtain vitamins of the B group, which are also included in natural-food supplements. Vitamins of the B group are essential for maintaining the nervous system and for healthy hair, skin, and nails.

▲ Baker's yeast cells with buds forming. When a bud reaches maturity, it breaks from its parent and repeats the cycle. Sometimes, however, the division does not succeed, and in such instances, branches of cells grow.

| SEE ALSO: | ALCOHOL • BEER AND BREWING • BIOTECHNOLOGY • FERMENTATION • MICROBIOLOGY • WINEMAKING |

Zeolite

The zeolites are a group of natural and synthetic aluminosilicate minerals, similar in composition to clays and ceramics. They are characterized by low-density crystalline structures in which cavities are interconnected by narrower channels. In the natural state, the cavities are occupied by water molecules and ions of alkali and alkaline earth metals, such as sodium and calcium. Because the water in these cavities evaporates readily on heating, there is an impression that zeolites boil—in fact, the word *zeolite* derives from the Greek words *zein* (to boil) and *lithos* (stone).

In nature, zeolites form by the metamorphosis of marine and river sediments or of volcanic debris. Metamorphosis is a process of chemical and structural change induced by prolonged exposure to high pressures and temperatures, as occurs when minerals are buried deep under ground. Zeolites form under relatively mild conditions compared with other minerals: pressures of 200 atmospheres (3,000 psi) and temperatures around 400–575°F (200–300°C) are sufficient.

Examples of naturally occurring zeolites include chabazite ($CaAl_2Si_4O_{12} \cdot 6.67H_2O$), heulandite ($CaAl_2Si_7O_{18} \cdot 6H_2O$), and natrolite ($Na_2Al_2Si_3O_{10} \cdot 2H_2O$). The type that forms in a given deposit depends on the materials present and factors such as temperature and pressure.

Modern zeolite chemistry started in 1933, when Richard Barrer, a New Zealander by birth, took up a research scholarship at Cambridge University, England. Barrer chose to investigate the sorption of gases by solids, especially in chabazite. Over the following decades, Barrer investigated the properties and crystal structures of natural zeolites and also developed methods for producing synthetic zeolites, for influencing their structures, and for modifying their chemical properties. These techniques were crucial to the development of numerous technologies based on synthetic zeolites, such as shape-selective catalysis and water softening by ion exchange.

Structure

Zeolites owe many of their properties to the channels and cavities within their structures. These features occur because of the tendency of silicon and oxygen to form the strong covalent Si–O bonds that are the basis of minerals, such as quartz, and ceramics, such as glass.

All these materials are based on silica (silicon dioxide, SiO_2), a compound in which each silicon atom is joined to four oxygen atoms that lie at the corners of a tetrahedron. Each oxygen atom is

▲ A sample of stilbite from east Iceland. Stilbite is one of some 40 zeolites that occur in nature. In its natural state, the channels in stilbite are occupied by water molecules and calcium ions; the result is a typical formula of $CaAl_2Si_7O_{18} \cdot 7H_2O$.

shared by two silicon atoms, and it helps in the visualization of zeolite structure to think of the oxygen atoms as being pivotal joints that hold adjacent SiO_4 tetrahedra together.

In these terms, the pores that run through zeolites can be thought of as consisting of rings of typically four, five, or six SiO_4 tetrahedra each, stacked together to form hollow shafts 2.2 to 8.0 Å (0.22–0.80 nm) in diameter. These pores can run along one, two, or three dimensions through a zeolite and can be straight or wavy (the pores in the industrial catalyst ZSM-5 are wavy, for example). Where several pores meet within a zeolite, the result is a cavity whose dimensions can be much greater than the individual pore diameters, lying in the range from 6.6 to 11.8 Å (0.66 to 1.18 nm). For comparison, the effective diameters of simple molecules, such as nitrogen (N_2) and water (H_2O), are around 3 Å (0.3 nm).

The structural framework of a zeolite does not consist entirely of silicon and oxygen, however: the aluminum content of a zeolite also resides in the walls of the pores and cavities, because a proportion of the SiO_4 tetrahedra is replaced by AlO_4 tetrahedra. Similarly, the SiO_2 formula is replaced by AlO_2^- groups, the negative charge arising because aluminum is in the +3 oxidation state, whereas silicon is in the +4 oxidation state in these compounds.

The presence of aluminum therefore leads to a net negative charge in the framework of a zeolite, and that negative charge is spread among the oxygen atoms of the framework. In order to maintain electroneutrality, the negative charge due to each aluminum atom must be balanced by a positive charge on a cation. Rather than forming part of the zeolite framework, however, those cations reside loosely in the pores and cavities.

In natural zeolites, the neutralizing cations are of metals such as calcium, magnesium, potassium, and sodium. M^{2+} cations, such as Ca^{2+} and Mg^{2+}, neutralize two aluminum-occupied sites each, whereas M^+ cations (Na^+ and K^+) neutralize one.

Synthesis

Zeolites are prepared by a technique called hydrothermal synthesis, which mimics their formation in nature. The starting material is a waterborne gel that contains sources of alumina (Al_2O_3) and silica (SiO_2), as well as hydroxides of the cations required for electroneutrality, such as sodium hydroxide (NaOH).

The mixture is heated to around 320°F (160°C) in a sealed container, so pressure builds up in the container. Over a period of two or more days of heating, crystals of zeolite form, and they can be separated from the remaining waterborne components by filtration and washing.

Templating. During the formation of a zeolite, aluminosilicate assembles itself around ions that determine the shapes of the cavities and pores in the final product. Richard Barrer realized that there was scope for influencing the structures of zeolites by including organic cations such as tetraalkylammonium ions. The salts that provide these cations are called template compounds, and they provide for much greater variety of pore and cavity geometries than can be achieved using metal ions alone. The technique also made possible the formation of low-alumina (high-silica) zeolites. The template compound for ZSM-5, for example, is tetrapropylammonium bromide, which provides $(C_4H_9)_4N^+$ cations.

Calcining. The next stage in the preparation of a zeolite is calcining, whereby the crude zeolite is heated to around 950°F (500°C) in a stream of an inert gas, such as nitrogen. The process first removes water molecules from the cavities, and they are followed by the decomposition products of the template cation: volatile amines, alkenes, and more water. The product of calcining is a zeolite whose pores are free of water but occupied by cations of the alkali used in the synthesis mixture—sodium ions, for example.

▼ A crew member on NASA's shuttle *Columbia* prepares a metal sample tube for the Zeolite Crystal Growth (ZCG) experiment. The sealed tube will be placed in a furnace where hydrothermal synthesis will take place. Crystal growth in zero gravity promotes the formation of flawless zeolite crystals from the reaction mixture.

Ion exchange. While the sodium-neutralized zeolite is itself appropriate for some applications, such as water softening, other applications require the removal of sodium ions and their replacement by other ions. This switch is achieved by ion exchange, whereby the zeolite is flooded with a solution that contains the desired ions in high concentration or with a weaker solution of ions that have a strong affinity for the zeolite.

The acidic form of the catalyst, in which protons replace neutralizing cations by bonding to oxygen atoms in the framework, are made by ion exchange with ammonium salts. Calcining removes water and ammonia, and the protons are left in place in the zeolite. The protons are then acidic in nature, a useful state for catalysis.

Absorption applications

In their earliest applications, zeolites were used as drying agents in laboratory work and industrial processes. The most suitable types are high-alumina zeolites, which have a greater affinity for water than high-silica zeolites. A class of zeolite called Linde type A is most suitable for such applications, since its internal surface area—the area of the internal walls on which species can absorb—can be as great as 275,000 sq.ft. per oz. (900 m²/g); when fully laden, water can account for up to 25 percent of the weight of such a zeolite.

Type A zeolite also has a high affinity for metal cations. It was used to mop up radioactive metal ions in the nuclear incidents at Three Mile Island and Chernobyl and is routinely mixed with treated nuclear waste to help contain active material in the event of container rupture.

High-silica zeolites, such as ZSM-5, are useful in selectively absorbing organic compounds from a water-based environment. One application is in the removal of toxic chlorinated hydrocarbons from groundwater. Once the zeolite has reached its capacity, the absorbed material can be removed by heating the zeolite and then collected for destruction in a controlled environment.

There is potential for high-silica zeolites to act as hydrocarbon traps for cold starting of internal combustion engines. Catalytic converters start to work only when they are hot, and hydrocarbons escape in the exhaust stream during the first few minutes after starting. Zeolite traps have been proven capable of absorbing 35 to 70 percent of those hydrocarbons and then releasing them to the hot converter as the zeolite warms up.

Molecular sieving. Molecular sieving is the ability of zeolites to selectively absorb substances according to size and polarizability. One application is in the extraction of nitrogen from air. Linde type X zeolite, ion-exchanged with lithium

SYNTHETIC ZEOLITE ZSM-5

Possibly the most important synthetic zeolite was patented by Mobil in 1972 as a catalyst for use in hydrocarbon conversion processes. Known by the product code of ZSM-5 (Zeolite Socony Mobil number 5) variations of this zeolite have been put to use in improving process efficiencies and reducing waste products for numerous oil-refining and feedstock-manufacturing chemical plants the world over.

The generic formula of ZSM-5 is $Na_nAl_nSi_{(96-n)}O_{192} \cdot 16H_2O$, where n is usually between 1.5 and 9, so there are at least 10 silicon atoms for each aluminum atom. The high silica content contributes to the affinity of this zeolite for the hydrocarbons whose reactions it promotes, especially when the sodium ions of the zeolite are replaced by protons.

Another key factor in the effectiveness of ZSM-5 is the size of the pores in its structure. At around 5.5 Å (0.55 nm) in diameter, these channels favor reaction products that are either straight-chain alkanes of up to 11 carbon atoms, or else aromatics whose substituent groups lie on opposite sides of the aromatic ring. The narrowness of such molecules allows them to pass through channels that retain bulkier products until they react to form more streamlined molecules.

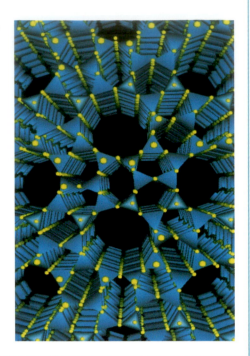

▶ This computer-generated graphic of the structure of ZSM-5 shows the channels through which molecules must pass to reach catalytic sites. The tetrahedra represent SiO_4 and AlO_4 groups, which are held together by shared oxygen atoms, shown in yellow.

ions, preferentially absorbs oxygen molecules from air. Hence, the output stream when air passes through a bed of this zeolite consists almost purely of nitrogen. The oxygen-saturated zeolite is regenerated when necessary by heating to remove oxygen. This process is more energy efficient than the distillation of liquefied air.

Water softening. The largest-volume application for type-A zeolite is as a substitute for polyphosphate bulking agents in washing powders. Sodium zeolite A assists detergents by absorbing water-hardening ions, such as calcium ions, and replacing them with sodium ions. The main benefit of using zeolites in this application is in avoiding the ecological damage caused by releasing polyphosphates in wastewater.

Sodium zeolite A is also used in water-softening devices for home and industrial uses. Flushing with concentrated sodium chloride (common salt) solution is sufficient to regenerate the zeolite ion-exchange column: the high concentration of sodium ions forces the water-hardening ions out of the zeolite. This exchange happens despite the greater affinity of ions such as calcium and magnesium for the zeolite pores.

Catalytic applications

High-silica zeolites, such as ZSM-5, find widespread use as catalysts in the oil-refining and hydrocarbon-processing industries. They are mainly used in their protonated forms, when they act as acid catalysts in reactions, for example, the cracking and isomerization of hydrocarbons.

Being solids, zeolites lend themselves to use in fixed-bed and fluidized-bed reactors, since they can easily be separated from gaseous products. Their great internal surface areas mean that an enormous active area fits into a small catalyst bed, and they are easily regenerated by roasting to burn off activity-reducing carbon deposits.

By far the most important feature of zeolite catalysts is the shape and size selectivity imposed on product mixtures. This selectivity occurs because the catalyzed reactions occur mainly in cavities within the zeolite, and these reactions are reversible. If the initial product of a reaction is too large or the wrong shape to leave through the pores, the product remains trapped until the reaction reverses and forms a product whose dimensions are more suitable for the pores.

The effective pore size of a given zeolite can be tailored to a particular target product by the inclusion of appropriately sized ions in the pores—ions of copper, transition metals, or lanthanide metals are typically used—and some of these ions have catalytic activity in their own right. More radical changes in the basic frameworks and catalytic activities of zeolites can be achieved by introducing sources of phosphorus or transition metals into the hydrothermal synthesis blend. These elements then become incorporated in the framework of the zeolite-type crystal.

SEE ALSO: AUTOCLAVE • CATALYST • FLUIDIZED BED • GASOLINE, SYNTHETIC • HYDROCARBON • OIL REFINING

Zinc

Zinc is a bluish-white metal with a hexagonal close-packed crystal structure. It is a little less dense than iron but not especially strong when pure. High-strength casting alloys are obtained by alloying with aluminum, copper, and magnesium. Zinc melts at 788°F (420°C) and boils at the comparatively low temperature of 1665°F (907°C).

Zinc is not found in the natural state, and the earliest metallic form would almost certainly have been in brass, an alloy of zinc and copper. Primitive metallurgists had learned to make brass by heating copper with zinc ores, but they did not understand the nature of the process, and if it happened that any free zinc metal was formed and not absorbed by the copper, it would have vaporized and been lost. It was not until the 17th century that substantial quantities of the metal were brought to Europe from China. It was about this time that the name *zinc* was specifically applied; the term had been used in Europe for over a hundred years to describe a variety of metals and ores. It is possible that the name is derived from the German word *Zinn*, which means "tin." The first zinc smelter in the Western world was set up near Bristol in the United Kingdom in the early 1740s by William Champion.

Production

The most important ore of zinc is its sulfide, called zinc blende or sphalerite, which is the source of more than 90 percent of the world's zinc. Zinc carbonate, ($ZnCO_3$) is another common zinc ore. The ores seldom occur in the pure form and are most often associated with lead or copper ores. The zinc concentrate (the ore after flotation) is usually roasted in air to convert the zinc sulfide or carbonate to the oxide:

$$2ZnS + 3O_2 \rightarrow 2ZnO + 2SO_2$$

zinc   air   zinc   sulfur
sulfide   oxide   dioxide

$$ZnCO_3 \rightarrow ZnO + CO_2$$

zinc   zinc   carbon
carbonate   oxide   dioxide

At atmospheric pressure, the reduction to zinc can occur only above the boiling point of the metal. For this reason, the reaction was traditionally carried out in horizontal retorts, and the resulting zinc vapor was condensed in clay vessels and iron pipes.

About 80 percent of the world's zinc production is by the electrolytic process. The roasted oxide is leached with sulfuric acid to produce an impure zinc sulfate solution that is then purified

to a high degree to remove such elements as cadmium, copper, cobalt, and iron. The purified zinc sulfate solution is electrolyzed in vast cell houses, with zinc of 99.99 percent purity being deposited at the cathodes, which are then mechanically stripped. This process, which was introduced in the 1960s, has since been further developed, and plants producing 200,000 tons (180,000 tonnes) per year are now common.

The other frequently used process, which currently produces approximately 12 percent of the world's zinc, is the Imperial Smelting Process (ISP) using metallurgical coke as the reductant.

The ISP is a zinc blast furnace with the principal reaction being

$$ZnO + C \rightarrow Zn + CO$$

zinc   carbon   zinc   carbon
oxide   (vapor) monoxide

Unfortunately, when burning carbon in air, both CO and CO_2 are generated and the reaction

$$Zn + CO_2 \rightarrow ZnO + CO$$

zinc   carbon   zinc   carbon
        dioxide   oxide   monoxide

also takes place. In the ISP, this problem of reversion is overcome by absorbing the zinc vapor onto lead droplets in the condenser. The molten lead containing approximately 2.5 percent zinc is then externally cooled from 1040°F (560°C) to 806°F (430°C), when a portion of the zinc comes out of solution and—being the less dense of the two metals—floats and is collected separately. The grade is lower than that produced by the electrolytic process, containing 98.75 percent zinc.

▲ High-grade zinc ingots, refined from one of the zinc ores—zinc blende or calamine. The first stage in producing high-grade zinc is to reduce the oxide in the presence of carbon; this reaction is usually carried out in horizontal retorts, and the resulting zinc vapor is condensed in clay vessels and iron pipes called prolongs. Further purification is achieved either by crystallization or redistillation.

The ISP will treat a mixed concentrate of zinc and lead, with a lead bullion (containing most of the copper, silver, and gold) being tapped off the furnace bottom together with the slag, the two phases being separated in a forehearth.

Zinc can be purified by distillation, and many plants still operate by taking advantage of the different boiling points of cadmium (1407°F, 764°C), zinc (1663°F, 906°C), and lead (3191°F, 1755°C) to effect a separation—with 99.99 percent cadmium and 99.99 percent zinc quality as end products.

Uses

About 50 percent of all zinc produced is used for coating iron to provide protection from corrosion. Brass manufacture absorbs a further 18 percent of world production annually.

One of the most important uses of zinc is in die casting, where molten metal is forced under pressure into a steel mold, or die, which is often intricately shaped. The resulting casting reproduces the dimensions of the die so precisely that little if any machining is needed to complete it. Its mechanical properties are also superior to a similar sand casting because the rapid solidification gives rise to a very small grain size. The preeminent use of zinc for die casting results from its combination of low melting point and adequate strength.

The optimum alloy is zinc alloyed with 4 percent aluminum, which can be hot-chamber die cast with minimal attack of steel dies and holding pots. It has a very desirable combination of mechanical and physical properties and is unsurpassed in its ability to take a variety of surface finishes, such as electroplating, powder coating, and anodizing. It is readily machined, and its good formability assists assembly and forming processes.

In addition, the foundry alloys (ZA8, ZA12, and ZA27) can be cast by a variety of methods, including sand and gravity and hot or cold pressure die casting. ZA12 is a general-purpose foundry alloy offering an excellent combination of physical and mechanical properties and castability. Notable are its hardness, machinability, and bearing properties. ZA27 is a very high strength alloy (TS 400–400 MPa) that is best suited to sand casting and cold chamber pressure die casting. It also has very good bearing properties. ZA8 can be hot-chamber die cast, and it offers the qualities of high strength, hardness, and improved creep properties.

Zinc alloys are manufactured from high-purity zinc (99.99 percent minimum) to avoid the phenomenon of intercrystalline corrosion promoted by small amounts of lead, cadmium, or tin.

Zinc die-cast components find wide application, particularly in the automobile industry and for building hardware, including both engineering parts and more decorative applications, where zinc's ability to take a variety of different finishes is unsurpassed by any other material.

▲ Hot-dip galvanizing of steel streetlight poles. About 23 percent of the zinc produced is used for galvanizing. The zinc coating oxidizes in the air to produce an oxide film that adheres strongly to the metal in two ways. First, it physically shields the metal in the galvanized article from contact with the surrounding air. Second, if the zinc coating is broken to expose the base metal, the zinc surrounding the break provides a type of cathodic protection for the metal.

Rolled zinc is used for dry-battery casings, engraving, stencils, and lithographic plates. It is also used for the cathodic protection of steel structures such as ships and underwater pipelines. Sheet containing 1 percent copper and 0.1 percent titanium finds application as a roofing material; the small amount of titanium forms an intermetallic compound with the zinc that greatly enhances the resistance of the material to creep deformation.

Like most metals, zinc dissolves in strong acids to give a zinc salt and hydrogen gas. A zinc–acid reaction of this sort is often used in the laboratory to generate small amounts of hydrogen. If the acid is hydrochloric acid, the reaction may be written as

$$\underset{\text{zinc metal}}{Zn} + \underset{\text{hydrochloric acid}}{2HCl} \rightarrow \underset{\text{zinc chloride}}{ZnCl_2} + \underset{\text{hydrogen}}{H_2}$$

The most widely used zinc compounds are zinc oxide and zinc sulfide; both are white pigments, and both are used as colorants.

SEE ALSO: Alloy • Brass • Casting • Electrolysis • Element, chemical • Metal • Metal cutting and joining • Metalworking • Surface treatments

Zoology

The U.S. government has established the Bitter Creek refuge to provide for the protection of the Californian condor. Reduced to only three birds left in the wild in 1986, a special breeding program managed to increase their numbers to 61 by 2000.

Zoology is the branch of biological sciences concerned with the study of animals, ranging from single-celled protozoa, such as amoebas, to the blue whale, which can measure more than 100 ft. (30 m) in length and weigh more than 150 tons (136 tonnes).

More than a million different kinds of animals have been named, but there are many that remain unidentified, particularly in tropical rain forests. Unfortunately, many of these animals may become extinct because of forest clearance before they are discovered and named.

Communication and behavior

Extensive research into the ecology and behavior of many species of animals has greatly increased understanding of their lives and needs. Scientists continue to learn how animals communicate with each other. Elephants, for example, use low-frequency sounds called infrasound. Although humans are unable to hear these sounds, they are audible to other elephants over very long distances. At the other end of the sound range, mice and bats use high-frequency sounds known as ultrasound for communication and, in the case of bats, for echo location to avoid obstacles and detect prey.

Whales and dolphins produce a wide range of calls to communicate with other members of their species. Humpback whales "sing," and their songs, which can be heard at least 20 miles (32 km) away,

probably help to bring whales together for mating. Studies of sperm whales have shown that each individual has a distinctive "voice."

Male frogs croak to attract mates, with the sound frequency varying between species and even between areas. If female American cricket frogs are taken from South Dakota to New Jersey, for example, they ignore the local males because they do not recognize their calls.

Not surprisingly, it is the groups of mammals most closely related to humans that show the highest forms of social behavior and communication. Although the grunts of East African vervet monkeys all sound the same to the human ear, those grunts contain information, often about events of interest to the other monkeys, such as the approach of another group of monkeys.

There have been several studies of communication by chimpanzees. At the Language Research Center at Georgia State University, chimps have been taught to "talk" to humans by pointing to sets of symbols. They can indicate objects and actions, but whether this is similar to language as used by humans is still under debate.

Chimps also show advanced behavior in other ways. Research from the Ivory Coast indicates that chimps may actively teach their infants—by showing them the correct way to crack open palm nuts, for example. Chimps also use tools; they can figure out how to use a stick to extract ants from an ants' nest. It appears that sick chimps can treat themselves, often by eating plants that contain antibiotics. When a chimp dies, a closely related chimp will clearly experience grief, though there is no demonstration of sympathy from unrelated chimps in the group.

Mysteries of migration

Many animals, particularly some birds and insects, undertake periodic migrations over huge distances, showing great feats of speed and endurance. Tiny ruby-throated hummingbirds, for example, migrate 620 miles (1,000 km) across the Gulf of Mexico, many completing the journey in 20 hours of nonstop flight.

One of the most spectacular mass migrations in the animal kingdom is that undertaken by the monarch butterfly. In the fall, these butterflies fly south from southern Canada and the northern United States to winter sites in California and Mexico, and in the spring, they fly north again to breed. By tagging thousands of butterflies, it was found that some flew as far as 1,800 miles (2,900 km).

It is still not known precisely how these animals find their way back to the same areas each year. Many migrating animals use the Sun as a compass for orientation to maintain a particular direction. They make use of an internal clock that compensates for the movements of the Sun during the day and keeps them on course. Birds can also use the stars for orientation. It is possible that birds and butterflies can detect and use Earth's magnetic field, perhaps with magnetic material contained in their bodies.

Many birds show evidence of an ability to navigate—they can reach a distant place even if displaced from their original route. This navigational ability indicates that birds know the position of their home site, rather than just its general direction, and have some type of internal map of the route imprinted on their memory.

Conservation

Knowledge of the behavior and the dietary, territorial, and other needs of animals provides essential background for their conservation. An animal cannot be conserved unless a suitable habitat is preserved for it to live in.

To aid these background studies on animals' lives, there is increasing use of new scientific techniques. One of them is the use of radios and radar to monitor animal movements. Radio transmitters are fitted onto collars while animals are temporarily immobilized, and then the signals are tracked by VHF radio or by satellites. Radios that weigh only $\frac{1}{40}$ oz. (0.75 g) can be fitted to small animals and birds. Other techniques include genetic fingerprinting to assess the genetic background of populations and computer modeling to predict changes in populations and suggest key measures for protecting them.

Radio tracking has been used to study mountain lions (cougars) and black bears in the United States. Numbers of mountain lions have been greatly reduced by shooting and habitat destruction, and they have become confined to a few wild recolonized former haunts. Tracking studies in Idaho and New Mexico showed that mountain lions are very territorial; with the size of their territory determined by the available food supply, the numbers that can live in a given area are limited. The studies also showed that mountain lions did not significantly reduce the size of herds of deer and elk because most of their prey is either very young or very old rather than breeding age.

Despite a ban on commercial whaling since 1986 and the declaration of the Southern Ocean as a whale sanctuary, 7 out of the 13 great whale species are still endangered or vulnerable, even after decades of protection. The North Atlantic right whale is threatened with extinction because of collision with shipping and entanglement in fishing gear, and the Western North Pacific gray

▼ Bull elephants in Kenya. Scientists are investigating the possibility of using birth control as an alternative to culling herds that have become too large for their habitats.

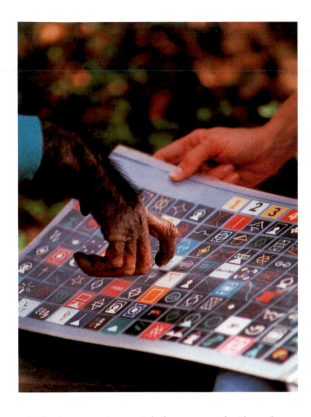

whale is at serious risk because of oil and gas development in its feeding grounds.

Satellite tagging of marine animals such as whales, seals, porpoises, and turtles enables scientists to track the movements of endangered or vulnerable species and also relays information about the behavior of particular species.

Marine animals are fitted with a tag that has an antenna that is used to send a signal each time the animal surfaces. The signal is picked up by satellites circling Earth, which collect, process, and disseminate data worldwide. The information relayed includes time, date, latitude, longitude, dive depths, dive duration, and the amount of time at the surface in the last six hours. A number of weather satellites maintained by the U.S. National Oceanographic and Atmospheric Administration (NOAA) are equipped to pick up the data about marine animals.

Elephant herds in parts of Africa present a complex conservation problem. As many as 10 million elephants roamed Africa 500 years ago, but by the end of the 1970s, numbers had fallen to well below 1.5 million. By 1998, population estimates for the whole continent ranged from a little over 300,000 African elephants to about 487,000 individuals.

Many elephants have died from poachers' bullets. Since 1989, a ban on the trade in ivory has reduced the threat from poachers to some extent. However, there is evidence that, despite the ban, poaching elephants for ivory remains a problem in West and Central Africa, and it recently seems to be increasing elsewhere in Africa. Large

amounts of ivory continue to be smuggled to North Africa for export to Asia.

Elephants are still menaced by human population pressure and by loss of habitat across much of their range. In some game reserves, their numbers are too large for the available land area and they may damage their own habitat. Elephants are shot in some reserves in southern Africa to reduce populations, but zoologists now realize that elephants grieve over their dead and remember such disturbing events, so it is vital to find more humane ways of population control. The possibility of using birth control as an alternative to culling is under investigation.

Success stories

Although many animal species remain threatened with extinction, more and better scientific studies have resulted in success stories with some of them. One of the most spectacular comebacks has been that of the Californian condor. By 1986, it had declined so drastically that only three birds were left in the wild. By 2000, however, thanks to a successful captive breeding program, the population had risen to 61 in the wild and 99 in captivity.

The condors' decline was originally due to the reduction in numbers of bison, their main food source. Later many were poisoned by the pellets of lead shot or the pesticides in the animal carcasses on which they feed. In 1987, the last three wild birds were captured and placed with 24 others already in captivity in southern California. As breeding techniques have improved, so the captive flock has in turn flourished.

One problem with these hand-reared condors is that they are liable to bond with their human rearer rather than with other condors, so the

keepers wear glove puppets carrying models of the heads of adult condors. Newly released birds have to learn how to scavenge in the wild, so before two were released in 1992, 13 Andean condors were freed in the same area. The Californian condors could learn how to survive from these related birds.

The spectacular whooping crane is at the center of a remarkable effort by U.S. and Canadian conservationists, which raised its population from an all-time low of 21 wild birds in 1944 to 300 birds in wild and captive flocks by 2000. The measures that have contributed to this success have included the careful management of the small population of wild cranes that annually migrates the 1,860 miles (3,000 km) from Canada's Northwest Territories to the Gulf Coast of Texas, the rearing of cranes in captivity, and the establishment of an additional wild population using sandhill cranes as foster parents.

Captive breeding is an increasingly important tool in the conservation of endangered species, and scientific advances are increasing the survival chances of more and more animals. In these breeding programs, it is important to maintain a diverse gene pool, so it is essential to know the genetic structure of the captive population.

New scientific techniques in biochemistry and genetics are aiding this research. Genetic fingerprinting enables an animal's parentage to be identified and the degree of genetic diversity in a particular population to be determined. Artificial insemination and transfer of embryos are other techniques that may be used.

Another example of success with captive breeding was that of the first aye-aye born in captivity outside its native Madagascar, which was being reared at the Duke University Primate Center in North Carolina in 1991. This curious animal is one of the most endangered species of lemur. It has a very long middle finger, which it uses to locate and extract animal larvae (its favorite food) from timber. However, all the efforts of captive breeding will be in vain unless suitable areas of habitat, into which the bred animals can eventually be released, are preserved.

Insects

The largest group of animals are insects, with more than a million different kinds already named and many more still to be identified. Some insects are pests, but scientists are increasingly looking to control them without resorting to insecticides that may pollute the environment.

Insects use scents to attract mates, to mark trails to good food sources, and to warn their companions of danger. Female moths attract male

► The codling moth caterpillars cause substantial amounts of damage to apples and other fruit each year by burrowing into them and leaving holes. Researchers are attempting to devise methods of controlling the moth.

moths over very long distances by emitting a scent that elicits a response only from males of that particular species. The males have very sensitive detectors on their antennae that can react to a single molecule of the scent, called a sex pheromone. Chemists have identified the structure of some pheromones and are able to synthesize them, leading to a novel method of pest control.

The caterpillars of the codling moth burrow into apples, pears, and walnuts. Researchers in California are attempting to control this pest by preventing the moths from mating. One solution is to flood the air with the artificial pheromone of the moth so that the male moths can no longer find the females by following distinct trails of the scent in the air.

In Africa, desert locusts form voracious swarms that consume an amount of vegetation equal to their own body weight every day. A swarm covering 386 sq. miles (1,000 km²) will eat about 80,000 tons (72,500 tonnes) of foliage a day. Satellites are used to give early warning of the buildup of swarms so that rapid action can be taken against them.

► A drugged and tagged seven-month-old mountain lion in Yellowstone National Park. Radio collars help keep track of the animal's movements.

SEE ALSO: Biotechnology • Genetic engineering • Life • Marine biology • Parasitology • Reproduction • Sonar • Taxidermy • Veterinary science and medicine

Index